PATTON'S *LAST* GAMBLE

General George S. Patton, Jr. PATTON PAPERS, LIBRARY OF CONGRESS

PATTON'S
LAST
GAMBLE

THE DISASTROUS
RAID ON POW CAMP
HAMMELBURG
IN WORLD WAR II

DUANE SCHULTZ

STACKPOLE
BOOKS
Guilford, Connecticut

Published by Stackpole Books
An imprint of Globe Pequot
Trade Division of The Rowman & Littlefield Publishing Group, Inc.
4501 Forbes Boulevard, Suite 200, Lanham, Maryland 20706

Distributed by NATIONAL BOOK NETWORK
800-462-6420

British Library Cataloguing in Publication Information Available

Library of Congress Cataloging-in-Publication Data

ISBN 978-0-8117-1990-2 (hardcover)
ISBN 978-0-8117-6595-4 (e-book)

∞™ The paper used in this publication meets the minimum requirements of American National Standard for Information Sciences—Permanence of Paper for Printed Library Materials, ANSI/ NISO Z39.48-1992.

Printed in the United States of America

CONTENTS

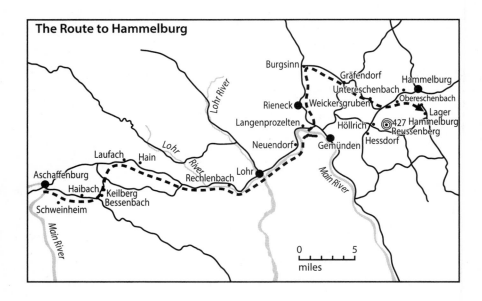

The Route to Hammelburg

Burgsinn

Gräfendorf

Hammelburg

Untereschenbach

Obereschenbach

Rieneck

Weickersgruben

Langenprozelten

Lager

427 Hammelburg

Höllrich

Reussenberg

Neuendorf

Gemünden

Hessdorf

Laufach

Hain

Lohr

River

Rechlenbach

Lohr

Aschaffenburg

Haibach

Keilberg

Bessenbach

Schweinheim

Lohr River

Main River

Main River

0   5
miles

Patton's raid on Hammelburg "was the most controversial military decision of his career, and one that many would argue ranked as his worst."

CARLO D'ESTE, *PATTON: A GENIUS FOR WAR*

Patton's mission "began as a wild goose chase and ended as a tragedy."

GENERAL OMAR BRADLEY

"This mission doesn't have a chance and we both know it. If this task force does make it back, it'll be a miracle."

COLONEL CREIGHTON ABRAMS

"From start to finish, the whole exercise was a tragic fiasco. It would certainly have cost Patton his career had it not been quickly covered up and its survivors sworn to silence."

ALEX KERSHAW, *THE LONGEST WINTER: THE BATTLE OF THE BULGE*

American tank crashes fence to the cheers of Allied prisoners as task force drives deep into enemy territory to liberate POWs at Hammelburg. US ARMY SIGNAL CORPS, NATIONAL ARCHIVES (SC387230)

Tank forces liberate Army officers from Hammelburg prison camp. US ARMY SIGNAL CORPS, NATIONAL ARCHIVES (SC387232)

I HAVE JUST PISSED IN THE RHINE

George Patton walked confidently across a hastily constructed pontoon bridge over the Rhine River leading from France to Germany, looking like the conquering hero he was. He stopped halfway over, checked to make sure the photographer was ready to record the historic event, and then undid his fly. "Time out for a short halt," he said to his aides. "I have been looking forward to this for a long time." Later that same day, he sent a message to General Eisenhower at his headquarters. "I have just pissed in the Rhine."

Then, when he got to the end of the bridge and started to set foot on German soil for the first time, he pretended to stumble, fell down on one knee, and grabbed some mud and dirt in each hand. Holding both hands up for everyone to see what they held, he proclaimed proudly, "Thus, William the Conqueror." He was recreating the gesture made by the Norman duke who, when he set foot on British soil in 1066 for the first time, said, "See, I have taken England with both hands."

Patton knew his history. Three months earlier, he had said, "I've studied military history all my life. Georgie Patton knows more about military history than any other person in the United States Army today. With due conceit—and I've got no end of that—I can say that's true." And he also knew how to make his own history.

He was once again at the height of his power and glory that month of March 1945. A week before he crossed the Rhine, he had written in his diary that he and his victorious Third Army were "the eighth wonder of the world." He was not exaggerating, at least not by much. He had done the seemingly impossible time after time, becoming one of the most famous generals in American history.

The year before, in August 1944, while driving through a battlefield in France strewn with hundreds of bloated and blackened dead soldiers amidst fields of burned-out tanks, he had turned to his aide and said, "Just look at that, Codman. Could anything be more magnificent? . . . Compared to war, all other forms of human endeavor shrink to insignificance. God, how I love it."

Three months before crossing the Rhine, on December 26, he had broken through German lines to relieve the besieged American troops at Bastogne in one of the most brilliant military feats of the war. He had quickly shifted three divisions of his Third Army 90 degrees to the north and sent them through roads covered with snow and ice in only forty-eight hours, to the astonishment of everyone.

Then, in March 1945, his tanks covered 65 miles from their former front line in only two days, speeding along on a single highway from the German Siegfried line, in a column that was only about 25 feet wide, all the way to the Rhine. His flanks were entirely unprotected, but Patton did not concern himself with that.

He happily let the Army Air Corps worry about his flanks, and they obliged, strafing and bombing every enemy target they could find, and doing an excellent job of it. The important thing for Patton was simply to keep moving relentlessly, as far and as fast as possible every day. And so his tanks and men stopped for nothing, not even, so it was claimed, for a retreating German parachute division, which they beat in a race to the river. And Patton's force crossed the river with the loss of only twenty-eight men.

But more important to Patton, he had beaten his hated British rival, Field Marshal Bernard Montgomery, who had been preparing for days to make a massive crossing of the Rhine farther north. So swift was Patton's crossing and consolidation of a huge bridgehead on the other side that nobody at headquarters knew about it yet. The next morning, March 23, Patton telephoned his immediate commander, Gen. Omar Bradley, and shouted over the phone.

"Brad," he said, "don't tell anyone, but I'm across."

"Well, I'll be damned," Bradley replied. "You mean, across the Rhine?"

"Sure am," Patton said. "I sneaked a division over last night. But there are so few Krauts around there they don't know it yet. So don't make any announcements. We'll keep it a secret until we see how it goes."

The news did not stay a secret for long. A few hours later, Patton's liaison officer at Bradley's headquarters proudly told the press about Patton's crossing of the Rhine. By then, it did not make any difference because the Germans had found out on their own, and the next day they sent 150 fighter planes to strafe and bomb Patton's troops and the pontoon bridges they had built across the river. The German attack did little damage, however, and that evening Patton called Bradley again and screamed even louder over the phone in his curiously squeaky, high-pitched voice.

"Brad, for God's sake, tell the world we're across! We knocked down thirty-three Krauts [aircraft] today when they came after our pontoon bridges. I want the world to know Third Army made it before Monty starts across."

"This operation is stupendous," he wrote to his wife, Beatrice. Congratulations and praise poured in from Eisenhower, Patton's fellow generals, President Roosevelt, Secretary of War Henry Stimson, and Winston Churchill. Public opinion polls conducted back home in the States showed that Patton was consistently rated as the most popular of all of Eisenhower's generals. Even the enemy, Field Marshal Gerd von Rundstedt, said later that Patton was the best American general of them all.

Newspapers and magazines devoted huge coverage to Patton—more than to any other general in the European theater, which irked both Eisenhower and Bradley. Two weeks after he crossed the Rhine, *Time* magazine did a cover story on Patton, reporting an alleged incident involving Eisenhower. "When asked where the fast-moving Patton was, Ike replied, 'Hell, I don't know. I haven't heard from him in three hours.'"

On March 25, Palm Sunday, the day after Patton pissed in the Rhine, his beloved 4th Armored Division raced ahead to the next natural barrier, the Main River. The first unit to reach the river, Combat Command B, was led by newly promoted, thirty-year-old Col. Creighton Abrams, who was one of Patton's favorite officers. His men found a railroad bridge still standing, though they could see bombs that the Germans had strapped to the girders. It was ready to be blown up to stop the American advance.

Men of the 10th Armored Infantry Battalion, led by Lt. Col. Harold Cohen, made their way cautiously out onto the bridge and, one by one, disarmed the bombs. The battalion then went over the bridge and set up a defensive perimeter on the other side.

Patton's men were once again deeper into Germany than any other Allied unit, and both Abrams and Cohen, as well as a bad case of hemorrhoids, were about to play leading roles in what happened next. It seemed that nothing could stop Gen. George Smith Patton Jr.

"Patton was a hero," historian Michael Keane writes, "to his men, to his superiors at SHAEF [Supreme Headquarters, Allied Expeditionary Force], to the public, and to the press. In the experience of George Patton this could only mean one thing—something bad was about to happen. Patton himself wrote to his wife on March 23, 'I am really scared by my good luck.' He was right to be worried. Perhaps the most controversial episode of Patton's career was about to unfold."

That was when he decided to take the biggest gamble of his career and put into effect what one army historian called "the most fascinating yet enigmatic military escapade in the European theater during World War II." It was a mission to a POW camp located 60 miles behind German lines in a tiny town few Americans had ever heard of, called Hammelburg.

If the mission to Hammelburg failed, and the real reason behind it became known, he would end his illustrious army career in absolute disgrace and shame. He would go down in history as one of the most reviled military commanders of World War II for having deliberately exposed his men to mortal danger for what everyone would know was a highly personal and selfish reason on his part. Even if the mission succeeded, he could still be vilified for risking several hundred lives to save one man who might not even be at Hammelburg.

The consequences would be far worse than what happened to him after the slapping incidents two years before in Sicily, which had almost cost him his command. Indeed, they did for a while. In August 1943, during the campaign to take Sicily, Patton visited two field hospitals a week apart and grew irate both times at seeing two soldiers who were not physically wounded but displayed signs of combat fatigue, a concept in which Patton definitely did not believe. One man was shivering and crying, and when Patton asked him what was wrong, the soldier replied that it was his nerves, that he could not take the shelling anymore.

"Your nerves, hell, you are just a goddamn coward," Patton yelled. "You yellow son of a bitch!" Patton told him he was a disgrace to the army and ought to be lined up against a wall and shot. "In fact, I ought to shoot you myself, you goddamned whimpering coward!"

He pulled out one of his ivory-handled pistols and waved it close to the terrified soldier's face. Then he turned to the hospital CO and told him not to admit the soldier and to get him out of sight of the others. By then the soldier was crying even more, and Patton slapped him across his face once and then hit him again so hard as to knock off his helmet.

The story got out, of course, and Patton was roundly criticized by the public, Congress, and even retired generals, including Pershing, who had been instrumental in fostering Patton's early career. Per Patton biographer Carlo D'Este, Eisenhower wrote to Patton using "the strongest words of censure written to a senior American officer during World War II."

Newspaper columnist Drew Pearson sensationalized the story in his highly popular radio program. Patton was forced to make embarrassing public apologies to the two soldiers he had slapped, to the hospital staff who had witnessed the events, and then to all the thousands of troops under his command. It was one of the most humiliating experiences in Patton's long military career.

Bradley later described Patton as being in almost a suicidal condition by then and wrote that he had wanted to get rid of Patton after what happened on Sicily, and never have anything more to do with him. Eisenhower, however, realized how much his army needed a commander as aggressive as Patton once they invaded Europe. "Patton is *indispensable* to the war effort," he wrote, "one of the guarantors of our victory."

In order to satisfy critics and the public back home, Patton was placed in exile in England and given no combat command for the next eleven months. To Patton's chagrin, Bradley was chosen to command American ground forces in the forthcoming invasion of Europe at Normandy. The job might well have been Patton's had he not behaved so abominably at those hospitals in Sicily.

He continued to believe, however, that what he had done was for the good of the army. "I am convinced that my action in this case," he wrote in his diary, "was entirely correct, and that, had other officers had the courage to do likewise, the shameful use of 'battle fatigue' as an excuse for cowardice would have been infinitely reduced."

He survived that embarrassing setback to his career and again became a national hero, but he knew he would not be so fortunate if word got out about the real purpose of his mission to Hammelburg. The war in Europe was going to end in a matter of weeks, and he would not be needed anymore. His service, his career, his reputation, his role in history would all be in jeopardy. But that did not stop him.

The incidents in Sicily could be explained away, his defenders argued, by the stress he was under at the time leading his successful campaign there. They could even be described as a one-time overreaction on the spur of the moment. His defenders said it was simply Patton being his usual impetuous self. Even one of the soldiers he slapped seemed to almost rally to Patton's defense when he said, "I think he was suffering a little battle fatigue himself."

The Hammelburg operation would, in sharp contrast, be recognized as a deliberately planned, conscious decision made for a highly personal and selfish reason that had nothing to do with defeating the Germans and ending the war.

Patton was willing to take such a gamble to save just one man. The man was a lieutenant colonel, a graduate of West Point who had been captured in North Africa two years earlier, in 1943, by Erwin Rommel's famed Afrika Korps. He was a tanker and former cavalry officer like Patton.

When he was listed as missing in action not far from the major American defeat at Kasserine Pass, Patton was frantic with worry and personally sent a graves registration team to comb the dead in search of this one man at the battle site. They did not find him. Patton himself walked among the debris of the battle and picked up an ammunition clip from what was left of an American tank; he sent it to the man's two young children to serve as a memento of their father if he did not return.

Finally, several weeks later, the man's name appeared on a prisoner of war list of the Germans. John Knight Waters was Patton's son-in-law. Patton would later deny to everyone, including Waters, that he knew Waters was at Hammelburg, and, indeed, he did not know for certain that he was there. Patton would also claim that the purpose of the mission had been to rescue *all* of the POWs at Hammelburg, not just one man.

Patton was so worried about public criticism and possible censure for what he was about to do that he classified the mission as top secret, meaning that nothing was to be said to the press and that his men were not to talk about it to anyone.

The mission to Hammelburg would last only forty hours over two nights and a day from start to finish, a blink of an eye in the many months and years that World War II in Europe lasted. It was only one of hundreds of decisions Patton made during the war. Yet, it stood out enough for Patton's biographer to describe it as "the most controversial military decision of his career, and one that many would argue ranked as his worst."

Before it even began, Creighton Abrams and Harold Cohen, who had to plan the raid, both called it a suicide mission. So did Capt. Abe Baum, the man chosen to lead the rescue force to Hammelburg. Sgt. Nat Frankel, a tanker who made it through the war in Patton's 4th Armored Division, called the mission "stupid and selfish."

Patton's gamble, as Bradley later wrote, "began as a wild goose chase and ended as a tragedy." Bradley called it "foolhardy" and said it was "doomed from the start." He was right.

CHAPTER 2

ONE LAST CHANCE TO BE A HERO

GEORGE PATTON WAS USED TO GETTING HIS OWN WAY FROM HIS CHILD-hood on. And what a way it was. "When I was a little boy at home," he wrote years later, "I used to wear a wooden sword and say to myself, 'George S. Patton, Jr., Lieutenant General.'" While there were some missteps and setbacks along the way, mostly of his own making, and times when he was sure his career was over, he eventually got his three stars and became a lieutenant general. Then he went beyond his childhood dream and got the fourth star of a full general.

"I must be the happiest boy in the world," Patton thought to himself as a child. When looking back as an adult, he confirmed, "I was probably right." He was born in 1885, on November 11, the date on which the First World War would later end, to very wealthy parents in southern California. Their sole mission in life seemed to be to spoil him and to never punish or chastise him in any way for anything he did. And they were not the only ones to do so.

His mother's sister, Annie, who had been desperately in love with Patton's father, moved in with them and became "Aunt Nannie" to baby George, whom she always referred to as her boy. She "completely dominated the Patton household. Her nephew could do no wrong, and in her quiet but controlling way she forbade any sort of criticism of Georgie," according to Carlo D'Este.

Aunt Nannie, and his mother, even moved to West Point for the five years he was a cadet (having failed his first year) to make sure they were available in case he needed anything. No wonder he became used to being the center of attention, a role he constantly needed to re-create for the rest of his life.

Sigmund Freud, the father of psychoanalysis, who was also the center of attention as a boy in his home, wrote, "A man who has been the indisputable favorite of his mother keeps for life the feeling of a conqueror, that confidence of success that often induces real success." And Patton had essentially two mothers to make sure he was always the center of attention. But when that role was threatened, no matter the source, or how old he was, he became intensely surly, angry, and depressed.

At the age of twenty-six, for example, he found it very hard to come second when his wife, Beatrice, had their first child, called Beatrice and nicknamed Little Bee. Suddenly, he was no longer the focus. His wife had to devote more time to the baby than to him, and he felt lost, jealous, and resentful of the child who, to make matters worse, was a girl and not the boy he had hoped for. He expressed his feelings in a letter to his beloved Aunt Nannie. "The accursed infant has black hair is very ugly and is said by some dastardly people to resemble me which it does not because it is ugly."

He eventually had a son, but only after another daughter was born. He never got along very well with his daughters, whom he resented for not being boys as well as for taking time and attention away from him. After one of them misbehaved, he asked his wife in front of them, "How did such a beautiful woman like yourself ever have two such ugly daughters?"

In an interview in 1985, his son, who was by then a general himself in the army, and daughter Ruth Ellen recalled how "scared to death of him" they had been as children. Even as late as 2004, at the age of eighty-nine, Ruth Ellen wrote that as a child, "I thought he was an ogre. Everything I did was wrong."

He was a strict disciplinarian with them. He once tried to teach the girls how to play tennis, behaving as though they were privates in the army going through basic training. They both vowed to each other that they would never play tennis again. When observing one daughter ride a horse, he yelled at her to get off so he could show her how it was done. As he rode off, she said, "Dear God, please let that son of a bitch break his neck."

Patton had grown up not only extremely spoiled and well looked after, but also very rich, and his father had no hesitation in giving the boy anything and everything he wanted, including two horses of his own when he was ten years old and a sailboat built for him when he was thirteen. The family lived a life of luxury, which Patton was able to maintain for the rest of his days.

In 1910, a year after he graduated from West Point, he married Beatrice Ayer, from a prominent New England family even wealthier than the Patton family, and they too were extremely generous with their money to George and Bea for the rest of their lives. Before the wedding, Beatrice's father wrote to him, saying, "From now on I'll take care of making the money. You take care of winning the glory."

For his sixteenth birthday, his Aunt Nannie gave him a ring "of gold in the form of a scaly snake wrapped around itself, and in the head were set ruby chip eyes and a glittering sapphire topknot." He wore it every day for the rest of his life and later added his West Point ring, a gold-set diamond given him by Beatrice, and a marriage band showing two hands wrapped around a golden heart. Not many career officers wore four such large, ostentatious rings.

British military historian Charles Whiting writes that there was "something arrogant [and] aristocratic" about George Patton. Whiting goes on to describe how, no matter how remote and primitive the army base Patton was assigned to, he "could always afford the finest accommodations in the nearest town, motoring back and forth to duty in the latest and most expensive automobile available. [He particularly liked Pierce-Arrows.] He ran a string of polo ponies at a time during the Depression when the average Army Officer of the same rank was lucky to have a single ancient steed at his disposal."

And when a far less wealthy and privileged commanding officer would order the young Patton to take his polo ponies off the base, he would simply take them all to the nearest private livery stable and pay for them at his own expense. "In short," Whiting concludes, "the Pattons' private life was aristocratic and upper class, a black-tie affair in the best society; his professional life was the contrived, rather shabby middle-class one of the Army." Of course, such a lifestyle aroused considerable jealousy and resentment among his fellow officers who were less fortunate in their circumstances, but that did not seem to bother Patton.

When he was still a poorly paid lieutenant, he bought a 50-foot schooner named *Arcturus* (the brightest star in the Northern Hemisphere), had it shipped from New England to California, and then spent a month with friends sailing it to his new post in Hawaii. Bea signed on as cook, even though she had never cooked a meal in her life. For two years as a young lieutenant, he and Bea spent their summers in Europe, shipping his car along on the same ocean liner on which they sailed. The cost of taking the car was twice Patton's monthly salary.

One of the times when he was stationed at the most glamourous of all army posts, Fort Myer, across the Potomac from Washington, DC, the Pattons rented a house so large that it required a housekeeper, a governess, a cook, and six servants to run the place. Patton was driven back and forth to the base every day by his chauffeur. He wrote to his father to explain his need for his own driver by noting that everyone else had one, and that he and Bea would not be able to maintain their proper social standing without one.

Fort Myer was the ideal spot to meet and socialize with influential high-ranking officers as well as leading congressmen and cabinet members. He used to say that being stationed there was like being "nearer God." Of course one had to have the right clothes, social standing, and bearing in order to be accepted by that level of society. George and Bea Patton fit right in, playing polo and tennis; going to foxhunts, steeplechases, and horse shows; and attending lavish dinners and parties, as well as hosting their own for Washington's prominent leaders.

They were eagerly accepted into two of the most important private clubs in the Washington area: the Metropolitan Club and the Chevy Chase Club. Both were considered very difficult to get into, but not for the Pattons.

For a different kind of relaxing and entertaining, Patton bought his second boat: a two-mast, 80-foot schooner that he kept moored nearby at the Capital Yacht Club for sailing in the Chesapeake Bay. He called it

When and If and said he and Bea would sail around the world in it when he retired.

Because of his fine horses and social standing, he found himself going horseback riding almost every morning with Henry Stimson, who had been secretary of war in World War I, then secretary of state in the 1930s (and would be once again secretary of war in World War II). Through the Stimsons, the Pattons met virtually all of the highly placed members of the Washington establishment.

Patton's lavish spending and upper-class social life led to his developing influential relationships with a number of high-level people. He had no hesitation about using his money, or his family, to expedite those relationships. While still a student at West Point in 1905, he wrote to his father in advance of his parents' visit to the academy, to do whatever he could to cultivate the goodwill of the officers. He told his father that if he could get "on their good side," that could increase his chances of promotion.

In 1939, in command at Fort Myer, Patton invited the newly promoted army chief of staff, George C. Marshall, to stay in his quarters on base while Marshall's house was being renovated. Marshall accepted and the two men apparently had a good time "batching it," as Patton wrote to Bea.

He also bought eight silver stars from a prominent New York jeweler and presented them to Marshall as a gift for his promotion, and often took Marshall out sailing on his schooner. Marshall was about to make major changes in the officer corps of the army, including forcing into retirement most officers of Patton's age.

On July 27, 1939, during Marshall's stay in Patton's quarters, Patton wrote to Bea, who was away with the children, "You had better send me a check for $5000.00 as I am getting pretty low." That was a little over three times what the average American made in a year. The dollar equivalent to that amount in 2017 is more than $85,600.

Given his upbringing and social standing, it is not surprising that George Patton felt a sense of superiority over others, most of whom he considered to be quite beneath him socially, mentally, and morally. While still at West Point, he wrote to his father, complaining about his fellow cadets and noting, "I am better than they are . . . someday I will show and make them feel how infernally inferior they are."

In another letter he told his father that "I belong to a different class, a class almost extinct or one which may never have existed yet." By his behavior he made it clear to his fellow cadets that none of them measured up to his own sense of self-worth, which left him pretty much alone. "Unable to hide his disdain, he was deemed arrogant and remote."

When he was growing up in Southern California, he looked down on those around him, including Mexicans, black Americans, and American Indians, as his social inferiors. As his world expanded and he traveled more, it seemed as though every other nationality or race of people he came into contact with was also deemed inferior.

His dislike of Jews was expressed in letters as early as 1913, when he and Bea had to share a table on their first cruise to Europe with a Jewish couple. In World War I, he wrote to his younger daughter describing the heroic self-sacrifice in battle of a Jewish West Point graduate, bragging that the academy could instill positive values in anyone, even a "dirty little Jew."

At the end of World War II, when he was on occupation duty in Bavaria, he had to deal with thousands of displaced persons, many of whom were Jewish survivors of concentration camps. Despite having seen the conditions in the camps, Patton deplored the behavior and appearance of the survivors and got angry when he had to turn "decent German families" out of their homes so that such Jewish "scum" could have a place to stay, making no allowance for the conditions under which they had been forced to live. "My personal opinion," he wrote, "is that no people could have sunk to the level of degradation these have reached in the short space of four years."

In addition to feeling superior to other groups, he also came to actively hate them. The list of those he disdained grew as the war continued and he came in contact with people from more countries. It started with Englishmen and then included all North Africans and Arabs, then Sicilians and Italians, Frenchmen, Germans, Russians, politicians, and even cartoonists, as a result of the work of Bill Mauldin. And GIs who forgot to wear neckties when they were on the front lines.

Whiting concludes that Patton's life "seemed to have been motivated by pure naked hatred," which as the war drew to its close gained the upper hand over him.

While Patton enjoyed many advantages in life from his childhood on, he was also beset by problems that, while not excusing his behavior, may have had a role to play in some of it. The first one was dyslexia, a learning disorder characterized by difficulties with reading, writing, and spelling.

D'Este describes additional problems related to dyslexia that may have applied to Patton, including sharp mood swings, obsessiveness, impulsiveness, feelings of inferiority, and a tendency to boast. Dyslexics like Patton commonly feel the need to be as least as good as, but preferably superior to, everyone else, which results in a tremendous drive to achieve, to be the best in whatever they do. If one is in the army, that means becoming not just a general, but a better general than any other.

And if dyslexia were not enough to deal with, Patton also fell off of horses a lot and apparently suffered several concussions. In one incident, two days after he suffered a spectacular fall while playing polo in Hawaii, he was sailing his yacht off the coast of Hawaii and turned in confusion to Bea, asking her what had happened.

As historian Martin Blumenson described it, "The last thing he remembered was falling off his polo pony [two days before]. A doctor confirmed that he had a concussion. After that . . . he could no longer hold his liquor well. If he had a few drinks in the privacy of his home, he was likely to become tearful and maudlin, reciting poetry and reminiscing about his boyhood in California."

Patton also suffered from bleak moods and intense bouts of depression that worsened as he got older. He had once hoped to be a brigadier general by the age of twenty-seven, but at the age of twenty-nine, he lamented the fact that he was not even a first lieutenant yet. The older he got, the more obsessed and worried he became about showing signs of age.

In 1934 his first daughter married John Waters, the man Patton would later try to rescue from Hammelburg. His other daughter watched him as he walked the bride down the aisle and later wrote that she would "never forget Georgie's face. He looked just like a child who is having his favorite toy taken away. All his determination to remain forever young was being undermined by having a daughter getting married. He was forty-nine years old and he had still not won a war. . . . He looked stricken to the heart."

The next year he turned fifty and refused to get out of bed on his birthday. All of his worst fears were coming true. His career seemed to have come to a halt, his West Point uniform no longer fit, he wore glasses, his hair was thinning and turning gray, and his stomach billowed out in front of him. His depression and anger grew even worse and he started to drink far too much, sometimes to the point of making a spectacle of himself in front of his fellow officers.

Then, in 1936, Jean Gordon, a lovely, charming, and intelligent twenty-one-year-old member of the Ayer family stopped in Hawaii on a Pacific cruise. She was the daughter of Beatrice's half sister, a close friend of Patton's daughters, and the same age as one of them. She served as a bridesmaid at both of their weddings. Her father had died when she was seven, and she and Patton, thirty years her senior, began an affair.

"Georgie was mad at Ma for ceasing to be his adoring public . . . he was scared of getting old and dissatisfied with his static career," his daughter Ruth Ellen wrote. "To have an unusually attractive girl, his own daughter's age, make a play for him was just what his starved ego needed."

His wife and family knew what was going on, as did most of his colleagues, because he was not discreet in carrying on the affair (or other more casual ones over the years). When the cruise ship took Jean away, Beatrice Patton told her daughter, "It's lucky for us that I don't have a mother, because if I did, I'd pack up and go to her now." Then she added, "Your father doesn't know it . . . but right now he needs me more than I need him."

[*Note:* During World War II, Jean Gordon went to Europe as a Red Cross Donut Dolly with Patton's Third Army and their affair apparently continued. A few weeks after Patton's death in 1945, Bea confronted Jean in a Boston hotel room, pointed a finger at her as though holding a pistol, and uttered an old Hawaiian curse: "May the Great Worm gnaw your vitals and may your bones rot joint by little joint." Not long after, Gordon killed herself in a friend's New York apartment by turning on the gas stove. The *Washington Post* reported on January 9, 1946, that she died "surrounded by pictures of her famous uncle, General George S. Patton, Jr."]

Patton remained depressed after Gordon left Hawaii, with his unfulfilled dreams of being a hero and with his family torn apart by the affair. And he saw little hope for any change in the future.

———

The pampered, spoiled, troubled rich boy who was used to having his own way in everything, and felt so superior to others, had only one goal in life, one vision, one dream for himself: to become a mighty warrior who would win major victories and go down in history as one of the world's greatest generals. Above all, he needed to win, at whatever he did and at all costs.

He decided early on that he had to look and behave the way a successful general would. He spent "the remainder of his life honing that image by becoming profane, ruthless, and aristocratic. His famous scowl became so successful a part of his persona it seemed as if he had been born with it permanently engraved on his face," writes D'Este. He prided himself on being able to "curse steadily for three minutes without repeating himself once," according to nephew Fred Ayer Jr.

Noted Patton scholar Martin Blumenson states that "Patton was always interested in glory, adulation, recognition and approval. He believed passionately in the virtue of becoming well and widely known. What he wanted, above all, was applause. And for him that meant winning. Not only wars, races and competitions of every sort, but also winning out over himself, overcoming what he regarded as his disabilities and weaknesses."

He once wrote to his father that he was afraid of being a coward. Years later, he took another bad fall from one of his horses while jumping hurdles and landed on his head. Though clearly shaken, he immediately got back on the horse and led it at a fast pace over the hurdles again.

"Do you know why I made my horse take those jumps?" he asked a junior officer who was watching. When the officer suggested the reason was to discipline the horse, Patton replied, "Not at all. I did it just to prove to myself that I am not a coward."

On the rifle range at West Point, it once was his turn to work in the pits raising and lowering the targets and recording where the bullets hit. Suddenly he climbed up and stood out in the open, with bullets flying all around him. He was testing his courage, proving to himself that he was not a coward. He passed the test that day, but there were to be many more. In 1943 he wrote to his wife that "I still get scared under fire. I guess I will never get used to it. . . . I do hope that I will do my full duty and show the necessary guts."

Patton developed his dreams of military glory as a child listening to heroic tales of the Civil War, including those told to him by the famous Confederate guerilla leader John Singleton Mosby, who was a frequent guest at the Patton home. His step-grandfather also told the boy all about his exploits in the rebel army, and his grandfather on his father's side was a Confederate hero who was killed in Pickett's Charge.

As a boy, he and Mosby spent hours recreating Civil War battles in which Mosby reenacted his own roles and Georgie played Robert E. Lee, brandishing his wooden sword while riding his pony, named Peach Blossom. Every night Patton and his mother prayed at her bedside while looking up worshipfully at drawings of what he assumed were God and Jesus. He was surprised to find out later that they were Lee and Stonewall Jackson.

By the time he was a teenager, Patton had read every book he could find about military heroes in all ages and was an accomplished rider. Early on he developed the idea that the greatest glory of all would be to die on the field of battle, but only, of course, as a famous general.

He convinced himself at an early age that that would be his destiny, which would be a repeat of what had happened to him in his earlier lives. A firm believer in reincarnation, he viewed ancient battle sites as familiar ground on which he had fought before, going all the way back to the second century BC, when he was a Carthaginian dying on the battlefield in what is now Tunisia.

When he visited the site during the North African campaign, Patton knew without a doubt that he had been there before. "It was quite simply an article of faith that he had lived before as a warrior and would continue to do so in future lives," argues D'Este. In whatever era he lived, and he had lived in many in his own mind, he had always been a fearless leader of men in war.

While Patton's financial and social positions certainly helped him to advance in his career, he also worked very hard to become a professional soldier, a model leader of men, and a sterling example of physical prowess. At the age of twenty-seven, while stationed at Fort Myer, he was selected to compete in the Modern Pentathlon at the 1912 Olympics, to be held in Stockholm.

The competition was designed to test the fighting ability and endurance of a man of war. It consisted of five events: pistol shooting, swimming, fencing, riding in a steeplechase, and running cross-country. Patton went on a strict diet for two months and cut out smoking and even drinking while he pushed himself in all five areas. He came in at a respectable fifth place out of twenty-four contestants.

The most famous of the competitors, and the one who received the most press coverage, was Jim Thorpe, the noted American Indian athlete. Patton was also mentioned in magazine and newspaper articles and army publications, all of which helped to further enhance his stature and recognition in the army.

Patton was particularly taken with fencing. The following summer he got permission to go to France to study under the world's leading European fencing master, who was in the French cavalry. He and Bea sailed to Europe, where he spent five weeks in training. When he came home, he wrote an influential report about the superiority of the technique he had learned and was named Master of the Sword in the US Army.

He wrote other papers on the use of swords in modern warfare and then developed a new sword for the cavalry, which was named the Patton Saber in his honor. And he was still only a second lieutenant, just four years out of West Point. He had achieved a lot in a very short time.

In 1915 Patton used his influence to arrange a transfer to the 8th Cavalry in Fort Bliss, Texas, to serve under Brig. Gen. John J. Pershing. Pershing's nickname was "Black Jack," given to him by West Point cadets when he served there after having commanded the all-black 10th Cavalry Regiment out west. It was meant derisively.

Patton quickly got promoted to first lieutenant and became an aide to Pershing (who began an affair with Patton's sister) and then went south into Mexico on Pershing's punitive expedition to stop Pancho Villa from crossing the border and killing more Texans. In a preview of the armored cavalry warfare to come, Patton led ten soldiers in three old Dodge touring cars in a blazing gunfight, killing three of Villa's soldiers.

As Blumenson described it, "Patton's men strapped the bodies across the hoods of their cars and returned to camp with their trophies. In the absence of anything else resembling news, the correspondents with Pershing played up the incident. For two weeks newspapers across the nation featured Patton's photograph and exuberant remarks, as well as Pershing's satisfaction [with his young aide]." Patton's dream was coming true, it seemed; he was becoming a famous warrior.

A year later, in 1917, Patton went to France with Pershing when America entered World War I. Patton joined the Tank Corps and was there for the first American offensive of the war at Saint-Mihiel in September 1918. His tanks approached a bridge in a barrage of heavy shelling but stopped when the men saw that the bridge was loaded with demolitions ready to be set off. Patton blithely walked across the bridge and nothing happened. The bridge did not blow up, and his men quickly followed him and captured a large number of German soldiers on the other side.

Weeks later, during the Meuse-Argonne offensive, Patton's tanks and the infantry that accompanied them were pinned down by a heavy barrage of machine-gun fire. Patton later wrote to his father that he was "trembling with fear" and afraid to move when suddenly an apparition appeared in the sky; it was all of his ancestors who had been killed in previous wars speaking to him and urging him forward. Patton then stood up, waved his walking stick over his head, and shouted, "Let's go!" Only six men out of one hundred stood up and started going forward with him. One by one, they were all hit, except Patton, who said later, "I felt a great desire to run."

He kept walking forward until he was hit in the thigh, but even then he continued on about 40 feet more before falling. His orderly dragged him into a shell hole where he stayed for several more hours, directing the battle, until he allowed his men to carry him back to an aid station. Patton's first major war was over and he had covered himself with glory. By November 11, 1918, he was a full colonel, awarded the Distinguished Service Cross and the Distinguished Service Medal.

But then came peace. As happens after every war, the army was cut drastically, and for more than two decades, until the next war, Patton's life grew stagnant. He was only thirty-three years old when World War I ended, and the prospects for his future were bleak. Patton, like most officers, was reduced in rank to his prewar rank of captain. Promotions were extremely slow, even with the connections and contacts Patton had made and the awards and decorations he had received for his exemplary service during the war.

Blumenson describes the interlude thus: "During the interwar period, Patton was little known outside the Army. Among the officers he was regarded as a polo player, a horseman and a yachtsman whose hijinks, exuberance and grandstanding were the mark of an eccentric, a playboy, a socialite."

He was angry and bored and behaved in outrageous ways, both at home and at work, and remained far too outspoken and critical of his fellow officers. He even criticized senior officers in official reports—not a way to guarantee friendships or promotions. He had still not achieved the destiny that he knew should be his, and his worry about growing old and losing his mental and physical advantages haunted him.

Yet, through those difficult years between the wars, he somehow managed to continue to push himself to develop professionally in his career. He read every book and article he could find on the nature and history of warfare, no matter how obscure. He wrote a number of important and well-received articles in army publications. In 1937 he managed to write a prescient paper called "Surprise," in which he quite accurately predicted a Japanese attack on Pearl Harbor.

He got high grades and excellent performance reviews when he attended the cavalry's Advanced Officer School, and he was one of few to win the Distinguished Graduate award from the demanding Command and General Staff School at Fort Leavenworth. In those difficult years between the wars, when Patton was struggling with his personal, family, and career crises, when many considered him too overbearing, aggressive, and outspoken, he nonetheless received superior ratings from his commanding officers.

One report described him as "an officer of outstanding physical and mental energy who . . . is absolutely fearless and [can] be counted upon for great feats of leadership in war." Another evaluation called him "ambitious, progressive, original, professionally studious; conscientious in the performance of his duties. . . . An officer of very high general value to the service." And one of his last peacetime reviews, given at Fort Myer, called him a "vigorous, forceful and conscientious officer, whom I consider an outstanding leader."

Patton remained depressed, however, still consumed with unfulfilled dreams of being a hero, and with his family torn apart by his affair with Jean Gordon. There seemed to be little hope for any change in the future. His situation suddenly improved markedly, however, in 1938, when he was stationed once again at Fort Myer.

He and Beatrice were able to resume their grand-scale social life and mingle with the most important people at formal dinner parties, foxhunts, and polo matches. In that same year he was promoted to colonel. A year later Marshall became chief of staff and began picking and choosing those officers whom he felt would be the best leaders in the coming war. That was when he accepted Patton's invitation to share his house while Marshall's quarters were being renovated. "A snappy move," Patton bragged to Bea about the invitation. "Of course it may cramp my style but there are compensations."

In October 1941, two months before Pearl Harbor, he was made brigadier general and given command of the 15,000-man-strong 2nd Armored Division. His picture appeared on the cover of *Life* magazine, and he was quoted as saying, "All that is needed now is a nice juicy war."

Only six months later, with the country now at the war he had waited so long for, he was made a major general with two stars on his collar and, at age fifty-six, given command of the ground force of 24,000 American troops for Operation Torch, the invasion of North Africa. It was what he had been waiting for all of his life. "The eyes of the world are watching us," he told his troops, and to President Roosevelt he said that he would return either "a conqueror or a corpse."

On November 8, 1942, Operation Torch went off well against the Vichy French forces and Patton was ordered to plan for the invasion of Sicily, which would be the next step in the plan to defeat the Germans. But then, on February 14, the still-green American troops suffered a major defeat at Kasserine Pass at the hands of Erwin Rommel's much more experienced Afrika Korps. Patton was ordered to take command of the II Corps to replace Maj. Gen. Lloyd Fredendall, whose incompetent leadership had contributed to the defeat.

Patton quickly took charge in his own memorable way and set about to restore the morale of the defeated troops. Omar Bradley, who was appointed to be his deputy commander, described the scene: "With sirens shrieking Patton's arrival, a procession of armored scout cars wheeled into the dingy square opposite the schoolhouse headquarters of II Corps. . . . In the lead car Patton stood like a charioteer. He was scowling into the wind and his jaw strained against the web strap of a two-starred steel helmet."

He immediately issued a number of orders to tighten discipline. They included fines for not dressing properly, such as appearing without a necktie or leggings or having unpolished boots or a helmet chin strap unfastened (even when soldiers were in the latrine). Drivers were fined for not having the right air pressure in their tires or the right level of oil in their engines.

"Patton sure scares the shit out of me," one young officer said, and the men quickly developed a hatred of him, but in the process they became more united and morale rose. That was when he got the nickname of Old Blood and Guts. "Our blood and his guts," they said, but they fought better when they next met the Germans.

By March 1945, after he had the glory of pissing in the Rhine and was celebrated as a national hero, becoming again the warrior general he had longed to be since childhood, he wondered what came next. The war in Europe was coming to a close. He knew that Douglas MacArthur would never allow someone like him, who had gotten so much publicity, into his Pacific theater of war to fight the Japanese. The glory there went only to MacArthur; he was not about to share it with the likes of Patton. Patton's war would soon come to an end, and he faced the prospect of retirement or assignment to dull, tedious occupation duty or a training command back home. None of those options was a happy prospect.

Unless the Germans could pull off another Ardennes offensive and he could save the day again by coming to the rescue of surrounded American soldiers as he had done at Bastogne, the war would simply wind down very soon with him no longer the center of attention. Perhaps that was why he decided to take the gamble of trying to reach the POW camp at Hammelburg. Saving several hundred American POWs would be a glorious way to end his war.

If he succeeded, and if John Waters was at Hammelburg and among those he was able to rescue, perhaps he might be forgiven by his family for all the pain he had caused them over the years. It could be his one last chance to be a hero.

CHAPTER 3

THAT IS SOME SORRY ASS

THE COUNTDOWN TO HAMMELBURG BEGAN ON FEBRUARY 9, 1945, THE day Patton found out that John Waters was one of 1,500 American prisoners being forcibly marched by the Germans from their POW camp in Poland to somewhere in Germany, to avoid their being liberated by the advancing Russians. The trek had begun almost three weeks before, on January 21. The march took five weeks and covered some 300 miles in the midst of a brutally cold winter. Some men died of starvation and disease, some were shot by their German guards, and others simply disappeared from the column, including three who made it to Moscow.

The runaways reported the details of the forced march westward to Maj. Gen. John R. Deane, head of the US Military Mission to Russia. Among the names of the POWs they gave to Deane, men who were still alive when they had escaped, was Waters, whom Deane recognized as Patton's son-in-law. He sent the information to General Eisenhower, who passed it on to Patton.

No one knew whether Waters had survived the march or exactly where in Germany the POWs were being taken. Two weeks after the message from Moscow, Secretary of State Cordell Hull sent a telegram to Patton confirming that the US government had no knowledge of Colonel Waters' whereabouts, or even if he was still alive.

But as Patton studied his maps of the German territory in the path of his Third Army, he decided that the most likely destination of the POWs was the camp at Hammelburg, only 60 miles from Patton's front line.

Patton believed that Waters was there with the rest of the officers from Poland, and that he would send out a task force to free him, and of course all the other prisoners being held with him. His decision might have also been influenced by his jealousy of all the publicity Douglas MacArthur was getting for a raid he had set in motion just ten days before to free over 500 American POWs from the Japanese prison camp at Cabanatuan in the Philippines.

Patton did not like being replaced in the headlines, and he reportedly said "that he would make MacArthur look like a piker." Hammelburg was thought to hold a thousand more American officers than were liberated at Cabanatuan. If he could free them, he would beat MacArthur, and perhaps save his son-in-law in the process. It clearly seemed worth the gamble to him.

By March 23, when Patton's Third Army had crossed the Rhine, Patton wrote to his wife, "We are headed right for John's place and may get there before he is moved." Two days later he wrote to her again: "Hope to send an expedition tomorrow to get John."

Two years earlier, in 1943, the news had come through that John Waters was listed as a POW, and no longer as killed or missing in action. The man who was closer to Patton than anyone in the army, his aide, Col. Charles Codman, wrote a letter to Patton's wife, expressing the mood around Patton's headquarters: "It certainly lifts a dark feeling we all had. . . . Next job on the calendar is to get him back." It was now time.

On March 24, 1945, Patton flew to XII Corps headquarters to tell his senior commanders to get the mission underway, only to find them arguing against it. Not that their objections made any difference to Patton. The mission to Hammelburg was on whether they liked it or not.

Patton had met Waters sixteen years earlier, in 1929, when he returned to West Point for his twentieth reunion. He had his family with him, and, in order to make sure that his eighteen-year-old beautiful but shy daughter, Bee, had a good time, he asked that she be escorted to events by the most outstanding cadet of them all.

The man chosen was the handsome, well-spoken, twenty-three-year-old John Waters. Son of a Baltimore banker, Waters had attended Johns Hopkins University for two years before deciding that he wanted to be a career army man; he went to West Point, where he was a leading student, athlete, horseman, and polo player. His goal was to be a pilot, but he did not score high enough on the vision test and opted instead to be a cavalryman.

John and Bee were attracted to one another immediately, but of course cadets were not allowed to marry and they had to wait for five years. When he graduated from West Point and received his commission, John asked Patton for her hand. "Waters," Patton replied, "I don't know you. Come back in three years." When Bee asked her mother for her blessing, Beatrice said, "You can't. You're much too young," and she burst into tears and slapped her daughter across the face.

She did give her blessing later. John and Bee were married in 1934, after the three-year waiting period Patton had imposed, in the same church where he and Beatrice had been married.

By 1943 Waters was a lieutenant colonel in command of a tank battalion in North Africa. When his outfit landed at the port of Oran, some days after the invasion, he showed his concern for his men by "liberating" ten barrels of red wine that he saw on the docks. It was enough to fill the helmets of every soldier in his battalion, which they proceeded to do.

Things were off to a good start but such high living did not last long once they got into the desert, where they were lucky to get some greasy mutton stew with hardtack for breakfast on Thanksgiving morning. Historian Rick Atkinson notes that with their "cigarettes long gone, the men rolled dried eucalyptus leaves in toilet paper and pretended they were Chesterfields."

Their equipment was not very good either. Waters's unit was equipped with undergunned, obsolete M-3 General Stuart light tanks, which were no match for German panzers. The M-3 was described as a "fast, agile deathtrap" that burst into flames whenever a German 75mm tank shell hit.

Atkinson again: "Crewmen tumbled from the hatches, their hair and uniforms brilliant with flame, and they rolled across the dirt and tore away their jackets in burning shreds. Others were trapped in their tanks with fractured limbs, and their cries could be heard . . . as they burned to death in fire so intense it softened the armor plate." In contrast, whenever a shell from a Stuart's 37mm gun hit a panzer, it barely dented the much thicker armor.

Their leadership was weak too. Gen. Lloyd Fredendall, CO of the 4th Division, who was fanatical about not having his men exceed the speed limit, spent most of his time in his deeply fortified bunker far behind the front. Once, when Waters took him to Oran in a tank, he saw the general "just peeking out over the tank turret, [and] it disturbed me. I was riding on the outside of the tank. I felt it was a weakness and a failure. . . . Somehow I felt he just didn't know his business."

Sometime in December Patton managed to visit Waters in the field and the two men had a happy reunion. Waters told him about the battles he had been in and how one time a German bullet tore right through his uniform without touching him. "I was very much pleased with his attitude," Patton said, "and also the behavior of the men, who were very glad to see me." It was the last time they would see each other for over two years.

On Valentine's Day, February 14, Waters's outfit was overrun by a German attack on their vulnerable position, a hill on the road to Kasserine Pass, where the high command had ordered them to go. General Fredendall had even forbidden them to conduct any reconnaissance of the area around their position.

Their fifteen remaining puny Stuart tanks were up against ninety fast-moving panzers. As Waters put it, "they just outnumbered and outgunned us." Waters's men were quickly surrounded and cut off. They tried to hide in narrow streambeds and gullies, but many were betrayed by the locals.

"I had noticed some Arabs," Waters told an interviewer after the war. "Those Arabs over there were despicable people. As soon as the battle line moved from one direction to another, they invaded the battlefield and started robbing from the dead. They saw us get annihilated and get cut off so they came.

"I got out from under this overhanging ditch and here was a German patrol being led by three or four of these Arabs . . . they brought the German patrol in on me. They were about fifteen feet away from me . . . they shot at me and the burst from a burp gun went right on by me. They shot from the hip, otherwise they would have cut me right down and that would have been the end of that. It was about 4:00 in the afternoon, I guess, that I was captured."

He was marched down the hill to a German mobile command post where several German officers were sitting around listening to American dance music on the radio of a captured American half-track. They were very happy and boasted to Waters how they would win back Tunisia by the next day. "Tomorrow," they told him, "we will win the war."

They treated him well and took him in a motorcycle sidecar to a holding area fenced in with barbed wire and patrolled by German guards. He was then taken by truck with other POWs to the city of Tunis, where they were placed in small classrooms of a school. The next day large groups of American and British prisoners were marched out to the airport.

"The Germans were bringing in Italians in their tri-motored German Fokker aircraft. They would disembark the Italian infantry, would not even stop the engines, and then put us on board," Waters recounted in an oral history. They were flown to the town of Capua in Italy, close to Naples, and stayed there for several days. Then Waters and two other American officers traveled by train north through the Alps to a British POW camp outside the town of Eichstadt, near Frankfurt. All the while he and the others continued to be well treated.

At Eichstadt, Waters was interrogated for the first time by an English-speaking German who started out the questioning by saying, "We know who you are. You are General Patton's son-in-law. We even have your picture." Waters was amazed at how much they knew in detail about the complete organization of his outfit. He refused to tell them anything beyond his name, rank, and serial number, and his interrogator did not press the point or threaten him in any way. The two men talked a lot over the coming days and weeks, but Waters never revealed anything of military importance.

Finally, some four months after his capture, in June 1943, Waters and a number of other American POWs were sent 450 miles to the northeast to a camp designated as Oflag 64 (Officers Camp 64) outside of the town of Szubin in Poland. And there he would remain for the next year and a half, until his long march to Hammelburg.

Maj. Gen. Manton Eddy, CO of XII Corps, was not happy. For one thing he thought he was dying. Army doctors told him he would not live much longer if he did not have surgery for his extremely high blood pressure, which he refused to have as long as there was a war going on. (He lived until 1962, having relented later in the war.) And if the prospect of dying were not bad enough, now he had George Patton telling him to carry out an impossible-sounding mission to some place called Hammelburg.

Eddy had been in the army since 1916; he had fought in France in both wars, and in North Africa and Sicily in the second one, so he was used to following orders, even those he was vehemently opposed to, like the one he had just received. That day Patton wrote in his official diary, "[I] directed Eddy to send an expedition to the east about 60 miles for the purpose of recapturing some 900 American prisoners alleged to be held in a stockade there."

Reluctantly, Eddy placed a call to Brig. Gen. William Hoge, the CO of Patton's favorite outfit, the 4th Armored Division, a job he had been in for only four days. The fifty-one-year-old Hoge, a veteran, like Eddy, of both world wars, had led the construction of the 1,500-mile ALCAN highway in Alaska in only nine months at the beginning of World War II. After that he had commanded the 9th Division in France at the Battle of the Bulge and then captured the famous bridge at Remagen, the only intact bridge over the Rhine. And he had done that against orders.

When Hoge came to the phone, Eddy wasted no time getting to the point. "Bill," he told him, "George wants a special expedition sent behind the lines to pick up 900 prisoners at Hammelburg."

Hoge was a tough, no-nonsense commander, but he also had a larger than usual concern for the welfare of his men and did not believe in spending their lives needlessly. In addition, "Hoge had never liked Patton," according to *Raid!*, Baron, Baum, and Goldhurst's 1981 book on the Hammelburg mission. "He found the controversial commander to be mean and vainglorious, his habit of browbeating his subordinates unnecessarily a nettlesome, distracting waste of time."

Hoge's men were exhausted. They had been in constant combat for the previous thirty-six hours taking the bridge across the Main River at Aschaffenburg. Also, they were spread thin over a 25-mile front, and his men and the whole of Patton's Third Army had just been given orders to turn to the north. Hammelburg was toward the east.

And finally, he believed that sending a small force so far behind enemy lines was unnecessarily dangerous. They could easily be cut off and destroyed. And for what? What was so special about the POWs at Hammelburg to warrant taking such a chance? At the rate the Allies were advancing, Hammelburg would be overrun in a week or so anyway. Why the rush now? Hoge did not bother to point out his concerns to Eddy. He simply said that Patton's order was impossible to carry out, and assumed that the matter would end there. He should have known better.

That night Patton noted in his official diary that both Eddy and Hoge had argued against the raid on Hammelburg. However, for the public record, he gave a different interpretation of their reasons for objecting, making it seem as though they were doing so on his behalf, to protect his reputation. He wrote that they "were reluctant to do this because they said if I failed, I would be severely criticized. However, I do not believe that fear of criticism should prevent my getting back American prisoners, particularly as in the last death struggles of the Germans, our men might be murdered." He made no mention of their real reasons for arguing against the raid or his real reason for promoting it.

At 7:00 that evening, General Hoge had an unexpected and unwelcome visitor who had no problem getting in to see the general even though he was only a major. His name was Al Stiller, and he was one of Patton's most trusted aides. Actually, Stiller was more of a bodyguard and he was rarely out of sight of Patton. The story was told that Stiller practically worshipped Patton, and once, when the general was nervous before a talk, he looked down and saw Stiller looking up adoringly at him.

"You little son-of-a-bitch," Patton said. "You're supposed to guard me, not look at me!"

He had served with Patton as one of his original tank crewmen in World War I. After that war he became a Texas Ranger and always wore his trusty old Colt .45 with several notches carved into the grip to show the number of men he had shot and killed. He was not very tall compared to Patton, who called him "Shorty."

When Patton was due to leave for the invasion of North Africa, he received a telegram from his old sergeant asking if he could come along for the new war. Patton said yes, and Stiller showed up wearing his World War I uniform complete with leggings. Patton quickly got him a new outfit and off they went to war.

After Stiller saluted General Hoge, he announced rather tersely that he was there to go along on the raid to Hammelburg.

"But I thought the idea was shelved," Hoge said in surprise.

"No, sir," Stiller replied, "The general wants it to go on as planned."

The next morning, March 26, Patton showed up at Eddy's headquarters. The chief of staff told him that Eddy was not there.

"Pick up the phone and get Bill Hoge," Patton said sharply. "Tell him to cross the Main River and get over to Hammelburg."

"General," Eddy's chief of staff said, "the last thing Matt [General Eddy] told me before he left was that if you came by and told us to issue that order I was to tell you that I wasn't to do it."

Patton would ordinarily explode with anger at any man who talked to him in such a manner, but not this time. He spoke calmly and quietly.

"Get Hoge on the phone and I'll tell him myself."

"Bill," Patton said over the phone, "I want you to put this little task force together. Now get on it."

Patton went on to describe the details of how he wanted the operation to proceed, but Hoge persisted in objecting to the plan. "My people are exhausted," he told Patton. "The division is only at half strength as it is."

Patton refused to relent and at one point told Hoge, "Bill, I promise I'll replace anything you lose: every man, every tank, every half-track. I promise."

Hoge thought Patton sounded nervous and even more excitable than usual, his voice even higher pitched, but toward the end of the conversation, Patton tried to strike a triumphant and victorious note: "This is going to make the MacArthur raid on Cabanatuan look like peanuts, Bill."

Hoge gave up trying to object to the raid, but when the call from Patton ended, he called Eddy back and protested again. "What's so darned important about Hammelburg and a handful of prisoners of war?" Eddy had no answer to give to Hoge, or to himself.

Major Stiller, who had been listening in on the call to Patton, saw the look of bewilderment and concern on Hoge's face and quietly told the general what it was all about. In the words of Charles Whiting, "The 'Old Man' wanted Hammelburg liberated because his own son-in-law, Colonel John Waters, was a prisoner of war there. That was the purpose of the whole raid. . . . General William Hoge looked at the little major in blank, utter amazement while, outside, the background music to the war, the artillery barrage, rumbled on unnoticed. So *that* was the reason."

Hoge knew he could never tell anyone about this, not even the man he would assign the mission to, Col. Creighton Abrams of Combat Command B.

Everyone liked and admired thirty-year-old Abrams, who had grown up with the childhood nickname of "Tootsie." Patton considered him his top tank commander, on a par with himself. The son of a railroad mechanic, Abrams had always excelled in whatever he did. In high school he was the captain of his football team, president of his class, editor of the school newspaper, president of the scholastic honor society, and voted the boy most likely to succeed.

He graduated from West Point in 1936 with only mediocre grades but was well liked as the class prankster, playing practical jokes on anyone he could find. He was also a star of the academy's football team and was once listed in a Yiddish-language newspaper as a member of a proposed Jewish all-America football team. He was the only Methodist to make the list, but a lot of people continued to assume that anyone with a last name of Abrams must be Jewish.

He chose the cavalry and rose quickly after the war began. In combat he led his men from the front tank and always gave credit to them instead of hogging the limelight for himself, as many officers did. He led the relief into Bastogne to save the encircled 101st Airborne, which resulted in a cover story in *Life* magazine that made him a household name.

Abrams was a tough, aggressive leader who never hesitated to tell off anybody, regardless of rank, if he thought they were doing wrong or defaming his men. A few days before, he and his men were taking some bridges over a river when the Germans blew one of them up before the Americans could get across. Abrams got some men on the other side to establish a bridgehead, then ordered his engineers to build a pontoon bridge.

While waiting, Abrams took a break with Lt. Col. Harold Cohen. The two men were sitting on a log, eating eggs and drinking some schnapps, when General Hoge, then only two days into his new command, came along. Hoge looked around, saw the destroyed bridge, and asked, "What happened here, that you missed the bridge?"

Abrams made a half-hearted attempt to stand at attention while staring at his new commanding officer.

"General Hoge, I'd like to tell you something, sir. You've only been here with us for two days. Now I want to get something straight with you. You're talking to the champion bridge-getters that there are in the army. Now when we can't take a bridge, it can't be had. We don't want to be criticized by somebody who has only taken one."

Lesser men had their careers ruined for saying things not half as insulting as that, but Abrams got away with it without any repercussions. Hoge walked away and never said anything about the way Abrams treated him. He knew that Abrams could be counted on to get the job done, and that was more important to him than his vanity. The incident said a lot about both men.

When General Hoge called Abrams to tell him about the raid Patton was demanding deep into enemy territory, he was sure that Abrams would object on the same grounds he had. He was right. Abrams barked that the distance to Hammelburg was too long for the small force Patton wanted.

"If we have to go that far," Abrams said, "I want my whole command to go. Hell, a combat command can go anywhere."

His combat command was made up 4,000 men, 150 tanks, and its own field artillery, engineers, and logistical support. It could barrel through almost anything, but Hoge told him no, adding that Patton wanted a much smaller force and that it had to be ready to leave that night. Abrams replied that he wanted to make his case directly to Patton.

"You'll get your chance," Hoge told him. "General Patton is planning to come down to your command post later this morning."

As Abrams prepared his arguments against the raid, he knew deep down that even he had no chance of winning against Patton, and so he decided on the man who would lead the much smaller task force behind German lines. He was a tall, lanky combat veteran whom Abrams liked and respected more than just about any other officer in his command. If anyone could carry out the mission, he knew that Cohen, CO of the 10th Armored Infantry Battalion, would, or die trying.

Cohen, who was twenty-nine years old and spoke with a deep Southern accent, was from Spartanburg, South Carolina, where his family owned a textile factory. He had enlisted in the army in 1942. After getting through Officer Candidate School (OCS), he rose rapidly in rank thanks to his aggressive fighting ability. Abrams once said that he trusted no man in combat more than Cohen.

He did have one problem, though it had not interfered with his fighting the Germans so far. He was in constant pain from advanced bleeding hemorrhoids. They were so bad that he had to sit on an inner tube while riding in his jeep. And they were getting worse. All that day, while getting across the Main River and occupying Aschaffenburg, he had been sweating even though it was very cold, and several times he had felt as if he was going to faint.

Cohen was also exhausted from the previous days of engaging in heavy combat while trying to find a bridge across the Main River. He had found three of them, but before his men could cross, the Germans blew them up—one with an American tank halfway across.

Finally, he got his men over the fourth bridge, after his men cut the wires to the bombs strapped onto the framework of the bridge. Cohen led them into Germany near the town of Aschaffenburg and was trying to get some rest when he received a radio call from Abrams on March 26.

"Prepare your battalion for a special combat mission for General Patton, ETD [estimated time of departure] 1700." That was only a few hours away. Not long after, Abrams called Cohen to make sure he had received the message.

"I want you to disengage and withdraw," Abrams told him.

"I ain't never heard you talk like that since I've known you," Cohen said, surprised at being told to withdraw when he had just achieved his objective. Abrams repeated his order, but Cohen stubbornly challenged it.

"I'm in the middle of this goddamn town. How in hell can I do that?"

"I'm telling you in plain talk," Abrams said. "I just sent you a message to prepare for another mission. How are you going to do that without withdrawing?"

Cohen reluctantly withdrew his men and tried to get a few more hours of sleep before crossing back over the Main River.

At 2:00 P.M. Patton, Al Stiller, and General Hoge arrived at Abrams's headquarters and then moved on to Cohen's command post an hour later. When they were all assembled, Patton asked who was going to lead the mission to Hammelburg. Abrams said that he wanted to lead it and take his entire Combat Command B with him.

"You are not going," Patton said, "and neither is your combat command. This is to be a small force. Now, answer my question. Who is going to lead it?"

Abrams knew there was no point in arguing with Patton.

"Hal Cohen," he said, "10th Armored Infantry. If he's well enough. His piles are giving him a lot of trouble."

Patton repeated the word *piles* with an amused expression on his face, and then said to get a doctor as quickly as possible so they could find out if Cohen was up to the task. While waiting for the battalion surgeon to show up, Patton gave them a bit of hemorrhoid history.

"I don't want any dammed hemorrhoids lousing up an important mission," Whiting quotes Patton. "Napoleon's hemorrhoids defeated him at Waterloo. He couldn't sit a horse for long and had to direct the battle from his tent. If Cohen's ass is hurting, I don't want him going."

When the doctor arrived a few minutes later, they went into another room and Patton told Cohen to pull down his pants and bend over. The doctor took one look and made a whistling sound to indicate how bad the hemorrhoids were. Patton looked too.

"That is some sorry ass," Patton said. "My God, they're the size of golf balls."

He then told Abrams that Cohen could not go, asked him who he had in mind for a replacement, and reminded him that the mission had to start that night—in just a few hours, in fact.

"Excuse me, sir," Cohen said, even though the question had been directed at Abrams, "but I already have someone in mind and I'm sure Colonel Abrams will approve."

"Well," Patton asked impatiently, "who?"

Cohen pointed to a tall, twenty-four-year-old captain on the other side of the room and gave his name: Abe Baum. Abrams nodded and said that Baum was an excellent choice and that he had a highly impressive combat record. Patton motioned for Baum to join him off to one side and spoke softly to him so the others would not hear.

"Listen, Abe," Patton said to him. "It is Abe, isn't it? I thought so. You pull this off and I'll see to it that you get the Congressional Medal of Honor."

Baum did not hesitate with his reply, as disrespectful as it might have seemed. "I have my orders, sir. You don't have to bribe me."

Patton said nothing as he started to leave the room. Then he turned around and gestured toward Al Stiller. "Major Stiller will fill you in on the details."

The mission to Hammelburg, to be carried out by what came to be called Task Force Baum, was ready to begin.

CHAPTER 4

WHEN WILL THIS END?

BEFORE HE WAS SENT TO HAMMELBURG, JOHN WATERS SPENT A YEAR and a half as a POW at Oflag 64, near the Polish town of Szubin, some 200 miles northeast of Warsaw. It had been a boys' school before the war and at the center was a large, white, three-story stucco house, which the Kriegies called the White House.

The highest-ranking officers lived there, and Waters shared a room with three others. The room had its own toilet, a rarity in a POW camp, as well as a washstand. Surrounding the White House were a number of brick, stucco, and wooden huts where the rest of the 1,500 officers lived. Lt. Brooks Kleber, who had been captured at Normandy, said in an interview in 1985, "We lived in dormitories. We were not overcrowded. We had cubicles made out of beds and lockers. Our mattresses were stuffed with straw, which was tolerable."

Another former Kriegie, Capt. Roger Shinn, taken at the Battle of the Bulge, recalled in his 1972 book the day he and others entered the camp after days of marching and being crammed into filthy, freezing boxcars across war-torn Germany. After all that, Szubin seemed "almost less a prison than a haven." The German assistant commandant gave a speech "in which he welcomed us, told us that everything possible would be done here for our comfort and enjoyment, and that we in turn must obey orders strictly."

The Americans were in charge inside the barbed wire. The Germans controlled everything outside. Szubin had the reputation of being one of the best of all the German POW camps, but it was still a prison and none of the men knew how long they would have to serve time there.

Because of his rank, Waters found himself second in command of the Kriegies, with a no-nonsense former sergeant in World War I, Col. Tom Drake, as the senior officer. He ran the camp just like any American army base would be run back home. "I admired him," Waters said. "He was tough. He wanted everybody to soldier in the prisoner of war camp, and we did. He kept the morale of our people up. He required us to sleep on our trousers to keep them pressed. He required everybody to shave every day. He required us to keep our clothing in as good a shape as we could. He required us to exercise every day. He really inspired *esprit de corps* among our prisoners of war."

After a year at Szubin, Drake was repatriated because of severe ulcers and was replaced as American commander by Col. Paul Goode, known as "Pop," who had been captured in Normandy. Waters had known him at West Point, when Waters was a cadet and Goode was a member of the staff. He was just as tough and strict as Drake had been. Waters remained second in command.

The officers liked Colonel Goode, who went so far as to get a set of bagpipes to help keep up morale. Not everybody liked the noises he made trying to play the thing, but they did appreciate why he kept doing it, to keep up their spirits. And it helped.

The men kept a short-wave radio hidden from the Germans that allowed them to get the latest news from BBC broadcasts, which they trusted far more than the German radio news. Only a few of them listened, then they spread the news around camp to small groups one at a time using the code "The bird is going to sing." "Bird" was their name for the radio.

The daily lives of Waters and the other POWs were helped immensely by the YMCA, as represented by a Swede named Henry Soderberg, who visited the camp every two to three months. He brought in enough supplies and equipment for the men to have a variety of recreational programs to help them pass the time. "We had an incredible amount of activities," Kleber recalled. "We had a 3,000-book library. We had 'Szubin Prep,' which took its name from the closest town, in which high school and college-level courses were taught by the prisoners. We had a jazz band, a classical orchestra. There was a baseball league and a touch-football league."

They even published a daily one-page newspaper they called the *Oflag 64 Item*, with the slogan "Get wise—ITEM-ize." The issue of March 2, 1944, talked about the opening of the spring season of the Oflag 64 Theater, featuring *The Man Who Came to Dinner*, a three-act comedy written by George Kaufman and Moss Hart that had opened on Broadway in 1939.

That issue also described the beginning of the spring landscaping and gardening season and noted that Lt. Royal Lee had received the one-thousandth package from the States to arrive at the camp. It contained three cartons of Chesterfield cigarettes, which Lee was looking forward to trading for rations.

The Red Cross made sure that each man received a food parcel once a week to supplement the meager rations the Germans provided. The meat was taken out of all of the parcels and combined for use in the mess hall, but each man kept everything else for his own use, including milk, chocolate, cheese, and raisins. The Germans gave them a kind of foul-tasting ersatz coffee that some used to shave with, along with a sixteenth of a loaf of bread each day.

Lt. Jay Drake remembered that "barley was added to many of our soups. Along with the barley you also got the meal worms which, when cooked, sank to the bottom of your bowl. Since you could not afford to discard any food you never looked into your bowl as you spooned out the last of your soup." Despite the help from the Red Cross, they were always so hungry that they ate the worms.

"You worried about food," Lieutenant Kleber said after the war. He lost thirty-five pounds in Oflag 64. But lack of food was not the only problem the men faced each day despite all the programs and activities available. The greatest enemy they faced was boredom or apathy, particularly when the brutal winter set in. It was too cold to do much outside. Some men just lay in their beds all day in winter, too dispirited to participate in any of the activities that brought them out in warmer weather. Morale plunged along with the temperature.

The German guards left them alone most of the time. Some even became friendly. There was only one report of a guard ever hitting a POW, and in that case the American officer who saw it later wrote that the POW deserved what he got for behaving the way he did. The man was "an ass," he said.

Waters remembered that they "could 'tame' almost any German soldier if we gave him a D-bar [the four-ounce chocolate bar made by Hershey that came in Red Cross parcels] and cigarettes . . . those poor bastards were hungry. They were smoking dried blossoms from the basswood tree with a little bit of tobacco mixed in with it. They had no decent soap; they had no chocolate bars; and with the D-bar and the cigarettes . . . we could get just about what we wanted from the German enlisted men."

Lt. Robert Corbin, who had been captured in the battle for the German city of Aachen on the day after Thanksgiving in 1944, liked to tell the story of their bridge tournaments, which often went on for six hours at a time. Whenever a German soldier came into the room, "the first thing we would do in the camp was to say, 'Goon coming in!' Everybody would stop what they were doing and stare at this Goon as he walked around looking at our barracks. And I can tell you that the Germans always felt a little uncomfortable with forty or fifty pairs of eyes staring at him but this was our routine."

The POWs found out about the Normandy landings from three guards who came running into the camp, excited and happy at telling them the news before they heard it on the BBC. "Those poor bastards had been on the Russian front," Waters said, "those poor damn cripples who were guarding us. They had every 4-F'er of the worst sort, they was so poor. Frozen feet, frozen fingers. Broken arms and legs, but the Germans, those three Germans couldn't get in there fast enough to tell us that the US had invaded. They were so pleased about that. And they were fed up with that war, and with Hitler, the lower-ranking ones."

The prisoners were deliriously happy about the D-day landings, and many thought that the war would surely end soon and they would be free again. But the war did not end soon, and another winter came. On October 1, 1944, Waters wrote a cryptic line in the little notebook he called Remembrances. "And so another month begins. When will this end?"

Soon it was time for another sad Christmas and the start of yet another year, and there was still no end in sight to captivity. "Morale got lower and lower," Kleber wrote. "The Red Cross parcels stopped. Weather got colder. The guards told us the Russians were getting closer. Sometimes we thought we heard fighting."

By the middle of January, they began to see endless streams of refugees going by the camp, heading to the east. All day long, every day, they filed past: on foot, bicycles, wheelbarrows, and wagons piled high with mattresses, chairs, children, chickens, anything they could salvage.

It looked like the whole world was trying to get out of Poland. The POWs watched the never-ending columns with mounting excitement. Then, on January 20, 1945, the Germans told them to get ready to move the following morning. They too were going to try to get out of Poland.

~

When Patton left Abrams's headquarters, Abrams, Cohen, and Baum stared at one another, wondering what the hell was going on. Finally, Abrams looked at Major Stiller, whom Patton had left behind, and asked him point-blank what was so special about the place called Hammelburg.

"There's a POW camp there with 300 American officers in it."

"And?" Cohen asked impatiently.

"And," Stiller said, "Patton wants them liberated."

Cohen, Baum, and Abrams stared at Stiller with doubt and skepticism written all over their faces. They began firing questions at him, and looked even more skeptical at his answers. When they pointed out that their vehicles did not have sufficient range to go for 60 miles and back without refueling, Stiller nonchalantly suggested they take extra cans of fuel along with them, or simply capture more from the Germans.

When they looked at the maps Stiller provided and asked where, exactly, the POW camp was in relation to the town of Hammelburg, he did not have an answer. Nor was the precise location indicated on the map. Stiller told them they could always get that information from German soldiers they captured, or civilians in one of the several towns they would have to pass through to get to Hammelburg.

Baum asked where the rest of the division would be, in the hope that the main body of troops and tanks would be following closely behind them, so that he might be able to count on them for support. Stiller quashed that idea quickly by pointing out that Patton's army would be moving to the north while the task force went off to the east. They would be on their own.

When Baum asked exactly how many POWs they would find at Hammelburg, Stiller said he did not know for sure. The number of 300 he had said before was just an estimate, more of a guess, really. Baum pointed out that if there were a lot more prisoners, they would not have enough vehicles to bring them back, to which Stiller replied that they would have to use captured German vehicles. Finally, after there were no more questions to ask, Stiller got up to leave, but then turned around and announced that he would be going along with the task force.

There was a moment of shocked silence in the room before Baum said that he thought he was going to be in command of the mission. Stiller quickly assured him that he would, indeed, be in command. Then he shocked the three army men even more.

"The general wants me to get a taste of combat. I'm only going along for the laughs and a high old time."

That announcement only added to the suspicion of the other three. Everyone knew that it was not going to be a high old time, that generals' aides did not usually go along on combat missions, and that Stiller already had more than enough in the way of combat experience from World War I. In addition, just a few nights before, Stiller had been in one of the boats crossing the Rhine under fire. He did not need another "taste of combat." But there was nothing more to be said. What Patton wanted, Patton got.

When Stiller left the room, they all agreed that something was fishy about the whole thing, but that "orders were orders" and there was nothing they could do about any of it. As Baum got up and started to leave to prepare for the mission, he smiled at Abrams and Cohen and said, "Don't think you can get rid of me this easily. I'll be back."

After Baum left, Abrams angrily slammed his fist down on the field table Cohen had been using as a desk.

"What the hell is this all about?" he asked Cohen. "It just doesn't make sense. We are always asking men to take risks, but they are calculated risks. They know they have a chance. This mission doesn't have a chance and we both know it. If this task force does make it back, it'll be a miracle."

"Did we ever do anything like this before?" Abrams went on.

"Never," Cohen replied. "Any time we ever sent someone out through the lines into enemy territory, we damn sure followed, and in force."

Abrams got even angrier. He got up, stalked around the room, and kicked a chair that dared to get in his way.

"Damn, I just don't like it," Abrams said.

"Look," Cohen said, trying to calm Abrams down. "We've already upped their odds of succeeding."

"How's that?' Abrams asked.

"We gave them Abe Baum. If anyone can get them back, Abe can."

For a street kid of immigrant parents from the Bronx, Capt. Abraham Baum had come a long way. At 6 feet, 2 inches tall and weighing 162 pounds, he was a formidable presence, aided by a crew cut, a thin mustache, and a no-nonsense look about him. He was described as a cocksure, shrewd, and efficient fighter who quickly earned the respect and loyalty of every man in his outfit. Like Abrams and Cohen, he always led from the front and never expected his men to do anything that he would not.

Martin Blumenson writes that Baum "knew what the war was about and he was going about winning it in the most direct way he knew. His instincts were right and his training had been thorough. Nine months of combat had hardened him." It was said that if Baum could not take an objective, then it could not be taken.

His life before the army had hardened him as well. He did not have an easy childhood. His father had been a penniless immigrant from Russia who became a dressmaker, but his business went downhill, as did the whole American economy, after the Great Depression began in 1929. Abe was eight years old then. He later dropped out of high school when his father's business went bankrupt and started working as a pattern-maker for women's dresses.

He worked for a small company where "he soon displayed an innate feisty streak," according to combat historian Gerald Astor. "Angered because his weekly pay of seventeen dollars . . . fell far short of the prevailing wage of ninety dollars for a skilled operator, Baum locked his boss in the designing room and refused to release him until he granted an additional twenty dollars a week." Baum won.

Baum's life changed on December 7, 1941, when the Japanese bombed Pearl Harbor and America found itself in a war for which it was ill-prepared. Baum told his father that day that he wanted to enlist. "If I was younger, I would go myself," his father replied. Abe went to the nearest US Army recruiting station the next day, only to be told that his blood pressure was too low to be accepted. But that was not the end of the matter. "The doctor said, 'Go outside and jump up and down and then come back,'" Baum recalled in a 2013 interview. "And that's how I got in."

He wanted to go into the air corps, but he flunked his vision test and so was slated for ground duty. When he was asked what he had done in civilian life, he said that he had been a patternmaker for women's dresses. All the sergeant heard was "patternmaker," because that fit one of the categories on the army assignment list (tool and die maker), which sent Baum off to Fort Belvoir, Virginia, for training at the Engineer Replacement Training Center. As he said later, he barely knew how to use a saw or dig a ditch and there he was going into the engineers.

Growing up in the Bronx, which was predominantly Jewish, Baum was not prepared for the anti-Semitism he found in what he called "a redneck outfit." The regulars did not like people from big cities or ethnics of any kind, and he ended up being put in the boxing ring with a 250-pound guy who did not like the idea of fighting another GI any more than Abe did. "When we didn't go at it," Baum said, "the sergeant got furious and he jumped into the ring. And said, 'Now I'm going to demonstrate.' Well, I put him in the hospital. I beat him up so badly."

The sergeant got his revenge by pitting Baum against a professional boxer who "hammered" him, according to Baum. Still, Baum held his own well enough that the head of the division boxing program asked him to join the boxing team. When he refused, saying that he had joined up to fight the enemy, not other Americans, he was put on every hard and dirty work detail the sergeants could find.

"I decided that I had to get out of this chickenshit outfit," Baum said. He met another New Yorker, Ralph Combs, who felt the same way, and he suggested that the only way out for them both was to apply to Officers Candidate School. Combs was a college graduate; Baum admitted that he had not even gotten through high school, but Combs persisted. When Baum put in his request to try for OCS, the first sergeant laughed at him—but eventually allowed him to file his application.

"Well," Baum said, "the day that I was supposed to go to the [OCS examining] board, the sergeant was going to fix me because he didn't want me to go. He gave me garbage detail, cleaning sixty garbage cans, too far from where I had to be to change my uniform. So I said 'The hell with it. I'm going to go the way I am.' And I smelled. . . . And when I opened the door, there's these three majors in a state of shock."

To his surprise, he was accepted for OCS, but when he got there, he found that his lack of education worked against him, and he failed two out of his first three exams in the first week. If he failed one more, he would be out, but a fellow student helped him get through the program. Thus Abe Baum, a patternmaker for women's dresses, was commissioned a second lieutenant and assigned to the 4th Armored Division. He was going to war.

The 4th Armored Division, then under the command of Maj. Gen. John Wood, landed on Utah Beach a month after D-day, on July 11, 1944, and went into action not long after among the infamous hedgerows around the town of St. Lo. "Naturally, I was afraid," Baum said after the war. "But there was so much to do that you didn't have time to think about your fear. My father had always taught me to discipline myself, to exert self-control and not to let emotions interfere." He felt fortunate to have Captain Cohen as his immediate superior.

"Harold was, let's put it, street smart," Baum said, "[though] not to the type of street I came from." Baum knew that Cohen came from a more privileged background, but added that they both adjusted to difficult situations and knew what they were doing, despite their different backgrounds. Baum later described Cohen as "a very good battalion commander. He had good quality, a good leadership ability. The men loved him."

The 4th Armored Division fought relentlessly through the hedge-rows and onto the open fields and reached the banks of the Seine by late August, just one month after they had arrived in France. They quickly became Patton's favorite outfit. By then Baum had earned two Bronze Stars and one Silver Star for outstanding combat performance. And along with the rest of the division, he felt confident in their fighting ability, if not in their equipment, which he said "was not usually as good as the Germans'. But we had more of it. When something was shot or broke down, we could replace it."

He felt greater confidence in his fellow officers and men, who were mostly from the Northeast. He experienced very little anti-Semitism, even though General Wood had deliberately chosen more Jewish officers than were usually found in any one outfit. When a visiting high-ranking officer from the Inspector General's office in Washington looked through his officers' roster, he said, "You've got a lotta Hebes." Wood replied instantly, saying, "I wouldn't have as good a division if I didn't have these men."

About a month after landing in Europe, Baum was advancing through a field near the Maginot Line when "sure enough, I blow up in the minefield. I heard a click. And then I turned quickly and the charge at the waist level blew. And I turned quick enough to get the charge throughout my buttocks and my legs. . . . And I ended up, I must have had maybe forty pieces of shrapnel throughout my body."

He was taken to a newly opened American hospital, where all the shrapnel was removed. Next door there was an Air Corps Rear Echelon Club, where there was "dancing, drinking, you know, really all of that." Baum loved to dance and was the hit of the parties with all the nurses until one night he danced so vigorously that all eleven stiches in his wounds popped open. After that orders were issued to all the nurses that anyone caught giving clothes to Captain Baum would be severely dealt with.

Normally, when released from a hospital, all officers and men were sent to a replacement depot and from there assigned to a different unit.

Baum was determined to go back to his own outfit, and so he arranged for a private from his unit to borrow a car and the insignia of a colonel and show up at the hospital to check him out "under orders" back to his own men. Abe Baum was sometimes a little free with the rules.

～～

The details of the mission to Hammelburg were worked out quickly that afternoon of March 26. There was no time to linger over decisions. The force would include eleven officers and 282 enlisted men, a total combat unit of 293 men, consisting of both tankers and infantry. None would walk; there was no time for that.

They would get to Hammelburg in fifty-three vehicles, including ten Sherman medium tanks, five M-5 Stuart light tanks (the same kind Waters had used in North Africa two years before), twenty-seven M-3 half-tracks, three 105mm mounted assault guns, along with six jeeps and a maintenance Weasel, an open vehicle on tank treads made by Studebaker. Two of the half-tracks were loaded with extra cans of gasoline.

The Shermans were taken from C Company of the 17th Tank Battalion and were commanded by 2nd Lt. William (Bill) Nutto. The lighter Stuart tanks came from D Company from the same battalion and were led by 2nd Lt. Bill Weaver. The self-propelled assault guns were commanded by T/Sgt. Charles Graham. Capt. Robert Lange led the twenty-seven half-tracks, taken from Company A of the 10th Armored Infantry Battalion. The nine-man reconnaissance platoon led by 1st Lt. Norman Hoffner rode in three jeeps, each of which had a .30-caliber machine gun mounted behind the driver.

One man chosen for Task Force Baum felt as though he was going home again, and he was not happy about it. T/Sgt. David Zeno had grown up about 10 miles from Hammelburg in a town where his father was a horse dealer. Zeno had left Germany at the age of sixteen in 1930, three years before Hitler came to power, because he recognized that there would be no future for Jews in Germany.

He became a butcher in New York, and when he was drafted and sent to Europe, he became a cook for then captain Creighton Abrams. By 1944 his unit had taken so many casualties that clerks and cooks became tankers, and Zeno was wounded in action on Abrams's mission to Bastogne. By March 1945, back to front-line duty, he found himself somehow assigned to Task Force Baum as, of all things, one of only two medics to take care of almost 300 men.

As Baum's outfit got ready for action that day, Zeno worried about what would happen if they took heavy casualties. How could he cope? And then, "Suddenly, as if in a vision, Dave Zeno knew they would be hit, and hit bad," in Charles Whiting's words. "Ever since he had been wounded on the Rhine, he could feel that sort of thing, almost as if he had some sort of divining device in his bones."

Another refugee from Hitler was also going along on the raid. PFC Irving Solotoff, whose parents had been able to get the family out of Vienna just in time, had seen lots of action. His job had been to go to German homes and tell the owners that they either had to make room for American officers to move in with them or move out and find somewhere else to live.

The night before the raid, he had been invited to go to a German brothel. Two young women had refused to leave their house, and when the madam and three more women promised him a riotous night for himself and five of his buddies, he decided that there were already too many homeless Germans. He ran back to his camp to round up five more guys when his CO stopped him and told him to report to Captain Baum, who needed an interpreter for a special raid. To himself, he said, "It's suicide to go with Baum on a mission like this."

The mission had a lot of strikes against it from the beginning. The men were exhausted, having slept only one night out of the previous four. There was no time for a thorough briefing prior to the mission. Baum had barely enough time to inform his key subordinates about where they were going and what they were supposed to do when they got there.

The terrain they would have to pass through was very rugged. Many of the main roads were bordered on one side by steep hills full of trees and on the other side by a river. The soldiers would have to traverse at least two bridges, which could easily be blown up by the Germans before the Americans could cross. An even worse possibility would be that the Germans blew them up *after* they crossed, preventing them from getting back.

No one knew for certain how many prisoners they would find at Hammelburg, or what their physical condition might be. If there were too many to ride back in the vehicles, then some of them would have to walk through enemy territory for the 60 miles back to American lines. Major Stiller had said they would have to deal with only 300 POWs, but his figure was way off.

There were actually five times that number, far too many to ride back on however many vehicles might be left in Task Force Baum. Those who were too weak would have to be left behind at Hammelburg for the Germans to recapture.

Another problem was insufficient fuel for the vehicles to reach the target and return, despite all the extra jerry cans they loaded on the half-tracks. To get back to American lines, they would have to find more gas from German sources, and no one knew where they were, assuming that any existed. In fact, no one knew much of where anything was because there were only fifteen maps for the 293 troops involved, and even some who had been given maps had little chance to study them before it was time to leave.

An analysis of the raid conducted a half century later by the Strategic Studies Institute at Johns Hopkins University concluded that "Task Force Baum would have to avoid the enemy to survive; stealth was another necessary ingredient for mission success. Yet, no alternate roads were planned if the primary route became untenable. Nor were any return routes identified for expeditious movement back to friendly territory. Portions of the route would leave the unit with no option but to fight any Wehrmacht troops in its path. . . . In sum, planning for the Hammelburg raid did not measure up to the difficulty of the task."

There simply had not been enough time for sufficient planning. Patton had ordered them to leave by that evening, and there was no changing his mind.

CHAPTER 5

THE JEEP WAS RED WITH BLOOD

GETTING THROUGH THE TOWN OF SCHWEINHEIM, ONLY A FEW HUNdred yards from the Americans' front line, was supposed to be easy. That was what everyone said. According to intelligence estimates, Task Force Baum would face only minor resistance getting through the first German town on their way to Hammelburg. "The town was reported not to have much in it," Cpl. Bill Smith, one of the tank drivers, said after the raid, "but when you hear that, watch out!"

It was up to Pancake and Tessier to make sure that Baum and his men got through Schweinheim and on their way to Hammelburg that night. Capt. Richard Pancake and Capt. Adrian Tessier were the two company commanders of Combat Command B chosen by Creighton Abrams to attack and secure the half-mile-long main street of the village of Schweinheim so that Abe Baum's men could quickly speed through it and continue on their way.

Pancake and Tessier were both experienced combat leaders who worked well together as a team. The radio code they used with each other was "Chicken, this is Shit." Some weeks before, Tessier had captured a German general who refused to surrender to a mere captain. Tessier told him that he could either surrender to him or stay where he was, permanently. The general said he would prefer to stay, and so Tessier shot him on the spot.

Before the attack was due to begin, Baum spoke to them both. "Pancake, Tess," he said, "I've got to get through there fast. You've never let me down. Get that goddamn street as fast as you can." At exactly 9:00 P.M., a massive artillery barrage opened up on the town and directly behind it Pancake's tanks and Tessier's infantry rushed forward, but they got bogged down right away. The town was far from empty of German troops, and the artillery barrage had not reduced their effectiveness.

The Germans opened up with Mauser machine guns, rifles, and deadly Panzerfausts, their much better version of American bazookas. The Germans fired so many Panzerfausts that the Americans later referred to Schweinheim as "Bazooka City." One German soldier stood up in the open, raised his Panzerfaust to his shoulder, and got off a shot at the lead American tank. It was a direct hit. The tank exploded and burst into flames, blocking the column behind it. Pancake jumped out of his own tank farther back and spotted the company clerk, Cpl. Lester Powell, at the wheel of one of the jeeps.

"Get that tank out of there," Pancake yelled to him. Powell, who had been an undertaker (among other things) before the war, pulled his jeep up next to the burning tank, climbed up on top, and went down inside the hatch. Four of the crew were dead and the fifth was unconscious with one leg blown off. Powell drove the still-burning tank off the road and onto the sidewalk, clearing the way for the rest of the tanks, and then pulled the wounded man out.

As he dragged the unconscious tanker back to his jeep, Powell was hit and badly wounded but he still managed to drape the wounded soldier across the hood of his jeep and drive him back to the nearest field station. "Pancake saw that Powell's jeep was red with blood," *Raid!* reveals. "The next thing Powell remembered was awakening at a hospital in England several weeks later; his actions at Schweinheim earned him the Silver Star and a Purple Heart."

Meanwhile, the second tank in line was hit by a German grenade. Thinking they had been hit by a Panzerfaust, which could quickly set the tank on fire, the crew got out and scrambled to safety. When they saw they had only been hit by a grenade, they started back to their tank but a German beat them to it. He started up the engine, swung the turret around to face the Americans, and opened fire.

While the battle for Schweinheim raged on, an increasingly impatient Baum was approached by Major Stiller, Patton's bodyguard, who made the obvious comment that they were behind schedule.

"We're late."

"I might not be able to reach Hammelburg before dawn," Baum replied. "We need the cover of darkness."

The success of the plan depended on being able to reach the POW camp before daylight without being detected by the Germans. Stiller asked him if there was another way they could reach Hammelburg. Baum shook his head. Any other approach would take much too long, giving the Germans more time to send in troops to stop them. Perhaps reflecting his increasing frustration about the whole mission, Baum came right out and asked Stiller why an aide to General Patton was going along.

"It's important to General Patton," Stiller said and then went on very matter-of-factly to say that Lieutenant Colonel Waters was one of the prisoners in the camp. *Raid!* presents Baum's recollection of the conversation:

"Who's Colonel Waters?" Baum asked.

"He's Patton's son-in-law. Didn't you know that?"

"No," Baum said. "How does Patton know he's in Hammelburg?"

"He knows," Stiller replied. "Johnny's been a prisoner of war for over two years and Patton has kept track of his movements all along. We're going to get him out. I'm the only one who knows what he looks like."

"Is that why you have your own jeep," Baum asked, "to drive him back?"

"We've got to get there first," Stiller said.

"I wasn't too happy about it," Baum said later. At the time, he was livid with rage but said nothing. He was worried about what his men would think if they knew the real reason behind the raid, and that they would blame him, thinking that he knew all along.

Fifty years later, in 1995, military historian Richard Whitaker interviewed Baum and wrote, "After hearing this [from Stiller], and knowing that 300 men were about to risk their lives for one man, [Baum] considered pulling the plug and aborting the mission. However, after collecting himself Baum hoped that the rest of his men would see it as he did, a job to be done." The mission to Hammelburg was still on, if they could ever get past Schweinheim.

The battle raged on in the little village, with the American infantry fighting from door to door and Abrams having to send in more troops. Author Charles Whiting sets the scene: "The foot soldiers ran to the first house. Swiftly the wooden door was kicked in. A grenade was lobbed. The inside of the kitchen exploded with a roar in a brilliant blinding flash of red and yellow. A sergeant shot forward, firing his grease gun from the hip. The kitchen was empty, save for a dead German lying in the debris of the floor. Raising his machine pistol, the sergeant fired a long rapid burst through the ceiling [to kill any Germans who might be hiding on the second floor] and then tackled the stairs. The first house was taken, but there were plenty more to come."

The tanks continued advancing down the street, when suddenly the rear tank was hit. The other tankers knew that if they were counter-attacked they would be trapped. They could not back up with a disabled tank blocking the single narrow road. This time the crew of the tank that was hit stayed inside and found that the engine still worked. The driver moved the huge gear level into reverse and gunned the engine. The tank roared backward at a high speed, clearing up the road jam.

By then it looked like every house in town was on fire or a heap of rubble from the tank shells, and a huge layer of smoke covered every-thing. German troops were still holding on, though, and Task Force Baum was getting more and more behind schedule.

Baum jumped in his jeep and raced toward the blazing town, where he yelled to Captain Pancake that he could not wait any longer; he had to get through the town *now*. They were already three hours late, which meant that they could not reach Hammelburg as planned, before daylight.

"It's no good," Pancake said. "I've got resistance in ten houses up ahead. Take another hour, I reckon."

"Goddamnit, Pancake, listen to me. I can't wait any longer. Get your tanks up on the sidewalks—about every twenty yards. We'll use 'em like signposts. We're barrel-assing through. Got that? Get those damn tanks going."

Baum next went to Captain Tessier and told him to get his infantry out of the way because Baum was coming through in five minutes come hell or high water. Years later Baum said, "They weren't able to completely clean the area for me to go through. So I got sick and tired. I waited three hours. And those three hours cost me surprise. And I went ahead and told them to get out of the way and we're coming through."

He took his place behind the sixth tank in his mile-long column and gave the order to go. "Well, we just barreled through. I mean, our instructions to everybody [were] not to stop for anything but just to go. And fortunately we went through. We got through without any problem." But "everything started to go downhill right then and there."

Cpl. Robert Zawada agreed with Baum's analysis in an interview many years later when he said, "The whole episode was a failure right there. That's where the mission failed."

The situation was actually worse than Baum or anyone else knew at the time. At German Army headquarters in Berlin, 250 miles away, scattered, vague reports were coming in of an American attack on Schweinheim. There were no accurate figures on the size of the American force, but they knew it was in Patton's area, and so they assumed that he was making another one of his quick and deadly attacks. The Germans knew they had to quickly mobilize and reinforce their troops in the area to meet this new threat. They had no idea they were dealing with only 300 American troops.

⌐◢━◣⌐

Lt. Col. John Waters never forgot the day he and his fellow Kriegies left Oflag 64 outside of Szubin, Poland, and started their long trek to the west. Years later he recalled the particulars: "We had blizzards; we had snow; we had subzero weather; we had rain; you name it and we had it. It was bitter. . . . The march resembled my idea of what it must have looked like when Napoleon's outfit was leaving Moscow."

It was January 21, 1945, two months before the battle at Schweinheim and the start of Task Force Baum's 60-mile run to Hammelburg. The Kriegies from Szubin, 362 miles away, would take five weeks to get there, and for much of that time, they were barely ahead of the advance of the Russian Army. A total of 1,350 POWs started the march; 490 of them would reach Hammelburg.

When they left Szubin, they joined the endless streams of hundreds of thousands of refugees whose columns they had been watching from the safety of the camp for days. Now they were refugees themselves. Waters described the scene: "Old men, old and younger women, and very young children with fear written in their faces, cold and freezing. Sitting in these wagons, full of hay, one horse pulling them on a shaft with no horse on the off side. . . . Those that couldn't ride, trudging along in the snow, done up in all their black clothing and just moving down the road."

The day before the march, the men had loaded up as much as they could carry from their store of Red Cross supplies in the way of food, clothing, and, of course, cigarettes. Lt. Jay Drake remembered, "I had a long Polish overcoat, socks used for mittens, long underwear bottoms used as a hat, face mask, and scarf. . . . We each took one blanket rolled and carried over our shoulder with the ends tied together at our belt line."

They left their camp walking through 6 inches of snow and well below zero temperatures. Those too weak or sick to make the trek were left behind in the hospital at Szubin, while an unknown number decided to hide in a tunnel they had dug and wait for the Russians to get there. By the sound of the firing, it would not be all that long.

The marching POWs spent most of their nights trying to sleep and get warm in barns. The first night, Lt. Robert Corbin decided to sleep with the sheep in the neighboring barn, thinking that it would be a lot warmer there. "The unfortunate part about it was that the sheep didn't sleep. They were awake all night," he later reported.

Some of the men (no one is sure of the exact number) were too weak and sick to keep up the pace in the freezing cold and snow. The Germans took them away in trucks or put them in boxcars and supposedly sent them to other camps. Of course no detailed personnel records were kept during the march, and so no one knows with certainty what happened to them.

Others decided to try to escape, which was not difficult to do much of the time during the march. "We saw them move off across the fields," Capt. Roger Shinn wrote years later. "How many reached freedom I don't know. It was not the guards who kept us from escaping in those days; we could have easily evaded them. But in the brutal weather, without food, a man might easily die. Certainly he would have to seek shelter. Few of us knew much Polish, German or Russian. And meeting an invading army is always dangerous, the more so when we know nothing of their language or tactics and little of their location. So most of us marched."

One morning about thirty prisoners decided to remain behind in the barn they had used the previous night, while the rest of the men lined up outside and marched away. When the lingerers left the barn and started heading back toward the Russians, they were found by a company of SS troops who, luckily, did not kill them on the spot, but instead returned them to the column. The next morning, when they assembled in front of another barn, the German commander ordered his men to spray the barn with machine-gun fire. No one tried staying behind anymore.

Those who managed to escape and be taken in by the Russians were sent on foot to Warsaw. From there they went by train on a series of often interrupted journeys to Odessa and then Greece. Finally, they were put aboard steamers and eventually made their way to America in late June, some six months after they had left Szubin. Most of those who remained German prisoners and went to Hammelburg got home sooner than that.

According to Shinn, the guards were "a conglomerate group, mostly of 4-F-ers unfit for combat duty. Many of them were from Austria or Poland and had no love for the Germans. Most of them were old, and some were physical wrecks. A number had been wounded in battle and assigned to this less rigorous duty. There were no more than two or three who had any enthusiasm for the war. Many of them became friendly with us before long."

The German commander during the march was Oberst Schneider, and the men agreed that he was not too bad, for a German. He sometimes ranted and raved at them but his bark was usually worse than his bite, and he was never deliberately cruel to them. Shinn remembered that he seemed to feel an obligation toward them, "which he took seriously. His notion of what he should do for us in the way of food and shelter was not a very high one, but he would not fail in it. And all the while, perhaps with an eye fixed on the future when we would be conquerors and he a prisoner, he tried to impress us with the efforts he made on our behalf."

Col. "Pop" Goode still led the Americans and was out in front every day despite his being so much older than the men. And he continued to insist that they behave in strict military fashion. Sometimes, seeing how weary he was, the German commander offered him a lift in his car to ease the strain on him, but Goode always refused. If his men had to march, then so would he. "He was an inspiring sight," Shinn said, "carrying under his arm, of all things, a set of bagpipes."

The Americans met a lot of civilians along the way as they passed through one town after another. The Poles were invariably quite friendly to them when they found out they were Americans. Corbin wrote about going through a Polish town where, "within minutes, they had opened their doors and literally whisked hundreds of us into their homes. I went into a home with two old Polish ladies and they hugged me and kissed me, saying, 'Americanish, Americanish.' They handed me a loaf of bread and wanting to reciprocate I gave them a pack of cigarettes. They immediately gave me another loaf of bread and so I gave them another pack of cigarettes."

In another Polish town, a young boy came up to the column of prisoners and asked if they had any soap. When Corbin gave him a piece of soap, the boy reached into his pocket and pulled out a pile of onions and handed it to him. The more soap the boy got, the more onions he gave in return. That night, Corbin said, they had a feast with Polish potatoes and onions. In other towns, Poles simply handed them food as they marched past, without asking for anything in return.

At yet another location, the people handed out so much cheese and bread to the Americans as they passed through that the German soldiers stationed there became angry. "As a small boy passed a piece of bread to a prisoner, a German lieutenant yelled at him. The boy turned to run, and the officer struck him with a 'potato masher' hand grenade. No wonder the Poles hated the Germans," Shinn lamented.

The men found less generosity when they passed through towns in Germany, but they were still sometimes able to barter for bread with cigarettes, of which they had a plentiful supply thanks to the Red Cross packages they had received in their camp in Poland. Cigarettes were better than money.

"We could have bought half of Germany for cigarettes," Corbin said. "Every Kriegie in Germany learned to say 'Cigaretten fur Brot.'" Even the guards longed for American cigarettes, and they often managed to get the prisoners extra food in return for some smokes. Waters said that the German civilians they saw "knew the war was lost. They knew it was over. They were dejected, yet inwardly happy. The military people knew it was lost, too."

Despite the bartering and generosity from Poles and even some Germans, the men were almost always hungry, particularly when they got into Germany. The German daily ration given to them consisted of a cup of ersatz foul-tasting coffee in the morning and one-third of a loaf of bread at night, together with very weak soup or boiled potatoes.

Hunger was "a haunting sensation," Shinn wrote. "It never left us. This was a hunger we had never known before. It was the hunger of men who marched every day, who could never fill their stomachs or find in food the energy they needed. We felt the weakness in our bodies and knew that we were getting thin. Sometimes we gnawed on 'cow-beets' that we found in barns, a vegetable never grown for human consumption. Then we stopped because we theorized that they made us sick, a shaky theory since we were sick much of the time anyhow. . . . Hour after hour on the march we talked of food. For food was our obsession."

"Toughest day yet," Colonel Waters wrote in his diary on February 22, one month after the march had begun. Historian Rick Atkinson adds more details: "Survivors studied their own stool like sheep entrails, for portents of illness; some chose not to wash rather than sponge away body oils that might provide a thin film against the cold. Starving men described the lavish meals they intended to devour when they got home, or concocted elaborate menus and lists of memorable restaurants where someday they hoped to dine again."

Once out of Poland and into Germany, the ever-shortening column headed north toward the Baltic Sea. They would march three or four days in a row, and then sometimes were allowed to rest for a day or two before starting out again. Waters and the others often had the impression that the Germans were not exactly certain of where they were going, or what they would find once they got there.

Waters said in a postwar interview that "the German colonel Oberst Schneider always said we'd be going down the road 12 more miles to this town and they are going to have a train waiting there. . . . Well, you'd go down the 12 miles and get to the town and there isn't a train in sight. There is no train coming. There is no train for our men. 'Okay,' he'd say, 'we are going on another 15 miles tomorrow. Going on to another station, yes, I'm going to lay on another train for you,' Oberst Schneider would say. 'I'll have it all there and pick you up.' No train. Well, we just keep doing that, and finally we went 300 miles."

They arrived at the little picture-postcard village of Siggelkow, near Parchim, about 100 miles south of Lubeck and Rostov on the Baltic coast. They stayed there almost a week and would have been happy to have stayed longer. "Siggelkow was our favorite town in all of Germany," according to Shinn, "the ideal place to vacation after our . . . march."

The men lived in barns located in the village, where there was a thriving black market and people more than happy to trade food for American soap and cigarettes. The Kriegies bartered for eggs, sugar, jam, oatmeal. In addition the guards fed them soup, boiled potatoes, and bread every day, and another batch of Red Cross parcels arrived. "We feasted," Shinn said. "All day long, until blackout, we cooked and enjoyed for the first time such delicacies as pancakes." Shinn even got to send a postcard home.

Oberst Schneider dutifully repeated the order he had often given during the march: that POWs were not allowed to trade or barter with civilians. The men listened, as they always did, and went right on trading out in the open in full view of the guards. The only time there was trouble was when a few of the men wandered off by themselves to a neighboring town to trade for even more food.

They were doing well until their knock on the door of one house was answered by a German soldier who lived there. They were given a dressing-down by Schneider, who told the men that they were behaving in an ungentlemanly fashion and had betrayed him once again after all he had done for them. He put them in solitary confinement for a few hours and nothing more was said or done about it.

Finally, on March 7, a train came and the prisoners' "holiday" was over. They marched a few miles to the railway station in Parchim and were herded aboard the familiar French freight cars of World War I vintage referred to as "40 Hommes ou 8 Chevaux." "You were just put in there and locked up," Waters said. "In some of the cars there wasn't room to lie or sit down except by taking turns at doing it. And they wouldn't let you off until they got good and ready, although the trains stopped frequently. Then they let you off a few at a time to go and relieve yourself and then get back on."

The conditions in the cars were terrible, and the men worried about being bombed, because Allied fighter planes roamed over all of Germany at will, strafing and bombing anything that moved. They particularly liked to go after moving trains because they presented a challenging target and blew up spectacularly when a locomotive was hit.

The temptation to try to escape ran high, but Waters and the others knew that the war was nearly over. "Why have a man shot at the very end when two weeks or three weeks more he could live through it," Waters reasoned. It was not worth the risk. The train rolled through central Germany, passing the bombed-out cities of Weimar and Magdeburg before stopping at the town of Hammelburg two days later, on March 9. The Germans kept them on the train overnight before unlocking the boxcars and letting them out. They marched for an hour through the lovely, gently rolling hills of Bavaria before Oberst Schneider assembled them all on a hilltop near the camp and gave them his farewell address.

"We have had a long and hard trip," he said. "You have walked 350 miles and the weather was very difficult. At the beginning of the trip I promised you that I would never leave you for a single day. I have kept that promise. Now . . . when you go through the gates, you will leave my command. I have thought of myself as your protector and have done all I could for you. I wish you all good fortune and a happy return home."

As the men turned toward the barbed wire of Oflag XIIIB, their new home, a feeling of oppression came over many of them at the look of the place. For the past five weeks, they had not been behind wire fences, and now a gate was about to close them in again in a camp that looked like their worst nightmares come true. They had never thought they would be homesick for Szubin, but many of them were just that when they saw what awaited them at Hammelburg.

CHAPTER 6

SOMEBODY KNEW WE WERE COMING

CONQUERING HERO LED THE WAY OUT OF SCHWEINHEIM HEADING EAST on Reichstrasse 8, Highway 8 on American maps. The tank's commander, S/Sgt. Robert Vannett, had been due to be rotated back to the United States two weeks before, but his closest friend, the outfit's sergeant major, talked him out of it so they could both be rotated together the following month. Now, as Vannett led the column through the dark, moonless night, he wondered if he had made the wrong decision.

The light tanks led the way, followed by the jeeps, the medium tanks, the half-tracks, the 105mm guns, and then the mechanical Weasel bringing up the rear. A large white star was painted on every American vehicle for quick identification; since these also served as a perfect aiming point for the enemy, they had been covered with daubs of mud. The roaring engine exhausts, shrill tank sirens, and clanking tank treads made a fearsome noise that spread out in advance of the mile-long column to announce its presence.

Tank commanders stood in their open hatches the way Creighton Abrams wanted all his tankers to do as a sign of support for the infantry who accompanied the tanks. He believed that tankers should have no more protection than the guys who went along with them on foot. For the first part of the run to Hammelburg, however, the infantry were riding on the tanks and in the half-tracks so the force could maintain speed. When they met the enemy, they would climb down to do battle.

At 12:30 A.M. on March 27, a mere half hour after they had left Schweinheim, the column raced through the village of Bois-Brule

Kaserne, taking small-arms fire but not slowing down. The tankers fired their machine guns at anything that looked like it might house German soldiers while the infantry tossed out grenades. Fifteen minutes later, they roared through Haibach/Gummersbach, where they received some sporadic fire but did not reduce their speed.

"When we entered a town," Baum said later, "if we got any fire I gave the command to fire. . . . All weapons were fired at suspicious places. No high-explosive shells were fired from the tanks at night while passing through the towns because the column would have to stop."

Sgt. Donald Yoerk, whose tank was named *City of New York*, remembered the peaceful scenes when they roared at top speed near another town later in the morning. In *Raid!*, Baum and his coauthors summarize Yoerk's viewpoint: He saw "German officers hurrying along the streets with their briefcases, civilians on their way to work and German soldiers exiting from bars with girls on their arms. He saw guards goose-stepping on sentry duty. As his tank whizzed by a hospital, Yoerk saw the windows filled with the smiling faces of pretty nurses who waved gaily." He waved back, feeling like a sightseer.

By 1:00 A.M., they reached Strassbessenbach, where they found German civilians out in the street to watch them pass. They stopped for a moment to ask directions and handed out cookies and cigarettes to the eager locals. No shots were fired. Everything was friendly, and a man gave them directions to Highway 26, their next destination.

As they left town, Baum gave orders to knock down all the telephone poles they came across to prevent any of those friendly Germans from calling ahead to announce the US presence to the German Army. The tanks slowed, swerving off the road at each pole, which they found easy enough to remove, seeing as German poles were much shorter than those in the States.

At the rear of the line of vehicles, Lt. Allen Moses, who had washed out of flight school and was now commanding a platoon of infantry, saw Captain Baum's jeep drop out of the column and race back to Moses's half-track. Baum was worried that, even though all the telephone poles were upended, the wires might still be intact, allowing calls to go through.

Baum ordered Moses to stop at each pole and use wire cutters to slice through the lines. In *Raid!*, Baum recalls that "Moses hated jumping from the half-tracks, because his helmet always thumped his skull. He thought that hundreds of thousands of men were going to be bald after the war because they had to jump from half-tracks, tanks, and 2½-ton trucks so often."

As the night wore on and the column continued to thunder through more towns, the men saw more and more white sheets hanging from the houses, signifying surrender. That was not a good sign. As PFC Bob Zawada, a radio operator, put it, "Somebody knew we were coming."

By 2:30 that morning, Baum and his men had reached the town of Laufach, where they stopped briefly to get directions from some civilians. Nearly 60 years later, in 2003, a German army officer, Lt. Col. Peter Domes, made a detailed study of the Hammelburg raid. He traced the route Baum had followed, mile by mile and town by town. Among the locals he met in Laufach was a woman whose mother had told her about the day the Americans came.

"It was three o'clock in the morning," the woman told Domes, "and my mother, who was a fifteen-year-old girl at the time, saw an endless column of tanks going by. They were twenty meters from her and she thought the war was over. Some soldiers asked another girl, an eighteen-year-old by the name of Josefine, for food and coffee. She replied that she hadn't got enough food for herself, and as for real coffee, well, she hadn't seen any of that for years. The landlord of an inn offered the soldiers some watery beer . . . they didn't think much of it."

As the column continued on through Laufach, they passed a German military base with what they later reported to be as many as 400 German troops assembled on the parade ground doing their morning exercises. Their rifles were neatly stacked nearby. They were so near, 2nd Lt. Bill Weaver said, that he could hear the German leader shouting commands. As they got closer, Sergeant Vannett opened up with his machine gun and began mowing down the enemy.

Later research by Domes reported that there were only fifteen German soldiers, not 400, and that only five were killed, along with one American. "The American casualty was left behind," Domes reported, "his body covered with a blanket and with a spade nearby. He is said to have had red hair and freckles, but his identity is unknown." There is no mention of a death in American reports of the raid.

However many Germans there were on the parade ground that morning, by the time Baum's tanks passed, some had retrieved their weapons and opened fire on the half-tracks. In one half-track, a German machine-gun bullet blasted the lid off of an ammunition can and hurled it against a soldier's helmet. "Now that pisses me off," he shouted. The lid struck the arm of the man next to him, leaving a burn almost a foot long. "Me too," he said. Sergeant Yoerk thought, "This sure isn't a secret mission anymore."

There was not enough room aboard the vehicles, and not enough time, to take any dead or wounded with them, a policy understood by everyone from the beginning. Wounded were given first aid by the medics, David Zeno and Andrew Demchak, and left by the side of the road in the hope that they would be found in the morning and taken to a hospital.

The column picked up speed after leaving Laufach. In the lead tank, Lieutenant Weaver spotted a line of German soldiers marching down the highway toward them. As he slowed and took aim, the Germans recognized the danger, dropped their weapons, and raised their hands in surrender. The Americans had the Germans place their weapons in the middle of the road, whereupon the lead tank ran straight down the road, squashing everything in its path. Using gestures and a few words in the German language, the Americans told the prisoners to keep marching west and surrender to the main force not far behind. Some of Baum's men wondered how far the Germans would go before they realized there was no American force coming for them to surrender to. Of course, if they met an SS unit, they might all be considered deserters for having thrown away their weapons.

Baum's column approached the next town, Lohr, at 6:00 A.M. It was light enough to see in the distance the now-familiar display of white sheets hanging from upstairs windows. But as they drew closer, they spotted a roadblock at the edge of town, a crude affair hastily constructed from an overturned truck and piles of telephone poles. Still, it was enough to make the road appear impassable.

The Americans could not go around it or over it, but before Baum could decide what to do, a shell from a German Panzerfaust hit the lead tank, one of the big Shermans. All but one of the crew survived and clambered out of the disabled tank while a second Sherman wheeled forward to take its place. The second tank fired its 75mm gun and cleared away the roadblock.

When Baum was asked years later how he reacted to the loss of a tank of the mission, he replied, "I ignored it. I mean, we just kept going. We ignored it. We didn't stop for anything." Many residents of Lohr did not ignore it, however, and fled the town. They ran across the bridge over the River Main, which the German Army had failed to blow up, conveniently leaving it available for Task Force Baum to use.

The Germans later claimed that the Americans sped through town firing into houses and shops to prevent anyone with a Panzerfaust from hitting another tank. One resident told interviewers in 2003 that his uncle had been given a huge black cigar by an American tank commander. When Baum was told that story, he said, "That must have been Lieutenant [William] Nutto—no doubt about it. He was always smoking those things."

In the brief battle at the Lohr roadblock, one man in the lead tank had been killed and several infantrymen wounded. As Baum and Major Stiller came upon the wounded men being treated by medics, Baum said to Stiller, "Is this the high old time you were looking for?" Stiller had no witty retort this time.

Once again, postwar interviews conducted by Colonel Domes in 2003 differ from the after-action accounts by the members of Task Force Baum. Instead of roaring through Lohr as the contemporary German report indicated and shooting up everything in sight, American reports claimed that Baum led his men around the town on a road that overlooked it and told his men not to open fire unless they were fired on first.

On the outskirts of Lohr, no more than a half mile from the ridge where Task Force Baum was traveling, Gen. Hans von Obstfelder was alerted by his aide, who pointed at the ridge and told the general that it was an American unit. Obstfelder, who had been given command of the forces in southern Germany only about two hours before, listened to the distant sound. He went back to his office, where he had been receiving scattered reports about an American advance coming through Schweinheim late the previous night.

He assumed that this had to be the same force and that they were headed toward the next town, Gemünden. He immediately ordered reconnaissance planes into the air to find and follow the column, and to determine the size of the American unit. He also radioed the German commander at Gemünden to tell him that Americans were headed their way. He ordered that the bridge at Gemünden over the conjunction of the rivers Main and Salle be prepared for demolition. If the Americans reached Gemünden, they had to be stopped there.

The pine forest that Baum's men were crossing through was so thick that it reminded Weaver, in the lead tank, *Conquering Hero*, of an endless display of Christmas trees. He found himself humming "O Tannenbaum," the traditional German Christmas melody, with Sergeant Vannett tapping his foot in time with the music.

Suddenly, Weaver stopped humming. He had spotted two German tanks followed by a convoy of trucks hauling 88mm antiaircraft guns. For a moment neither side reacted, then Weaver opened fire, hitting the German vehicles and raking the column of soldiers with machine-gun fire. Many of the German soldiers raised their hands in surrender, but it was too late. The American lead tanks drove through them, scattering equipment and bodies along the road.

As the American tanks and half-tracks sped by the wreckage, they were horrified to see the bodies of young, mostly blond teenage girls wearing uniforms. These were what the Germans called Flak Girls, recruited and trained to operate antiaircraft weapons due to the growing shortage of men. It was a sight the Americans would not soon forget.

As Task Force Baum passed the area surrounding Lohr, they saw a train to their left traveling at the same speed they were maintaining. The train had both freight and passenger cars, and German soldiers leaned out of the carriages and waved at them, mistaking them for their own. They recognized their error only moments before the Americans fired.

Lieutenant Weaver opened up with his 75mm piece and Sergeant Vannett sprayed the train with machine-gun fire. The first shell hit the locomotive's boiler, which exploded in a spray of steam; the two engineers leaped out of the cab. The second shell hit a boxcar full of ammunition. The explosion twisted the railroad tracks and left little else behind.

Moments later another train approached, racing toward the road ahead of the column. If it got there first, it could cut the Americans off. The second tank, Sergeant Yoerk's *City of New York*, opened fire and hit the locomotive in its undercarriage, bringing it to a dead stop, with the cars behind crashing into it. Task Force Baum sped up, heading for Gemünden.

It was now past 6:30 on the morning of March 27. They were far behind schedule but had covered almost 30 miles from their starting point at Schweinheim. They were now halfway to Hammelburg.

———

"Hammelburg was in bad shape when we arrived," Colonel Waters wrote. It was a little after 6:00 P.M. on February 26, one month before Patton's last gamble, when the men from Szubin marched from Hammelburg's railroad station down Hermann Goering Strasse and arrived at the gates of Oflag XIIIB.

It was not the physical condition of the camp that unnerved Waters and the others. It was the condition of the men, the American prisoners already in the camp staring at them hollow-eyed through the wire. "They looked scruffy, ragged and unkempt," Charles Whiting writes in *48 Hours to Hammelburg*. "They stood there in the cold wind that always blew across the bleak plateau, their hands burrowed deeply in their combat jacket pockets, their shoulders hunched, feet shuffling to keep warm as they gazed at the new arrivals."

At their worst the men who had marched from Szubin were certain they had never looked so bad. Waters and the others stared at their counterparts and took in the camp itself. It was made up of two separate but adjoining compounds. One held about 700 American officers, mostly from the 28th and 106th Infantry Divisions captured two months earlier in the Battle of the Bulge. The other compound held 3,000 officers from Yugoslavia who preferred to be called Serbs, who had been captured in 1941. Despite being prisoners of the Germans for four years, they were in better shape, physically and emotionally, than the Americans, and would prove to be generous in sharing their rations and equipment and helping them in every way they could.

The American compound consisted of seven old barracks of stone and wood originally built as stables for horses. On January 23, one month before the men from Szubin arrived, representatives of the International Red Cross had inspected the facility. In their report they noted: "Approximately 200 men were crowded into each five-room barrack, and although ventilation and daylight were adequate, each room contained only two drop lights of 15-watt bulbs. During the extremely cold weather, the men tried to keep from freezing by putting on all available clothing and huddling around the one stove furnished to each room. . . . The barrack temperature averaged about 20 degrees." Lt. William Falkenheiner of the 106th Infantry, captured in December in the Ardennes, attested that "compared to the worst US Army barracks, this one was dirty and primitive."

By that stage of the war, the Germans did not have enough food for their own people, and even less for POWs. According to the Red Cross, "The normal daily menu consisted of one-tenth of a loaf of bread, one cup of ersatz coffee, one bowl of barley soup and one serving of a vegetable a day. About three times a week a small piece of margarine was issued, and occasionally a tablespoon of sugar." The Americans were suffering from malnutrition, with some men losing as many as thirty pounds since their arrival at Hammelburg. A number of lives were saved by the Serbs, who generously shared their regularly received Red Cross packages.

In addition to food shortages, the American prisoners suffered serious health problems, including dysentery, trench foot, and influenza. There were twenty-seven doctors among the captured Americans, but they had no medicine, supplies, or equipment. There was a twenty-bed dispensary, but all the doctors could do was keep the seriously ill and infectious away from the general population.

Here again, the Serbs were helpful. They had a 450-bed dispensary and a medical staff that had four years' experience in treating the maladies that affected prisoners with their insufficient diet and lack of adequate heat. The head of the hospital was an outstanding surgeon well known in

Europe; his skills would soon mean the difference between life and death for John Waters and Abe Baum.

Oflag XIIIB was part of a larger German facility that had been in operation since 1893, when it was established as a training camp for the German Army. It was called Lager (Camp) Hammelburg, after the town 2 miles away. (It still bears that name today.) It became a prison camp for the first time during World War I, but in 1920 part of it became a children's home operated by Benedictine nuns. Before the German Army took it over again in 1938, more than 60,000 children had spent part of their life there.

By 1940, when Germany was at war, part of the facility became a camp for enlisted POWs from England, Holland, Belgium, France, Australia, and New Zealand. Renamed Stalag 13C, by 1941 the camp housed thousands of new prisoners from Russia, Poland, and Yugoslavia. By 1945, when Americans were held there, the guards were men considered too old or ill for combat or men who had suffered combat wounds, making them ineligible for further frontline duty. For the most part, they were no longer Nazi zealots and were as tired of the war as the prisoners were.

The Russian POWs suffered more than those of any other nationality, as they did in all German POW camps. At Hammelburg more than 3,000 Russian prisoners were killed or died from starvation and disease. One of the Russians held there for a short time was Yakov Stalin, son of the dictator. The Germans offered to send him back to Moscow in return for the release of Field Marshal Friedrich Paulus, who had been captured at Stalingrad. Stalin refused to make the exchange, telling the Germans, "You have millions of my sons. Free all of them or Yakov will share their fate." Stalin is also alleged to have said that he would never trade a field marshal for a mere lieutenant. It is believed that Yakov later committed suicide in the Sachsenhausen concentration camp by deliberately running into an electrified fence.

As the newly arrived Americans from Szubin stood at the gates of Hammelburg, Colonels Goode and Waters, standing at the head of the group, spotted an older but erect and impeccably dressed senior officer inside the gate watching them. This was fifty-six-year-old Gen. Gunther von Goeckel, commandant of Oflag XIIIB, who had lost a lung in World War I and tried to remain throughout both wars an honorable soldier. He realized, unlike many Germans in 1945, that the war was lost, and he treated the prisoners in accordance with the rules of the Geneva Convention, a task that had become increasingly difficult with shortages of food and supplies available to prisoner of war camps.

Goeckel was also worried about the physical safety of the prisoners in his charge. The Allied armies were getting closer, and he knew that the small Wehrmacht units stationed nearby would be no match for them. His concern was not entirely humanitarian. He was worried about his own safety as well—not from the enemy, but from his own side. He could be charged with dereliction of duty, even treason, if the POWs at Hammelburg were to be freed. His fear was confirmed two weeks later on March 10, when a directive from Gen. Alfred Jodl announced, "All prisoners of war have to be led back. Every prison camp commander who allows one prisoner of war to fall into the hands of the enemy will lose his head."

As Goeckel watched the new arrivals, he was surprised to see the ungainly line regroup in military formation. Colonel Goode, still carrying his bagpipes from Szubin full of radio parts, and Colonel Waters were determined to demonstrate to the camp commandant, and more importantly to the slovenly and unkempt American prisoners inside the barbed wire, that they were still American soldiers.

Whiting describes the scene: "Goode straightened up. Suddenly he forgot his burdens. He was going to show the Krauts and the watching Kriegies! He rapped out a command with the authority of decades of Army service behind it. The ragged column came to attention. Then in perfect formation the newcomers marched through the gate and down Hermann Goering Strasse, with Pop Goode, head held high, proudly stepping out at the head. Behind them the gate of Hammelburg Lager clanged closed with a note of hollow finality."

CHAPTER 7

LET'S JUST GET THE
HELL OUT OF THIS PLACE

ON THE MORNING OF MARCH 27, WHILE ABE BAUM AND HIS MEN WERE roaring past the town of Lohr, George Patton wrote to his wife, "Last night I sent an armored column to a place . . . east of Frankfurt where John and some 900 prisoners are said to be. I have been nervous as a cat all day as everyone but me thought it too great a risk. I hope it works."

He worried that he "would catch hell for ordering such a reckless mission," and endangering the life not only of his son-in-law, but also of his trusted aide, Major Stiller. Sometime later he visited Gen. Troy Middleton, commander of XIII Corps, and told him about the raid. "Troy," Patton said, "I'm in trouble again. This time I've really done it. I've sent Alex Stiller off to his death. I loved that boy like a son. Why did I let him talk me into letting him go along?"

When Middleton asked him what size outfit he had sent, Patton replied, "Oh, something like a reinforced company."

"A reinforced company!" Middleton shouted. "You needed at least a combat command for a mission like that."

When Patton returned to his headquarters, he made this entry into his personal diary: "I was quite nervous all morning about the task force I sent to rescue the prisoners, as we could get no information concerning them. I do not believe there is anything in that part of Germany heavy enough to hurt them, but for some reason I was nervous; probably I had indigestion." He would soon have a lot more.

According to Jonathan Jordan's *Brothers, Rivals, Victors*, on that same day, March 27, a reporter learned about the mission to Hammelburg and asked Gen. Omar Bradley about it. Jordan submits that "Bradley, frowning, gave no information about the raid, because he had none to give. But he promised to find out."

As soon as the reporter left, Bradley got on the phone to Patton and said the press was asking about some kind of raid on a POW camp, a mission that Bradley had never heard of. It did not take long for Patton to give in and tell Bradley what he had done.

He swore to Bradley that "he didn't know his son-in-law was interned at the camp, but whether he knew it or not was beside the point. The fiasco put Patton and, by extension, Bradley and Eisenhower, in a bad way with the press. The raid had turned into a public relations nightmare as well as an unnecessary disaster," Jordan writes. Bradley said that Patton "knew damn well if he asked me for permission I would have vetoed it."

Bradley repeated that point in his autobiography: "[Patton] did not consult me. Had he done so I would have forbidden it. Overriding all advice, Patton ordered the mission. It was a disaster."

Task Force Baum made its way to the northeast away from Lohr, heading toward Gemünden and a crucial bridge across a river. If the Germans blew it up before the column got there, they would have to take a much longer and dangerous route to Hammelburg. Everything depended on that bridge. The road took the men through a long, narrow valley, which increased Baum's concern about being ambushed by Germans firing down at them from the heights. Surely, the enemy had to know by then that an American force was on its way. And if the Germans had spotted them, they would know just how small the force was.

Baum ordered radio silence. If the Germans did not yet know where they were, he did not want to give away their location with a careless radio message. But just as he gave the order, he heard firing from the tanks at the head of the column, a clear announcement of their presence. The tanks were firing at a train of flatcars coming from the direction of Gemünden. The first shot hit the locomotive dead center, bringing it to a stop. Baum later said, "I estimate there must have been about twelve trains, each consisting of twenty cars. It was just getting light and it was there that I realized that I had run into something."

Charles Whiting continues where Baum left off: "One after another the gleeful tankers in the lead shot up the unsuspecting German trains, laughing and chuckling among themselves . . . like a bunch of silly school kids. A flak train hove into view. The light tanks took after it like hawks after a hen. They roared up to the locomotive, punctured its metal sides with several rounds of 37-mm fire and left it spouting steam from several gleaming holes." The infantry in the half-tracks threw dozens of thermite grenades at the stranded, burning trains as they roared by. In short order Task Force Baum destroyed at least a half a dozen locomotives, which were increasingly rare in Germany.

The Americans spotted some barges on the Main River being towed by a tugboat. The tankers swung their guns around and fired high-explosive and incendiary shells. Five barges blew up in flames. Some of the crew were seen diving into the river and swimming to shore. No one fired back at the Americans.

By then, at 7:00 A.M. the 27th, the task force had destroyed at least a dozen trains heading out from Gemünden. Baum concluded correctly that there had to be a large marshalling yard in Gemünden or right outside. So many trains could also mean the presence of many German troops being transported elsewhere. He ordered his tankers to fire at the tracks to render them impassable. However many other trains there might be, they would not be coming in their direction for quite a while.

Baum also realized that a large marshalling yard was a valuable target for the US Air Force. Breaking radio silence, he sent a message to the 10th Armored Infantry headquarters. The message was picked up and passed on by one of the two-man Piper Cubs, designated as the L-4 Grasshopper; they were shadowing the task force and being used as reconnaissance planes. Baum's message was acknowledged: "Message received. Over and out."

Baum stopped the column outside of Gemünden and studied the town through his binoculars. He was sure there were enemy troops there who knew about the Americans. He would have preferred to avoid the town altogether, but it was essential that he cross the Main River bridge if he intended to reach Hammelburg anytime soon. Otherwise, he would have to find a long, roundabout way through unfamiliar territory. Going through Gemünden was their quickest route, but first Baum had to know if the bridge was intact and under guard.

He went to his reconnaissance platoon, led by Lt. Norman Hofner, and told him to take his three-jeep outfit into town to check the status of the bridge. Hofner was good at his job, having been in recon work for nine months. Most men in a recon platoon did not last that long out front because, as one history puts it, "Working in a reconnaissance platoon is Purple Heart work and leading one is like playing Russian roulette."

Hofner's platoon made its way through the town, which appeared to be deserted. Apparently the residents had heard the explosions when Baum's men destroyed trains and barges, and now they were hiding. They did not have time to hang white sheets from upstairs windows. There were no German troops around and no roadblocks. Hofner thought it was eerily quiet. The men kept their eyes on the rooftops, searching for snipers, but they did not see or hear any shooting. Finally they reached the old stone bridge, whose foundation had originally been built by the Romans some 2,000 years before. And there they saw their first German soldiers.

The enemy was arrayed on the far side of the bridge, waiting for the Americans to try to cross. But there was a more immediate danger: dozens of flat black circular mines piled one on top of another, ready to be placed on the bridge to blow it up. It appeared that the Germans were too late to stop Task Force Baum.

Hofner pulled out a smoke grenade and tossed it onto the bridge. He told his driver to keep throwing them, and he ordered the other men to follow him. As the Germans fired at them blindly into thick clouds of smoke, the Americans grabbed the mines and began tossing them into the trees nearby. Some mines exploded but did not cause any injuries; nor was anyone hit by German fire.

Hofner raced back to the main column and told Baum that the bridge was intact but German troops were on the other side. Baum had no choice. He had to have that bridge, even if they had to fight their way across.

He ordered 2nd Lt. Bill Nutto's medium tanks to lead the way to the bridge, followed by an infantry platoon commanded by Lt. Elmer Sutton.

"Pin 'em down," he told Sutton. "Keep them pinned down until we're past."

Nutto, riding in the second tank, ordered the column forward through the deserted streets, his machine gunners firing anywhere the enemy might be hiding. Sutton's infantrymen moved along behind them. As they approached the bridge, they saw that Hofner's recon outfit had spread out; his men were pouring a steady stream of fire across the river. There was very little return fire.

Baum quickly assessed the situation and ordered Sutton's infantry to "go over the bridge and seize it," so Baum reported years later. "And at the time we didn't have any fire. There was nothing being fired on. And then we started . . . over the bridge. And then the Germans started firing."

Lieutenant Nutto heard the distinctive sound of a Panzerfaust, and then another and another followed by the roar of a German antitank weapon being fired from an old castle high on a hill overlooking the town. The lead tank in his unit exploded only a few yards from the bridge.

Author Richard Whitaker describes the moment as one of chaos: "Nutto watched as the stunned platoon leader, Lieutenant Raymond Keil, helped his badly burned crew out of the tank. At this point, panic ensued and the lead tank's sergeant, who had seen too much combat and been wounded twice, broke and ran for the rear, yelling, 'I've had it, I've had it!'" Baum told Nutto to move the stricken tank out of the way.

Nutto reported hearing fire from another Panzerfaust and, according to Baum and his *Raid!* coauthors, claimed he saw "the rocketlike projectile wobbling toward them. When it hit the street to their front, it threw up tar splinters, cement and steel fragments and searing pieces of its phosphorous head. Nutto felt them pierce his arms, his chest, his neck and his legs, He was on the ground wondering if he could take another breath. Sure he was dying, a vast disappointment washed over him: Damn it, I never screwed a girl with big tits, he thought."

He saw Baum fall also, with blood oozing from his right knee and hand. Baum's wrist was slashed deeply and the knee cut to the bone. Dazed, he forced himself to stand and noticed Nutto, lying all bloody on the street. Privates Solotoff and Zeno ran to help, but Nutto could not get to his feet. Baum sent them back to one of the half-tracks that had medics.

A radioman came up and poured sulfa into Baum's knee wound. He asked if Baum could bend it, which he was able to do, indicating that his leg was not broken. He waited while the radioman bandaged his wounds, watching his men cross the bridge.

Sutton and his infantry platoon were already on the far side. Two more men started running across. Suddenly the bridge rose up in slow motion. The Germans had mined it after all. The entire structure disappeared in a shower of wreckage and noise. Obviously Task Force Baum was not going to get to Hammelburg that way.

Major Stiller, Patton's aide, rode up and asked Baum the question on everyone's mind: "You want to go back?"

"We don't quit," Baum said. "Besides we can't go back. . . . If we go back the way we came they will hand us our ass. We gotta go ahead." He turned to his men and shouted, "Let's just get the hell out of this place!"

Years later Baum was asked, "What do you think the turning point was of the whole mission? When did it start to go bad, in your opinion?" "Gemünden," Baum said. "Once I was stopped, that's when it was bad."

———

"I remember the sense of absolute frustration, anger, humiliation, and shame," Lt. William Falkenheiner of the 106th Infantry Division said, when interviewed in 2014, some sixty-nine years after he surrendered during the Battle of the Bulge in December 1944. That was one of the largest surrenders in American military history, and the POWs who watched the men from Szubin march smartly into Oflag XIIIB at Hammelburg still felt the shame of it. "The morale [of the POWs already there] when we reached that camp," John Waters said later, "was almost non-existent."

After their surrender every prisoner felt depressed and lethargic, disgraced and even dishonored. Father Paul Cavanaugh, a Jesuit priest and chaplain in the 106th, wrote in 2004 about the condition of his fellow Kriegies at Hammelburg: "For the newly captured prisoner of war his battle is lost. He has failed in his mission. He has proved himself a failure and his efforts have come to naught. His soul is crushed with the weight of ignominy . . . humiliation and defeat. For us of the 106th Division this depression was universal. But recently committed to action, we crumbled before the first enemy attack and every individual shared in that disgrace."

The 106th Infantry was a hard-luck outfit. It was the newest, the greenest, and the only one with no battle experience, and it was placed in what was considered a safe portion of the American line east of Bastogne. No German attack was considered likely at that point and so, it was thought, the men could devote themselves to training and getting used to life at the front. They were not ready for combat.

Yet, as it turned out, they bore the brunt of the German attack that took the Allied command by surprise. Suddenly the 106th found itself hemmed in on three sides by experienced, well-equipped German units. Stunned, the senior US officers demonstrated no capacity for trying to unite their men to resist the German attack. These men, the soldiers of the 106th, made up the bulk of those Waters saw when he entered the camp at Hammelburg.

The 28th Infantry Division, located to the east of Bastogne, was also hit hard when the Germans attacked. The 28th had been in heavy combat since Normandy, six months earlier, and they were exhausted. Duty in the Ardennes was considered to be a rest tour for them, but they too were overrun and suffered heavy casualties; many of their officers were at Hammelburg when the men from Szubin arrived. They too suffered depression and anxiety that made it difficult for them to maintain morale and organize their life at Hammelburg into some semblance of a military unit.

Just getting from the front line to the camp at Hammelburg was an ordeal, and the trek cost many lives. They marched for days with little food in ice and snow through destroyed towns, while being bombed and strafed by American planes seeking German targets. The temperature kept dropping; it was the coldest winter in Europe in thirty years.

They were crammed into boxcars. As Falkenheiner described it, "This train ride lasted at least a week and there were some terrifying moments particularly at night when we were halted on some siding. We could hear the air raid sirens and were bombed. The train I was on was hit and a number of men were killed and hurt. During the bombing we would try to get out of the cars, but the guards would shoot anyone trying to leave the train."

On Christmas Day, when they were bombed again, the guards gave them the first food they had eaten in days. "It was a small piece of brown bread," Falkenheiner recalled, "and I learned later that sawdust was one of the ingredients. The terrible conditions of that week and the terror and helplessness of the bombings are impossible to describe."

The Germans did not paint white crosses on the tops of the railroad cars to identify them to American pilots as transporting POWs, and several of the trains experienced near misses and some were hit. A soldier in one of the cars later wrote a book based on his experiences as a POW. His name was Kurt Vonnegut; the book was called *Slaughterhouse Five*.

Father Cavanaugh spent a week after his capture crammed into a boxcar that had once transported horses and still had plenty of manure spread over the floor. The best the men could do was sweep it toward the edges with their hands and feet. They were too tired, weak from hunger, and downhearted over their surrender to care, no matter how revolting it was.

In one village they passed, there was a well, and the men were let out of the boxcars to get some water. Father Cavanaugh remembered that "many of the men were so weary they had not the energy, thirsty as they were, to get up off the cold stones on which they were lying to go to the well. We tried to get some pails to carry water, but none would be given us."

Sometimes they were hauled out of the trains, usually because Allied planes had destroyed the track ahead of them, and forced to continue on foot. Many men were so thirsty and hungry that they grabbed piles of snow, filthy though it was from tanks, trucks, and marching boots that had trampled it, and greedily stuffed it in their mouths.

Whiting details more harsh realities: "At each station at which they halted, they begged pathetically for food and water and wept openly when the guards, enraged by Allied bombing raids on German cities, knocked the helmets filled with water from their frozen fingers. Before the shocked eyes of haggard German *Hausfrauen*, they relieved themselves by the hundred wherever the train stopped and, when the guards would not allow them out any more as a result, they used the floors of the cars as a latrine."

Father Cavanaugh said that for those who walked, "Every step was a torture [but] slowly the column kept moving. Darkness and wind came together. Soon it started to drizzle and in our misery we even stopped counting the kilometers which marked the distance along the highway." They also stopped counting the days, since each seemed to be worse than the one before.

It took up to a month for the groups of those captured in Belgium to reach the various camps, including the one at Hammelburg, and no one knows how many died along the way, by starvation, disease, cruelty, American bombs, or as a result of simply giving up.

On Thursday, January 12, 1945, the first American officers to be captured at the Battle of the Bulge arrived at Oflag XIIIB at Hammelburg. "The heavily wired gates swung wide to admit us," Father Cavanaugh wrote. "We were counted again. The gates were locked behind us and we remained standing in the snow." Later they were taken indoors and told to take off all their clothing, everything except their dog tags, and every item was inspected before being given back to them.

They were taken in groups of one hundred into the barracks and given one thin blanket each, which measured about 3 by 6 feet. Chief Warrant Officer Harry Thompson remembered that the only faucet for drinking water was outside and that it was kept turned on constantly. Otherwise, the water would have frozen in the pipe.

"What a mess!" he wrote in his 2002 book. "If you needed water, it was very difficult with ice everywhere. You almost had to get on hands and knees and crawl to the water. We sure did not take chances of falling and breaking an arm or leg." He also remembered that the barracks were "so cold that we got into groups and bunked two or three to a bed for warmth. . . . The room was so cold that we stayed in bed most of the time just trying to stay warm. As a result of lying down so much, we grew weak."

Twice a day, at 8:00 A.M. and 5:00 P.M., they had to go outside for roll call, which took about forty-five minutes, during which they were not permitted to move around to keep warm. It was held on the camp's main street, Hermann Goering Strasse, even in the worst weather. "There were times," Father Cavanaugh attested, "when we felt the cold wind blowing through our thinning arms and limbs and were chilled to the marrow while the camp was searched—barracks, kitchen, lazaret [quarantine hospital], and latrine—for some missing Kriegie."

The days quickly settled into a boring routine. "Two roll calls a day, and three so-called meals. And in between, emptiness, empty stomachs and empty minds," Cavanaugh wrote. There were a few attempts to raise morale by organizing classes. There was a French class taught by a fluent French speaker, but only ten people showed up and before long "the class became something of a drudgery and died a natural death," again according to Cavanaugh. General von Goeckel described the prisoners as "unbelievably infantile" for their inability to retain some military discipline.

The problem was a lack of leadership in the camp from the senior American officers, including the nominal commander, Col. Charles Cavender. Although he was a West Point graduate (class of 1923) who had fought in World War I, he made no effort to establish leadership or run the camp in military fashion. A postwar report noted that "both the enlisted men and company-grade officers felt let down by their commanders, particularly Cavender and his staff. Creating a unified front against the Germans was virtually impossible" without proper leadership. Thompson recalled that several of the higher-ranking officers had "severe nervous breakdowns and just went incoherent. . . . They just sat in a stupefied condition and did not seem to recognize anyone or talk to anyone."

The low morale, the lack of leadership or cohesiveness as a military unit, the chilling cold, and inadequate food led to disease, malnutrition, and hopelessness. Dysentery was common; the American doctors had no proper medication for its treatment. "Day by day," Father Cavanaugh wrote, "I became weaker and thinner and more languid from the interruptions in sleep and hurried trips to the latrine." He spent a week barely able to get out of bed before the symptoms began to ease.

The irritating presence of lice also became a serious health problem. There was no escaping them. "I can't tell you what a horrible feeling it is to feel a creature crawling across your skin," one Kriegie said. "Every night before we turned out the light and went to bed, everybody would take their GI underwear and turn it inside out and go through and pick off all the lice they could find. They would also reach under their arms and so on and do the same thing."

The men became obsessed with food and spent hours talking about their favorite meals back home, writing down recipes and even menus from restaurants they had been to. Lieutenant Falkenheiner said, "We were all plagued with memories of past meals and food items we had taken for granted. This even included some of the Army food we had griped about. Some of us prepared detailed daily menus for meals we would have when we got home."

One Sunday Father Cavanaugh was escorted by a guard to the enlisted men's camp a mile away to say mass. On the way back to the officers' camp, he felt faint and had to sit down, just as a pushcart with their daily food supply passed by. The road was rutted and the cart swerved; a few potatoes rolled out and fell on the road. "I picked them up and ate them," Cavanaugh wrote. "This is the depth of humiliation, I thought. A priest eating half-rotten potatoes out of the gutter. I stayed in my bunk for the rest of the day."

All that made life at all tolerable for the Americans at Hammelburg, before the men from Szubin arrived, was the presence of the Serbians in the next compound. They not only shared their Red Cross packages but also passed small cups of coffee and slices of bread and sugar through the wire dividing the two groups. Some GIs, including Father Cavanaugh, managed to slip through the wire and visit the Serbs in their quarters, where they were often given food and intricate carvings. The Serbians also gave them two Ping-Pong tables, playing cards, and checkerboards, as well as medical assistance.

The lives of the Kriegies captured at the Battle of the Bulge changed on March 10 when the men from Szubin marched smartly into the

Hammelburg camp, led by Colonel Goode and Lt. Col. John Waters. Lt. Richard Baron watched them march in and "thought to himself that these new arrivals looked better after their long trek than the Hammelburg Kriegies who had spent the last three months in their bunks. Baron was sure he would never see men march as spiritedly again."

Goode and Waters saw immediately how bad the situation was at Oflag XIIIB. The POWs there were disheveled, unshaven, and slovenly in appearance and manner. Discipline had broken down completely. They were no longer a military outfit, and Goode and Waters immediately set about to change their lives for the better, determined to make them look, act, and feel like soldiers again.

On the day after their arrival, Goode and Waters held a formal inspection of each barracks. "They reviewed every rank," Baron said, "stopping to order men to shave, to dress in a military manner, to stand up straight. When asked why his shoes weren't shined, a young, slovenly second lieutenant laughed at the question. He was summarily confined to his barracks for one week. Army discipline had come to Hammelburg and with it morale began to improve."

One of the concessions Goode got from camp commandant von Goeckel was that each man would be issued a razor so he could shave himself daily. "Funny," Thompson wrote, "the differences a small thing like a razor can make. Simply being able to take a little pride in our appearance made each of us carry our heads a little higher and put a small spring back in our steps."

Goode and Waters also got von Goeckel to issue more food, distribute Red Cross parcels, cancel roll calls in snow or freezing rain, and provide better medical care. Waters set up a bulletin board listing a series of lectures and classes, and this time morale was high enough so that many of the men attended. Father Cavanaugh gave a sample schedule of courses and activities for one busy day:

0900 Hrs. Irrigation of Crops

1000 How to Make Ice Cream

1100 Economic Geography

1300 Child Psychology

1400 Roller Coasters

1500 Glee Club

1600 Catholic Mass

Bring Your Own Chairs.

Thanks to Colonel Goode's radio, which he had hidden in his bag-pipes, the men were kept up to date on the rapid progress of the Allied armies as they got closed to Hammelburg. They knew it would not be long before they would hear guns firing and see one of Patton's tanks knock down their barbed wire fence and set them free. All they had to do was to wait a few more weeks, or even days, and their war would be over.

CHAPTER 8

NOW THEY KNOW WHO WE ARE

THE ROAD ABE BAUM AND HIS MEN HAD PLANNED TO TAKE TO HAM-melburg was now closed to them. The bridge was gone, and so was more of the task force. As soon as the debris from the explosion stopped falling and the smoke cleared, Panzerfausts opened fire on the stopped column. In a matter of minutes, according to German reports, three of Baum's medium tanks were destroyed, and three of his men were killed and eighteen wounded. Before they could get out of Gemünden, thirty-seven more were captured. The Germans claimed they lost only three of their men.

Baum held the map in his wounded, bloody hand, looking for a way out. The roads behind them, the ones they had come this far on, were probably full of German soldiers by then. There would be no surprising them as they had done on the way to Gemünden. They would be on the alert now. Baum had to find another way to Hammelburg, and soon.

He quickly saw on the map that they would have to change direc-tions and head north to find another bridge over either the Saale or the Sinn Rivers. Unfortunately, the only road heading where he wanted to go was a good distance behind where the column was stopped. That meant that they would have to turn around by backing and filling, which is a slow process on narrow roads for vehicles with treads rather than wheels. It was after 9:00 A.M. when they finally all got in line to head out on the back road Baum had found.

At some point that morning, not long after getting out of Gemün-den, the lead tank in the column, *Conquering Hero*, ran into a German paratrooper, Lt. Hans Gutbell, and knocked him off his motorcycle. Miraculously, the German was not injured, and when he saw Captain Baum come toward him, he stood at attention and saluted.

Through the interpreter, Irving Solotoff, Baum learned that the man was going home on leave to get married. He also said that he was tired of the war and no longer believed in the Nazi cause and so was willing to surrender and cooperate. When he was asked how they could get to Hammelburg, he said there was a bridge 8 miles away in the town of Burgsinn that could take them there. If they could reach it before the Germans blew it up.

After the Americans were repulsed at Gemünden, German military headquarters there quickly radioed warnings about their presence to every civilian and military leader in the area. In the town of Hammelburg, the Nazi mayor (the burgermeister), Herr Clements, immediately telephoned everyone he knew to tell them to get out of town as fast as they could. He then sent the town crier through the narrow cobblestone streets ringing his alarm bell and yelling for everyone to leave.

According to Charles Whiting, "Chaos reigned in the narrow streets as the crowd of refugees hastened to the north and the east. Hurrying women, children and old men (there were few young ones left) rushed down the main escape route, their baggage loaded on little handcarts. There were also wagons, pulled by horses and slow plodding oxen, and laden with clothes, bedding, food and other household goods. Even pigs and chickens were loaded and taken away.... Soon the town was empty save for a few invalids and stubborn old men and women, who refused to leave. It [the town] lay there in the sunny, sleepy little valley waiting for what was to come."

Two miles south of the town, the commandant of Oflag XIIIB, General von Goeckel, had been awakened early by the sounds of battle from the direction of Gemünden. He had fallen back asleep, then woke up again, put on his uniform, and gone to his office to place a call to the nearest German Army headquarters, located at Nuremberg.

He asked if he could evacuate the camp and move the prisoners elsewhere. When that request was turned down, he asked for troops to protect the camp if the Americans came. He was told there were no more troops available for Hammelburg and that he would have to use his guards to defend the camp. When he protested that his guards were all old and infirm or otherwise unfit for combat, all he heard in reply was the click of the phone being put down at the other end. They had hung up on him. General von Goeckel was on his own.

———

Task Force Baum came to a fork in the road, and it was not clear on Captain Baum's map which way they should go. After pondering the choice for a moment, he told Lieutenant Yoerk to take his *City of New York* Sherman tank up to the top of the hill on the road to the left and see which way they should go. It turned out to be a dead-end narrow road. As the tank reversed, the crew heard a telltale grinding noise and the tank came to a halt.

One of the treads had come off and there was no way to repair it where they were. The crew placed one grenade inside the tank and another down the barrel of the cannon, and trudged back down the hill to the waiting column. Before they headed off to the right, the medics told Baum that four of those who had been wounded at Gemünden were not fit to continue. They needed more medical care than the medics could provide.

Baum had no choice. "Put them on the road," he told the medics. "Stick a rifle in the ground and a white bandage on it. The Germans will pick 'em up."

If the Germans found them in time and did not shoot them on the spot, they might have a chance of surviving.

The column moved off again and had not gone very far when they saw an American jeep coming up behind them, with the white star on the sides not covered over with mud like their own vehicles. It had a .30-caliber machine gun behind the driver's seat along with a large loudspeaker. It was not one of their own.

It was a psychological warfare unit from the Seventh Army that was lost, only the three GIs in the jeep did not know it. It was headed by Technician 3rd Class Ernst Langensdorf, who had learned German while growing up in Germany. His job was to broadcast propaganda messages to German troops, encouraging them to surrender, a job he had been doing since the North Africa campaign and then in Italy.

Langensdorf and his two assistants had started out earlier that morning and had wandered over 35 miles behind enemy lines, not quite sure of where they were. When they saw the smoke coming from Gemünden, they drove into town as far as the demolished bridge, but then left as fast as they could when they saw no American troops around. They ended up following the tracks left by Task Force Baum and caught up with the tail end of the column sometime after 10:00 A.M.

Langensdorf, always on the lookout for German troops to broadcast his messages to, spotted some trying to hide in the woods nearby. They had apparently run away from Gemünden when Baum's men showed up. Langensdorf immediately picked up his microphone and went into his well-practiced speech, urging them to give up, as the men of Task Force Baum listened and watched, both amused and fascinated.

"Surrender," he said, "before our troops have to kill you. Hitler is crazy, Germany has lost the war. You will be treated according to the Geneva Convention. It is better to surrender to the Americans than to the Russians." That final line was usually effective, now that the Russians were getting so much closer so fast.

Langensdorf had barely finished talking when German troops, unarmed and with their hands in the air, began coming out of the woods to give themselves up. He counted them as they came forward and was very pleased when he reached the figure of 300.

Langensdorf was less pleased, however, when he got into a conversation with one of Baum's tank commanders at the rear of the column. The tanker told him that they were from the Third Army and not the Seventh, as he had assumed.

"This isn't where I'm supposed to be," Langensdorf said.

He looked at the German troops and told them they would have to wait until the American army got there before they could become prisoners. They looked bewildered and disappointed as they watched the three men in the jeep turn around and speed off in one direction while the column of Baum's men headed in the opposite direction. They had thought the war was over for them, but it was not. Now they would have to surrender all over again.

⸺

The captured German paratrooper who was leading Task Force Baum to the bridge at Burgsinn, perhaps inspired by what the propaganda team had done, or simply trying to keep in the good graces of the Americans, told the column to stop. He jumped down from the lead tank, waved his white scarf in the air, and yelled in German into the forest that the war was over and that American tanks were coming.

Two dozen German soldiers came out of the woods with their hands up in surrender. The interpreter, Solotoff, told them to wait there for the main force, and continued on down the road. Twice more, the German paratrooper called to Germans hiding in the forest and got them to surrender. They too, were left behind, as the column roared on.

Shortly after that, the lead tank in the column almost ran head-on into a Volkswagen staff car containing SS general Oriel Lotz and two aides. The German driver slammed on the brakes and the captured paratrooper and Solotoff jumped off the lead tank and ran forward while the rest of the task force trained their guns on the startled Germans.

General Lotz took his time getting out of the car and then marched brazenly toward the lead American tank without putting his hands in the air. "We started to interrogate him," Baum said years later. "And the GIs didn't like too much to have him around." The men were openly hostile toward him, but the general stood straight and haughtily refused to provide any information beyond his name, rank, and serial number.

"I told them to put him on front of the half-track," Baum said, thinking that if they ran across other Germans up ahead, they might not shoot if they saw a German general in front. General Lotz climbed up on the hood of the half-track "with as much dignity as he could muster. His driver and aide saluted their chief as he bounced past them. One had salvaged the general's riding crop but could not get it to him," Baum and his coauthors recall in *Raid!* "Oriel Lotz was on his way. So was the task force. And it was much more formidable now that it had a German staff officer as a hood ornament."

Task Force Baum reached the village of Burgsinn at 10:15 a.m. and found the narrow old bridge still in place. And there were no German troops to be seen. No one in the town knew they were coming. If they had, it would have been easy to set up a roadblock at the main gate or anywhere along the streets, which were so narrow that the tanks just barely scraped by.

The tanks and half-tracks crossed over the bridge slowly, one at a time, with everyone wondering if the frail-looking structure would hold up under all that weight. It did, and when the column reached the other side, they were no more than 12 miles from Hammelburg. It would be an easy and quick run if there were no Germans in the way.

As they crested a hill heading toward Gräfendorf, the next and last town to pass through, they came across a group of German soldiers sitting peacefully by the side of the road, taking a break. They threw up their hands and surrendered immediately. Moments later a ragged crowd of what turned out to be 700 starving Russian POWs the Germans had been guarding came running toward the Americans across an open field. They were like an avalanche, overwhelming Germans and Americans alike and causing a huge traffic jam.

The column had to stop as the Russians swarmed all over them, hugging and kissing every American, climbing on all the vehicles and yelling in a language none of them understood. Corporal Zawada remembered them well: "I was leaning over the front of the half-track and all of a sudden this Russian jumps on the hood of the half-track and he just comes up and puts his two hands behind my neck and kisses me right on the mouth. It was disgusting." Baum described it as "a fiasco having them run around. That didn't help us a bit." The Americans could not move without risking running over dozens of screaming Russians.

The German guards looked terrified, and with good reason. Baum saw one Russian grab a knife and chase a guard into the woods. In the midst of all the confusion and chaos, General Lotz managed to slip away unnoticed. "All of a sudden, I turn around and look, and the general disappeared," Baum said in a 2013 interview. "What happened to him, I don't know. To this day, I don't know what happened to him."

They finally found a German guard who spoke some Russian, and he managed to tell Baum that the POWs were asking him if they could take over the town of Gräfendorf. Baum told them through the interpreter that they could take the town—"Why not?" he said—but not until he and his men had passed through it.

In *Raid!*, Baum's actions that morning are described in these terms: "He knew how badly the Germans treated Russian POWs: cruel neglect, torture, summary executions. He had a vision of pillage and fire and rape that made the Spanish conquistadores look like Boy Scouts on a jamboree. . . . He told the Russians that the Germans were their prisoners and that when they got to Gräfendorf, their first stop should be the police station where they would find weapons. The Russians cheered and laughed. Minutes before these men had been on the point of utter exhaustion. It was astonishing what freedom and the chance for revenge could do for a beaten man. The Russians had turned tigers."

Task Force Baum made its way along the narrow country road toward Hammelburg, having no idea what was happening behind them. It turned out that the people of Gräfendorf were safe, at least from the 700 Russian POWs who did not get the chance to wreak their vengeance on them after all. They were saved by General Lotz, who had so carefully slipped away from his position on the lead American tank when the Russians surrounded them. He hid in nearby woods, and when the Americans left, he quickly took charge, rounding up the guards and restoring order among the Russians, who were made prisoners once again.

Fifty years later, on March 27, 1995, an American historian, Richard Whitaker, revisited the route Task Force Baum took and stopped for coffee at a café in Gräfendorf. He asked the proprietor of the café if he remembered anything about an American tank column that came through town on that day a half century before.

The man became very excited, Whitaker wrote, and "told me that he was a small boy [in 1945], hiding in the basement below where we were standing, when the American tanks came rumbling through. He watched them from the basement window, and it was a sight he will never forget.

Another man who had been sitting nearby got up to tell me that he had also been a young man in the town of Burgsinn when the column passed by, and he recalled similar memories."

Neither man knew that the town had faced the possibility of being pillaged by hundreds of escaped Russian POWs. When Whitaker and the café owner stepped outside onto the street, however, the man remembered something else that had happened fifty years before. It was the only tragedy that befell Burgsinn during the war, and it was caused by other Germans.

The café owner "pointed to some second floor windows above the shop next door, and explained that his neighbors had draped a white sheet over the window sill in order to keep the Americans from firing on them. This worked fine until some SS troops came through the village later and, upon seeing the white sheets of surrender, proceeded to shoot the townspeople who had hung them up!"

—◆—

By 12:30 P.M., Task Force Baum was being shadowed by a single-engine, wood-and-canvas Fieseler Storch observation plane as they left Gräfendorf. The plane flew dangerously low over the column at about 80 miles per hour as the pilot counted the number of vehicles left. Every man in every vehicle opened fire on the plane, even the wounded in the half-tracks, but it miraculously escaped damage.

The plane flew past the front of the column and almost insolently waggled its wings twice and then flew back over it again from its head to its tail. When the pilot finished counting what remained of the task force—thirteen tanks, three assault guns, and seventy-seven half-tracks—he climbed to a higher altitude out of reach of the men firing from the ground.

"Now they know who we are," Major Stiller said to Captain Baum.

"They don't need a plane for that," Baum replied. "They want to know where we are."

He did not know it at the time, but there had been three Storches following them all morning, plotting their progress and their direction. It was only the third pilot who had the nerve to come down so low, as though daring them to shoot him down.

Baum also did not know that General Lotz, who had escaped from capture when the Russians mobbed the column, had reached a telephone and contacted Gen. Hans von Obstfelder, back in Gemünden. Lotz had overheard the Americans talking about their objective, the POW camp at Hammelburg, when he had been a prisoner, and he passed this vital information on. Now the Germans knew how large (or really how small) the unit was and exactly where it was heading.

General Obstfelder quickly began to spread the word about the American column and its destination. Among those other commanders he notified were General von Goeckel, the commandant of Oflag XIIIB at Hammelburg, and Col. Cord von Hoepple, who was in charge of the region around the town of Hammelburg. He also contacted Gen. Bernhard Weisenberger, in the city of Schweinfurt, east of Hammelburg, and ordered him to send whatever troops he had available to Hammelburg as quickly as possible. Task Force Baum had lost the vital element of surprise.

At 12:40 P.M., Baum led his men across a narrow bridge over the Saale River in the small village of Michelau. It was the last river they had to cross before getting to Hammelburg. Five minutes later one of the Sherman tanks developed engine trouble and had to be left behind, and not long after that, Baum realized they were lost. The German paratrooper they had captured had led them this far quite well, but now they found themselves in hilly, wooded terrain he did not recognize. He had no idea where they were.

They needed a new guide who was familiar with that area of the country. Shortly after, they came upon a man in his seventies standing in his garden next to the road, looking terrified at seeing American tanks. His name was Anton Forsch and he was visibly shaking as Irving Solotoff, the interpreter, walked up to him and spoke to him in fluent German, asking him to lead them to Hammelburg.

The man did not want to get involved. He was afraid of either being caught up in the middle of a battle or of what would happen to him if the authorities or his neighbors found out that he had helped the Americans, willingly or not. He protested to Solotoff that he was just a poor farmer, a good Lutheran, and harmless. And besides, he said, he had a heart condition.

When Solotoff told Baum that the man said he was too sick to go with them, Baum said, "Tell him he'll be a lot sicker if he doesn't get us to the highway to Hammelburg." The old man climbed into Baum's jeep and pointed which way to go, but after only a couple of miles, they reached a crossroads where he said he was lost. He claimed that he had never been that far away from his farm in his life.

When Baum yelled at him to tell him which way they should go, the man clutched his chest as though in pain. He was either feigning a heart attack or having a real one. Baum kept asking which road they should take, and the man finally pointed to one that led up a hill. Baum led the column that way only to find that it was a dead end. Now not only were they totally lost, but they also faced the long and difficult task of turning all the vehicles around again on a narrow road hemmed in by trees on both sides.

Baum ordered his driver and Solotoff to head back the way they had come to the last village they had passed, Weickersgruben, and find someone who knew the way to Hammelburg. When they got there, Solotoff ran into the village inn and yelled loudly in German that they needed a guide. Everyone inside looked terrified; no one spoke until one man blurted out the name of someone who lived just a few doors down, Bernhard Gerstenberger.

Solotoff pounded on Gerstenberger's door, then burst inside and dragged him out to the jeep and headed back to where the column was. When they reached it, Gerstenberger and the previous guide, Forsch, recognized each another right away.

"Bernhard," Forsch said frantically, "I don't know how to get to Hammelburg from here. You do. You are the best hunter and guide in the area, go with them. Show them the way."

Gerstenberger, looking at the tanks and American soldiers who surrounded him, knew they could kill him on the spot if he refused to cooperate. But he also knew, as all Germans did, that if it came out later that he had helped the Allies, his own people would kill him, or at the very least shun him for the rest of his life. He also had another more personal and pressing problem that he told Solotoff and Baum about: His wife back in Weickersgruben was pregnant and about to deliver any minute, and there was no one else to help her except him. Would they please let him go back to her?

Solotoff translated for Baum, who shook his head immediately. Gerstenberger was their only chance to find the way to Hammelburg. Baum was determined to not stay lost when they were so close and had come through so much.

Gerstenberger, realizing that he had no choice in the matter, got into the jeep while the old man, Forsch, who had led them that far and then gotten them lost, was allowed to go back to his home. Gerstenberger asked Forsch to please go to his house and tell his wife that he would be back soon. The column moved off in the direction their new guide indicated. At least he gave the impression that he knew what he was doing and where he was going. But even he got lost a few times, and the task force had to make several detours.

Finally, by 2:20 that afternoon, they reached the original route on Highway 27 they would have been on hours before if they had been able to cross the bridge at Gemünden. Along the way they came across two German soldiers who ran away as fast as they could. Gerstenberger was amazed and relieved that the Americans did not shoot them down. Perhaps, he said to himself, he would live through the day after all.

When they reached the top of another ridge, this one overlooking a long valley, Gerstenberger pointed down the valley and told Baum that was the shortest way to Hammelburg. For some reason Baum was not sure he completely trusted him and so he chose to go the other way on Highway 27. He later admitted that was a mistake.

"I didn't trust him," Baum said in 2003. "That was the one error I made. I made others probably. But I mean the one area that I am really responsible for was not to listen to him."

The guide then asked Baum if he could go back home to his pregnant wife. Baum stared intently at the road that crossed the valley, as though planning his next move, and seemed not to hear the guide's question.

As he started to give the order to move out, Solotoff asked him what he wanted to do about the guide. Baum said to let him go. Then he turned to Gerstenberger and said, "Mazel tov," which usually means "congratulations" in Yiddish but can also mean "good luck." Maybe Baum meant both.

The guide hurried back to his house just in time to help his wife give birth to a son. But then he had to leave again, still worried about being killed if German soldiers found out he had helped lead the enemy to their target. Saying goodbye to his wife and son, he hid out in the woods for the next two months, until the war ended.

As we have seen before, so much of what passes for truth and accuracy in history depends so much on who is telling the story that later becomes enshrined as history. In this case different accounts have given us two completely different names of the German who reluctantly guided Task Force Baum to within reach of Hammelburg. However, in the light of what was about to happen to Abe Baum and his men, it is not surprising that he and others could have ascribed the wrong name to a German who, for an hour or so, guided their path. Indeed, Baum and others probably did not even know his name at the time. It was not important to men who were fighting for their lives to know or remember the name of an enemy civilian with whom they so briefly came in contact. And so, in Baum's account of the mission to Hammelburg—published in 1981, some thirty-six years after the event—the guide was given the name of Bernhard Gerstenberger.

In 1995 Richard Whitaker, following the route Task Force Baum had taken fifty years before and meeting Germans and Americans who lived to tell the story, gave the name of the guide as Karl Sturzenberger. It was raining on the day Whitaker drove through the village of Weickersgruben, and on a whim he stopped next to three local men who were standing together out of the rain, smoking.

He asked them if they knew anything about an American raid that came through town in March 1945 and the local resident who served as a reluctant guide for them. "The answer was an excited yes!" Whitaker reported. "One of the men was among the Russians freed by CPT Baum and his men. He had elected to remain in the area after the war. He said we were only 50 meters from the home of Herr Sturzenberger."

Whitaker walked the third of a mile to the house, knocked on the door, and was greeted by Sturzenberger's grandson, who invited him inside to meet the family. Karl Sturzenberger, Abe Baum's frightened and unwilling guide, had died in 1991, but the son who was born that day in 1945, named Walter, was there along with three grandsons and Sturzenberger's wife, who had given birth that day in 1945.

As Task Force Baum got closer to Hammelburg, at least two German units were also rushing toward the same destination. They had been alerted by the phone call from General Lotz after his escape from the Americans. From Schweinfurt, some 20 miles from Hammelburg, Hauptmann (Captain) Richard Koehl, who had been a priest before the war, led his company of eight Panzerjaeger, tank destroyers sporting 90mm cannons, capable of destroying any tank the Americans had.

The tank destroyers were loaded on a train to save gas and drove right off when they reached the railroad station in the town of Hammelburg. Carefully studying his map, after receiving a call that the Americans were most likely headed toward the POW camp, Koehl positioned his tank destroyers on a ridge overlooking Highway 27 and settled back to wait.

From another direction 300 SS officer cadets were marching at a furious pace toward Hammelburg. They desperately wanted to get there before the Americans did, not just because they were at war, but also to prove themselves worthy of becoming officers. All of them had combat experience as enlisted men, but now they were preparing themselves to serve as leaders in the most feared, frightening, and elite outfit of all.

As part of their training to be officers, they learned not only how to kill, but also "the courtesies of the officer profession, including dancing lessons and the formalities of exchanging cards when visiting (this in the middle of the final disastrous year of the war with the enemy within the boundaries of the Reich itself)," according to Charles Whiting.

When dancing lessons ended, the cadets did physical training, part of which involved doing pushups over daggers placed beneath their chests. If they got careless, or simply could not keep up the pace, they would fall on their own knives. They were obviously highly motivated to stay on their toes and hands.

At the POW camp headquarters, Oberst (Colonel) Cord van Hoepple, in command of the area around the camp, was concerned about the reports he had been receiving about the American tank unit heading toward them. He spoke to the camp commander, General von Goeckel, asking him how many troops he had at his disposal to fight off the Americans.

"I have two hundred men," von Goeckel replied, "all of them old. They are armed with rifles salvaged from the Belgians five years ago. They have thirty rounds per man."

Hoepple realized that they would not be able to put up much of a defense with the camp garrison. Their success would depend on units being sent to the area, including the tank destroyers, the SS officer cadets, his own small cadre of less than 100 men, and a few hundred others in training around Hammelburg. It was not an impressive or a well-trained force.

Hoepple knew that better and larger units were on their way, but it looked as though the American raiding party would reach Hammelburg before they would. He would have to do the best he could with what little resources he had. And he would have to do it very soon. At 2:20 that afternoon, he received a message from a unit of forward observers he had positioned a few miles outside of town. They reported spotting a column of twelve American tanks heading his way.

At 3:00 p.m., Task Force Baum arrived within sight of Oflag XIIIB on the outskirts of Hammelburg. Captain Baum did not slow, but maintained the column's high speed as he gave the order to attack. At the same moment, Hauptmann Koehl, 1,000 yards away on the ridge overlooking the highway, gave the order for his eight tank destroyers to open fire.

CHAPTER 9

THIS OFFICER MUST BE SAVED

"That's the way a tank battle starts, Padre," Colonel Goode said to Father Cavanaugh. "I've heard enough of them to know."

It was 2:00 P.M. on Tuesday, March 27, and the two men were standing just inside the barbed wire fence on Hermann Goering Strasse looking out across a beautiful meadow with flocks of sheep grazing lazily on new shoots of grass. It was a bright, beautiful, sunny day with not a cloud in the sky and the first hint of warmth in the air, after so many months of cold, wet, dismal weather.

In the hills beyond the meadow, Cavanaugh and Goode watched German troops taking up positions and saw German tanks and other vehicles moving fast and a single ambulance making its way down the road. All along the barbed wire fence, hundreds of other Kriegies gathered to see what was going on.

"The rumble of guns grew louder," Father Cavanaugh wrote. "Even those with poor hearing were sure they could distinguish the caliber of the weapons; machine guns, bazookas, mortars, tommy guns, Panzer Fausts, etc." And the noise of battle was getting closer. It sounded as though it was coming from the other side of the ridge they could see in the distance.

The rumors and excitement had started two hours before, at noon, when Colonel Goode and Lieutenant Colonel Waters had listened to the BBC and also German news broadcasts and then spread the word about what they had heard. The German report spoke of an American breakthrough at the small town of Schweinheim, not far from Frankfurt.

The broadcast also went into detail about the battle at Gemünden where, it said, the American force was beaten back with the loss of fifteen tanks and other vehicles. Chief Warrant Officer Harry Thompson said, "We did not believe that they had knocked out fifteen tanks, though. That's a lot of tanks to be destroyed in one skirmish."

German radio also indicated that the American column was trying to get to Hammelburg, which greatly raised the spirits and morale of the POWs. Help was on its way, they told one another. They would be free again in a matter of hours. But then they heard about the report on the BBC that Hitler had ordered that all prisoners of war being held in German camps were to be executed. If that was true, then even if the American force did get to Hammelburg soon, they could all be killed only hours before being rescued.

And then a rumor passed quickly, from one man to the next throughout the camp: that Colonel Goode had been told that morning to report to the office of the camp commandant, General von Goeckel. It was true, as Goode later told Father Cavanaugh. "General Patton's boys are getting close," Goode said, "and the Germans are going to move us out of here. They first wanted to move us at five o'clock this morning. I got them to put it off until evening. Now I'm hoping to have it postponed to five o'clock tomorrow morning. If we can stall them off long enough, the Americans will get here before the Germans move us."

According to some sources, there was another meeting between von Goeckel and Goode a few hours after the first one. Colonel Goode had arrived back in his quarters at an unrecorded time that morning to find von Goeckel and member of his staff, as well as the Serbian POW commander, waiting for him.

The German commandant looked worried, as well he should be. Not five minutes before, he had spotted an American tank about 2 miles from the camp and correctly assumed that it was part of a plan to release the Hammelburg POWs. "An American task force has broken through the German front and appears about to attack the camp," he told Goode and the others.

He knew that his chances of resisting an attack were slim, given the old, infirm guards and militia units he had at his disposal, most of whom were unfit for front-line duty. Still, he had to do his best, and so he told Goode and the others that he would resist the attack as much as possible. He then reminded them that they were still his prisoners, which meant that he was still responsible for their safety and well-being. He also admitted, however, that before the day was out, the situation might well be reversed. He would then be their prisoner.

But until such time, he told them, he was in charge. He ordered Goode and the Serbian commander to tell their men to take shelter during the battle in the air raid trenches and cellars and to remain quiet and not to get involved in trying to help their rescuers. "It would be foolish, gentlemen to do anything stupid at this late stage of the game, which might have serious consequences."

—◆—

The Serb Kriegies were also excited by the sounds of battle getting closer, and they too had heard the rumors about an American attack force. One group who had been away doing farm labor passed along the word when they were brought back to the camp that they had heard shots fired in closer range.

Lt. Konstantin Jovanovic had spent most of the morning by himself, reading a book about German cities, behind the stables on the edge of the camp closest to the town of Hammelburg. He looked up to see the German deputy commander of the Serbian compound looking as if he was afraid of something and acting as if someone was chasing after him. He stopped in front of Jovanovic and shouted, "*Die Amerikaner sind da . . . gleich hinter dem Berg!*" [The Americans are here . . . just behind the hill!] He pointed in the direction of the town, and then "he ran away like a headless chicken," the lieutenant wrote in a 1977 letter.

Back in the American compound, the Kriegies went wild with joy and excitement. John Waters vividly remembered that moment: "All of a sudden we heard a lot of shooting and looked out and by God, there were the American tanks on this hill about two or three miles away. An American force. Gawd, did you ever see so many people jumping up and down and screaming and yelling and hollering and carrying on and running around and shaking hands, unbelievable."

Capt. Donald Stewart, one of the group from Szubin who had been captured in North Africa, looked out from his barracks window in another direction and yelled, "My God, they're raiding the mess. They're throwing the food out." The men who worked in the kitchen preparing their daily meals had been ordered to prepare food to be ready for the possible evacuation of the camp so they would have enough to take with them to wherever they might be sent next.

Instead, they began throwing it out through the windows and doors to celebrate in advance their being freed. After all, once the Americans got there, they would not need what they had been using for food. As Baum and his *Raid!* coauthors reveal, "Canned goods, Red Cross parcels, loaves of bread, vegetables and small casks of margarine began piling up in the street outside the mess. Cheering men streamed from the barracks, Stewart among them. Men were clustered around the cornucopia in a thick, impenetrable circle, the tallest among them leaping high like basketball players to snare the food sailing through the air."

Captain Stewart and other Kriegies who were not so tall found themselves crawling on their hands and knees through the others to make their way inside. Once Stewart got there, the only thing left was a burlap bag he found on top of a pile of coal. He had no idea what was in it, but he grabbed it anyway and ran back to his barracks. When he opened the bag, he found the best prize of all.

It was sugar, and he and a friend took turns using their one spoon to eat almost all of it on the spot. It was a feast they would long remember. When they finished, they kept thinking that if all went well, they would be free in a matter of hours and would never go hungry again.

—◦—

While Task Force Baum moved closer to Hammelburg, George Patton moved his headquarters from France into Germany for the first time. He took over a former German infantry base at the town of Idar-Oberstein, located 50 miles to the west of the Rhine River. He settled into the officers' quarters, which still had its full complement of regimental silver, exquisitely monogrammed and adorned with swastikas. As busy as he was, he made sure that his men packed up a huge carved eagle and sent it as a gift from him to West Point.

In the midst of planning the movements of three of his divisions, he kept trying to find out if there was any news about the mission to Hammelburg. But neither Creighton Abrams nor General Hoge had anything to report. Later that day he wrote in his personal diary, "We were very much disturbed because we could not get any information at all as to what happened to the task force sent east from the 4th Armored Division."

The opening shots the Kriegies in Oflag XIIIB heard came from Hauptmann Richard Koehl's eight tank destroyers firing their 88mm antitank guns at Task Force Baum, passing 1,000 yards away on Highway 27. The first salvo missed, falling short of the highway and tearing up huge mounds of earth from the open meadow.

Captain Baum and every man in the column knew instantly they had a problem. They could tell from the sounds of the explosions that they were up against powerful weapons being fired from a position above them. Their only defense was quick deployment and even quicker return fire. Baum raced to the head of the column in his jeep and ordered it to turn to the right at the next intersection. Unfortunately, turning there was difficult and time consuming for the vehicles with treads, and that direction led them closer to Koehl's tank destroyer at the crest of the ridge.

T/Sgt. Charles Graham, who had been in command of the three assault guns, led his unit about 500 yards up the hill to take on the German tank destroyers. While they were on their way, the main column, which had slowed to a crawl to make the turn, became an excellent target. The German gunners hit two of Baum's tanks and one half-track, a serious loss.

Graham's gunners opened up with their deadly 105mm cannon and quickly destroyed three of the German tank destroyers along with six trucks bringing more guns and gas to Koehl's men. Meanwhile, Baum's heavy Sherman tanks also opened fire on the tank destroyers, but their weapons were not as effective as those of Sergeant Graham's assault guns.

Baum watched in frustration and anger as the shells from the Shermans scored direct hits on the enemy and simply bounced off their heavier armor plating.

But a shell from a German tank destroyer hit one of the Sherman tanks and it did not bounce off. It tore right through the steel armor plating and exploded. "The tank's interior was a bloody shambles," historian Charles Whiting notes. "The solid armor-piercing shell had penetrated the front of the turret just near the gunner. Tracing a path along the metal . . . it had swung across the turret, still glowing a vicious red, wrecking everything in its path. Miraculously, it did not hit one of the crew save the gunner, whose shining red blood spurted out to splash the walls of the vehicle."

The inside of the tank bore bright yellow spots of flame getting closer to the powder-filled shells, and it was full of smoke and a gag-inducing acrid smell spilling out from the damaged batteries. The survivors made their way out through the damaged hatches only to come under fire from German machine gunners farther up the hill. Incredibly, all four made it without being hit. But a second Sherman right behind them was hit next and started to burn.

Task Force Baum was taking other casualties as they headed toward the top of the hill. Baum got angry when he saw some of the crews of his half-tracks abandon their vehicles. As the driver of his jeep weaved his way among them, Baum stood up amidst the exploding shells and machine-gun fire and held on tight as he yelled at the men to get back in their half-tracks and get on up the hill. They did, but more of Baum's men and machines were being hit.

Sgt. Donald Yoerk, whose *City of New York* had lost a tread and had to be abandoned, was riding in the back of a half-track with his gunner, George Wyatt. They bailed out when a shell hit the front and exploded. They continued up the hill on foot and came upon another tank that had been hit and saw two men trying to pull a wounded man out. He was dead, but they saved two more from inside the tank and then managed to start the engine and drive it up the hill. In the meantime, Hauptmann Koehl's remaining tank destroyers on the next ridge were running out of shells and fuel, and he pulled his vehicles out of the fight.

It was obvious to Koehl that the Americans were heading toward the POW camp, and so he took his unit on a course parallel to theirs but hidden from view in a valley. He was going to load up with more gas and ammunition from another supply convoy not far away and then wait for the Americans and try to ambush them when they left the camp and headed back toward their lines.

The rest of Task Force Baum made its way to the top of the hill and assembled around a huge French cross that had been erected in 1919 to honor French prisoners of war who had died at Hammelburg during World War I. While waiting for the rest of the infantry to arrive, Baum assembled his officers to brief them on what lay ahead.

Among them he was surprised to see Nutto, who had been wounded back at Gemünden, where Baum had also been hit but not nearly as seriously. Nutto was limping and was still wrapped in blood-covered dressings, but when Baum looked at him questioningly, Nutto replied that he could manage. Baum said nothing more and turned to his infantry officers to tell them to break up their platoons into squads of a half dozen or so each and to follow the tanks.

When Baum got back to his jeep, he found Major Stiller waiting for him. Baum knew that he was in command, but he hesitated a moment, recognizing that Stiller outranked him but also that he was only there because he could recognize Patton's son-in-law, and that he might want to go off on his own to find him.

"Now that we're here," Baum asked the major, "what are you going to do?"

Stiller gestured to the small groups of infantry gathered behind the tanks.

"I'll take one of the squads, if that's OK with you."

Baum nodded and Stiller pulled out his .45 and walked over to the nearest group of infantry.

From the top of the hill, Baum's men had their first view of Oflag XIIIB, which lay spread out at the bottom of a gentle incline some 1,700 yards away. They were barely a mile from what they had come all this way for, and Baum saw through his binoculars that there were very few guards or other German soldiers left in place around the camp.

Once they reached the camp, he knew they would have no trouble getting in and freeing the prisoners. But the battle still raged around them up on the hill.

He had to make sure he had beaten back those tank destroyers and small bands of infantry that continued to fire on them before he led his men down to the camp. He could not risk trying to take the prisoners away while still under fire. He would never forgive himself if some were to be killed in the very act of being set free.

But it was getting late. The battle was taking far too long, they were even further behind schedule, and their losses were mounting. He had lost three tanks; five half-tracks, one of which had held their fuel and ammo reserves; as well as three jeeps, along with an undetermined number of men.

He ordered Sergeant Graham and his remaining assault guns, along with a platoon of infantry, to stay behind them to provide covering fire from the rear. He arranged his remaining eleven tanks in a line, side by side, with the infantry, half-tracks, and jeeps behind them, and headed down the hill toward Oflag XIIIB. It was 4:10 P.M.

Inside the camp Father Cavanaugh started to prepare for mass at 3:30 in spite of the sounds of battle, which seemed to be getting closer. About a hundred men showed up for the service, held in a large room adjacent to the barracks. Cavanaugh began, as he always did, by hearing confessions, but then at ten minutes to four, he was loudly interrupted by the blare of the camp air raid sirens. Outside, orders were shouted for everyone to stay in their barracks and to keep away from windows and doors.

"Since no more can get here," he told the men, "I will start mass immediately and give you general absolution before Holy Communion." The men were not alone in their fear. "While I was vesting," he wrote later, "several shots landed very close to the camp. I began the prayers at the foot of the altar with trepidation." Suddenly a large shell exploded somewhere nearby in the camp and the men dropped to the floor while Father Cavanaugh got under the table he used as an altar. After a few moments of waiting breathlessly for another shell to land, but hearing only the continuing sounds of combat beyond the camp's fence, Cavanaugh slowly got up. "I stood up," he recalled, and "told the men to be calm (though I did not give them a very good example). And to remain kneeling.

"If anything happens," he continued," just stretch out on the floor. . . . With trembling hands I made the sign of the cross over the kneeling congregation. At the Lavabo (washing of the hands) the building shook with another explosion—a direct hit, it seemed. Again we were all prone on the floor."

The attack was getting closer by the minute.

"I kept pushing the task force over the ridge," Baum said, "onto the high ground where two companies of Kraut infantry were dug in. It took us two and a half hours to clean it up so the infantry and tanks could move in."

The German militia troops had dug a series of foxholes outside the camp's barbed wire fence and kept up a heavy round of rifle and machine-gun fire. In addition, more German troops were holed up in several concrete sheds and outbuildings on the camp's perimeter. They had more machine guns and at least one Panzerfaust.

The closer the Americans got, the more tightly their infantry bunched together behind each tank, which reduced their ability to maintain a steady and heavy rate of fire. The attack moved forward with agonizing slowness, and the tanks' cannons did not spread their fire but instead concentrated on a tall wooden water tower within the camp's perimeter, which they eventually hit, but which did nothing to reduce the Germans' defense capability.

After they shot down the water tower, most of the tank fire was directed toward the Serbian compound, which upset von Goeckel as well as Colonel Goode and John Waters, who were all watching the shells explode. The Americans did not want to see their friends among the Serbs, who had helped them so much, be killed by Americans. Something had to be done, and it was von Goeckel who recognized his responsibility, his duty, as camp commandant. He quickly made his way to Goode's room.

"Look," he said to Goode and Waters, "there is no point, we can't resist this force anymore. I don't have any forces here to withstand this attack. As far as I'm concerned, I'm your prisoner now."

He pointed out that the Americans were killing Serbs and that Goode and Waters had to get them to stop. The Geneva Convention forbade combat in a prisoner of war camp, and now it was their responsibility to protect the Serbs, not his.

Goode and Waters agreed and suggested that they send a group under a flag of truce to explain the situation to the American attacking force and get them to stop shooting. They had to persuade the Americans that the battle for Hammelburg was over. Waters volunteered to lead the group, and three other Americans and a German, Hauptmann Fuchs, acting as interpreter, agreed to go with him. The other Americans were Capt. Emil Stutter, and lieutenants George Meskall and James Mills.

Waters went back to his barracks and got out the American flag he had carried with him since his days in the camp at Szubin. Someone gave Fuchs a white sheet to wave over their heads in hopes that no one would shoot at them. Waters and Fuchs led the group through the camp gate with the other three in a line behind them.

They turned left once outside the camp and walked down a country road. As they passed a barn, Waters spotted a soldier wearing a camouflage uniform who looked to him like a paratrooper. He thought perhaps he was an American but he was not sure, and so he called out *Amerikanish* to identify his party as Americans.

"My poor German attracted his attention," Waters wrote years later.

He looked over there and saw us coming down the road. He ran over to a fence about ten yards away and saw that it was a German officer and [four] Americans, US flag and a white flag. I think he must have thought that the German officer had surrendered to us. So, he put his gun through the fence at the second rail, and pulled the trigger. The bullet hit me here on my right thigh, and hit the ischium bone [the back part of the hip bone] and then bounced up and hit the coccyx and came out my left buttocks.

Just one shot. And I fell down in the road. It felt like somebody hit me with a telegraph pole. There was no pain. There was no pain because I was numb from the waist down. And I said to him [the German who had shot him] "You son-of-a-bitch, you ruined my fishing."

That's what I said to him, I did. Because I was thinking and planning on going fishing, for a long time—after the liberation! That's a hell of a statement to make when you get shot but that is what I said.

No one in Task Force Baum saw John Waters get shot, but it would have made no difference if they had. It would not have changed the outcome of the attack, and no one but Major Stiller would have recognized Waters anyway. Only Baum and Stiller knew that his rescue was what the mission was all about. If he could not be saved, then there was no point to the raid.

And there was no way to rescue Waters now and take him back to the American lines because his wound was so serious. He later learned that "had the bullet been one-sixteenth of an inch higher, he would have been killed, or at best, paralyzed for the rest of his life." He desperately needed proper medical treatment immediately, but the German guard kept his rifle aimed at the others and was threatening to shoot the German officer, Captain Fuchs.

The guard told Fuchs to stand up against the wall and prodded him with his bayonet while Waters and the others watched. The guard may have thought the officer was deserting, the penalty for which was death, no matter the rank. Captain Fuchs gestured and spoke frantically, explaining to the guard that the commandant had surrendered to the Americans and that he had sent them to meet with the Americans and get them to stop shelling the Serbian compound.

Waters lay on the ground where he had fallen and the other American officers stood still with their hands raised, wondering if they would be shot too. Fuchs kept on talking, and finally the guard lowered his rifle and told them to go back to the camp.

The three Americans found a German orderly who got a blanket from von Goeckel's quarters, which they used to place under Waters and carry him to the civilian hospital in the town of Hammelburg. But when they arrived, they were told that the hospital was too full of sick and wounded Germans, and the staff refused to take Waters. It is possible that there actually was room for another patient, but not an American one. At any rate their refusal meant that Waters had to be carried in the blanket all the way back to the Serbian side of the compound and the hospital there.

The procession was met outside the hospital building by a Serbian officer who had become good friends with Waters, Capt. Dragon Yosefovitch. He quickly led them inside to what passed for an operating room and yelled, "This officer must live."

Chapter 10

MISSION ACCOMPLISHED!

IF GEORGE S. PATTON HAD BEEN AT HAMMELBURG THAT AFTERNOON OF March 27 with Abe Baum, some have suggested, it would have been easy to imagine him screaming, "Abe! Why the hell is it taking you over two goddamn hours to get from the top of this hill to the camp?" According to historian Charles Whiting, writing in 1970, General von Goeckel said just that after the war: that he did not understand why it took the Americans so long to reach the camp from the hill with the huge French memorial cross.

The German commandant said that when the American tanks hit one of the buildings in the Serbian compound, which went up in a bright burst of flame, "I expected then that they would overrun the wire fence guarding the camp. After all there was nothing to stop them. But to my surprise they did nothing. Instead, they remained at 500 to 800 meters' distance, firing their cannon from time to time."

Whiting goes on to note that "it is very hard to get at the truth of the matter. No one seems to be able to tell the inquirer what happened between 1700 hours and darkness . . . save that Baum's tanks, remaining outside the camp, fired continually into the Serbian compound."

No one corrected or even questioned those critical remarks until eleven years later, in 1981, when Robert Baron, one of the Kriegies at Hammelburg, and Abe Baum coauthored a book with the writer Richard Goldhurst. In it they presented their version of events. Baum and his men were totally exhausted, they wrote, having been on the move constantly, and surviving one battle or ambush after another since the previous night at Schweinheim.

Having come so far and faced down so many obstacles, the goal was in sight. They were so close to the wire fence they could see the prisoners inside watching and waiting for them. Captain Baum said that he had by then more than earned the right to be extremely careful as they approached the camp, to make sure that no further surprises—such as another ambush by a larger force—awaited them there. And so he proceeded with exquisite caution, one step at a time.

He set his men in motion from the top of the hill at a very slow speed of only 5 miles an hour, on the lookout for anything unusual. Baum rode in his jeep behind the wide line of tanks. They had gone only a short distance when one of Sergeant Graham's assault guns hit something that exploded into a huge bright flame and threw out so much smoke that it totally obscured their view forward. Baum's men cheered, thinking they had hit a German tank or a truck loaded with ammunition or gasoline. It turned out to be a haystack, but Baum had no way of knowing that, and he ordered the advance to slow down to a crawl.

When they got within 200 yards of the camp, they were hit by rifle and machine-gun fire as well as Panzerfausts. As the smoke from the still-burning haystack began to clear, Baum was able to make out a line of foxholes where the enemy fire was coming from, not far from the camp fence. He ordered his men to return fire, but then he noticed more shots and shells coming from some buildings and sheds and what looked like a stable on the edge of the camp.

Serbian lieutenant Konstantin Jovanovic, who had been quietly reading a book about German cities when the attack began, watched it all unfold from his high vantage point on the edge of the Serbian compound. He wrote that it felt like the earth was shaking: "Yellow tracers covered the whole sky. It was like a fireworks display. All the tracers ended up in the forest at the opposite side of the camp. Suddenly, there was the simultaneous counter fire from German machine guns."

Then he heard the roar of tank engines and the clanking of tank treads. Suddenly, the earth felt as if it were shaking again beneath him and the sounds of battle were now much closer. He hugged the ground as machine-gun fire and shells roared over his head and began hitting the roofs and walls of the Serbian barracks and the stable he had been leaning against.

"Hell," he thought, "they are aiming at me!" He suddenly worried that he was going to be killed at the moment he was about to be liberated after being a prisoner for four years. He said, "It was the worst situation which I experienced since the beginning of the war." But then the firing shifted and he raised his head and looked down the hill to see American tanks and infantry moving slowly toward the wire fence of the American compound.

Capt. Roger Shinn, captured at the Bulge, watched the battle from his barracks window and remembered seeing the first American infantryman come closer. "The silhouette of the American helmet on the hilltop was beautiful. The GIs looked wonderful. They deployed, fired and advanced, in the tactics that we knew so well. . . . Machine guns still rattled, shells exploded. One of the Serb barracks was on fire; a shell had landed there. It was curious to be a spectator in this fight. No fight had ever been more exciting to us; yet we could do nothing. So we watched."

As the infantry got closer to the compound, more of them were hit. "Men were dropping everywhere on the slope," Whiting notes. "Here and there a man cried out loud for a medic in shocked angry bewilderment that this terrible hurt had been done to him. But there were others who lay crumpled and still. . . . They would never move again, dying to save a man they were fated never to see."

The closer they got to the barbed wire fence, the more casualties they took. No one knows for sure how many were lost on that final assault. The official count was nine, but one American Kriegie said he counted twenty-five bodies on the slope leading to the camp.

❧

Baum looked closely through his binoculars and saw what looked like more German machine guns and Panzerfausts. He ordered the tankers to shift fire to the buildings. As the tanks turned a bit to the left, the infantry behind them found themselves out in the open, taking fire from the enemy in the foxholes. The tanks and infantry were still moving forward but at a very slow pace, to make sure they hit all the Germans in the foxholes.

More of Baum's infantry were getting hit, but the Germans began retreating as the tanks continued forward. Some of the men could see the flagpole inside the camp, and they saw the German flag descend down the pole and in its place a crude American flag being run up to the top. One of the tanks then charged toward the barbed wire fence as fast as it could go, hit it, and broke through.

A second tank pulled up beside it, turned to the right, and started running down the length of the fence, knocking down the wire and every wooden post. Lieutenant Jovanovic watched it and later called it the fulfillment of a four-year dream: "I could see it with my own eyes. A huge tank (later I was told it was a Sherman) drove toward the main fence and began to push it. The mess of wooden piles, barbed wire, signal and alert devices, began to move under loud bursting and cracking into the compound. The strong wooden piles at the gap left and right bent one after another like matches . . . and the whole fence was pushed deeper and deeper into the compound. Finally the tank [buried] this mess under its tracks and drove now into the camp compound. I couldn't wait any longer. I ran so fast along the embankment to this place."

When the tank came to a halt, one of the American Kriegies climbed up on it and yelled, "Got a cigarette, buddy?"

Inside the Serbian compound, John Waters was being operated on by a once-prominent surgeon in Belgrade who ran the Serbian POW hospital. Col. Radovan Danich and his assistant, a dentist named Giri Georgevitch, saved Waters's life and gave him the ability to walk again later with a combination of primitive equipment, expert technique, and attentive care. But it was a horrible time for Waters.

"I had violent hiccups. I would hiccup for an hour or two at a time," he recalled. "And I had diarrhea. I couldn't eat. I could not hold anything and if I ate anything it would go right through me. The hospital had some sort of a pain killer which was no pain killer at all. . . . So I just lay there. Dr. Danich kept this wound open so it was draining. That's all he could do. Keep it open with the table knife and paper bandages and let it drain." Waters was in no condition to be moved, to be rescued and taken back to American lines, which was what the mission was all about, but at least he was still alive.

———

Father Cavanaugh continued his mass throughout the rising sounds of battle outside and the occasional explosion that brought him and his congregation to its knees. In his 2004 book, he revealed the instant it all changed: "Just as I finished the last line of communicants, a tremendous shout of jubilation rose from the windows across the street. Loud talking, shouting and laughing came from men who had rushed from the barracks into the street."

"We're free! We're liberated!" they exclaimed. "You're not a Kriegie any longer."

The makeshift American flag had just been raised to the top of the flagpole, a signal for all to see. Within minutes white sheets were being hung out of all the windows facing to the east, by both the Americans and the Germans. Everyone wanted the attackers to know that the battle was over. Hammelburg was theirs for the taking.

That was when the first American tank burst through the barbed wire and came to a stop right outside the building where Father Cavanaugh had held the mass. "Liberated prisoners crowded around it," Cavanaugh wrote. "It was a grand sight. Better still was the appearance of Americans in combat dress. The tankers with their steel helmets, ammunition belts, field jackets and boots, and with rifles in their hands. Their ruddy faces and lithe bodies contrasted strangely with the drawn looks and emaciated frames and the dirty clothes of the Kriegies. From the wondrous recesses of the tank came cases of K-rations, which were distributed prodigally to the skinny hands that reached out for them."

Captain Shinn remembered years later the sheer joy and exuberance of the moment. And something else as well: "It was not only the glorious hope of freedom. For with this, perhaps even more than this, was the feeling that someone had come after us, that after months when we had not mattered, someone cared enough to come and get us. It felt wonderful to be Americans."

Amidst all the chaos and confusion, Maj. Al Stiller went from one barracks to the next, looking for Lt. Col. John Waters. He finally found him in the Serbian hospital and spoke to Waters's friend, Dragon Yosefovitch, and the two doctors who had operated on Waters. They told him how seriously he was wounded, what they were doing to try to save his life, and that there was still a possibility he would be paralyzed forever. Stiller did not indicate whether he was able to speak to Waters, but he left to rejoin the task force, knowing he had a terrible message that he dreaded delivering to General Patton.

The raucous celebration continued. "It was like Times Square on New Year's Eve," Baum said. The Kriegies went wild, yelling and cheering, jumping up on the tanks and hugging and even kissing their liberators. "We had to push them off," Sergeant Graham said. It was chaos as hundreds of prisoners, who now thought they were free, celebrated the day they had for so long believed would never come. They overwhelmed Baum's men and their vehicles. They carried their bedrolls and extra clothes and as many Red Cross cans of food as they could stuff in their pockets, ready to leave the camp.

Baum, still suffering from pain in his hand and knee from his wounds at Gemünden, looked on in despair at the wild scene and wondered why the POWs seemed to be totally without any discipline or organization. They were acting like a crazed mob completely out of control as far as he was concerned. When he had first reached the downed fence, he had been immensely pleased and relieved, but then he began to realize that there were far more POWs there than he had been told. There were supposed to be only 300 of them to try to get back.

Baum said nearly sixty years later that he was, at first, "elated at the fact that I got there. It was a miracle in itself. But I had understood that there were supposed to be three hundred POWs. And out ran fifteen hundred. That overwhelmed me. It was unbelievable. I could have thrown up when I saw them. I was frustrated and exhausted, and we hadn't had any rest for two days. It was sickening to see the condition of some of the POWs, skeletons of men. . . . I knew damn well I couldn't take those men back. And even if I did take some of them with me, I wasn't certain we were going to make it."

He knew he was going to have to tell the Kriegies the awful truth, that he could not take all of them back. There simply was not enough room on the number of vehicles he had left to carry them all. And most of them were too weak and exhausted to be able to walk all that distance on their own.

And there was something else that Baum realized in that chaotic and confusing moment. He was not even sure that he could get his own men back through 60 miles of German territory, given that the enemy now knew precisely where he was. They also knew the general route he would have to take to return to where he started.

He and his men were battle weary, worn out, and dispirited; his gas and ammunition supplies were running low; he was overwhelmed by the number of POWs and upset that he could possibly save only a small number of them. And Major Stiller had told him about Lieutenant Colonel Waters being shot and in critical condition. Baum would not be bringing Patton's son-in-law back to him. Nevertheless, he brazenly dictated a message to his radio operator to send back to the division headquarters. "Mission accomplished," it read. "It was the last message anyone was to receive from Task Force Baum," Charles Whiting tells us. "After that, there was nothing but silence."

———

After the POWs got over their initial excitement, a note of alarm spread through their ranks when they realized how small the attacking force was. And when they started talking to the Americans, they were shocked to find out that the soldiers were not part of a general advance as the prisoners had thought. The American army was not right behind them, just over the hill. It was still 60 miles away!

And then they began to see the poor condition of the outfit. Lt. Bill Falkenheiner, one of those captured at the Battle of the Bulge, wrote of the rescuers: "They appeared tired, apprehensive and unwilling to communicate with what must have appeared to them as a large group of unorganized rabble."

After not being able to persuade Colonel Goode to tell the Kriegies the truth about their supposed rescue, Baum realized that he had no choice but to tell them himself. He climbed up on the hood of one of the half-tracks and shouted for the men to be quiet. All eyes turned toward him, some men hopeful about finally being free and others fearful that he was going to tell them they were still prisoners.

"We came to bring you back to American lines," Baum said, "but there are far more of you than we expected. We don't have enough vehicles to take all of you. Those of you who want to go will have to go on your own." Gesturing over his shoulder to the west, he said, "When I left, the lines were about sixty miles back in that direction at the River Main. That's all I can tell you. The Seventh Army should be moving up closer by now. Some of you who want to go may be able to walk along with the column, but remember, we'll probably have to fight our way out of here."

The men looked at one another in stunned disbelief, and Captain Baum had to hold back the tears as he saw the disappointed, angry, sad, and forlorn looks on their faces. They milled around, yelling at one another about what to do, to go or stay. Some decided to go with the attacking force, and they climbed up on the tanks and other vehicles in such numbers that the tanks could not even turn their turrets.

According to some accounts, Colonel Goode also spoke to at least some of the men, and his comments were received no better than Baum's had been. Chief Warrant Officer Harry Thompson said that Goode sounded as disappointed and disgusted as even Thompson himself.

"That way is west, fellows," Goode said. "The task force does not have enough gas to get us back to the front or enough vehicles to transport all of us, so you are on your own." Upon hearing that, a number of angry and disappointed men started walking back to the camp. After a moment, however, most of the Kriegies trudged slowly behind Goode.

"We could not believe it," Thompson wrote years later. "They sent a damn task force to liberate us and did not give them enough stinking gasoline to get back to American lines!! What kind of crap was this?"

It was a downhearted, dejected group that straggled slowly back to the camp. Before it was all over, fully two-thirds of the Kriegies would return to Hammelburg to become prisoners of war again, so soon after believing they had been set free. Father Cavanaugh was one of them. He felt he had to go back for the sake of those who had come to depend on him for religious consolation.

"My duty was clear," he wrote. "I must go back too and see this thing through with them. . . . Captain John Madden and I reached the gaping hole left by a tank in the barbed wire fence shortly after midnight. There was scarcely a word spoken as we trudged along. In the compound we had inhabited for over two months an American officer on guard at the gate told us to go directly to our barracks and remain inside."

"We are not free yet, Father," one of the Kriegies said to him.

Captain Shinn could not make up his mind as to what to do. Expressing the feelings of so many of the men, he wrote: "The thought of prison made us shudder. Our imaginations tried to reckon with the possibilities of getting to American lines on foot. Sixty miles! Weak and half-starved as we were, we could never make it without food. I tried to get K-rations from the half-tracks. There were none left.

"We did not know where the American forces were. . . . 'Go due west,' someone said. But where was West? Clouds covered the stars, and no one could keep directions in these winding valleys. Without food and a map it would be a dangerous job, but worth the risk. Without them it seemed hopeless."

Shinn came across Colonel Goode and asked him what he thought he should do, but Goode refused to give him any advice, one way or the other.

"What are you doing, sir?" Shinn asked.

"I'm going with the vehicles," he replied. "I think I have done my duty."

"I think you have, sir."

Shinn stayed with the task force for a while, still trying to decide what to do, and then slowly headed back to the barbed wire, wondering if he was doing the right thing.

Capt. Benjamin Lemmer, another Kriegie captured during the Battle of the Bulge, tried to analyze his dilemma the way he might deal with a hand at poker. "Baum had put the cards on the table; there wasn't room for everyone. And the danger would be great for those who followed the column." The odds were high that the column would be attacked by Germans on their way back to American lines, and both Kriegies and task force members would die. As much as Lemmer hated the thought of being a prisoner again, he realized that there was a greater chance of staying alive at Hammelburg, and so he returned. When he got back to his barracks, he heard one of the other men say, "We're better off here. At least nobody is shooting at us. Besides, the war is almost over."

Lemmer and his buddies pooled the cigarettes they had been given by the tankers and, as they had been doing for months, cut each one into four equal parts so they would last longer. No one knew when they might be able to get more.

Lieutenant Falkenheiner was determined not to go back to Hammelburg. He was finally free and intended to stay that way. "A friend and I decided we should take our chances with the task force," he later recalled. "It was not a wise decision, but we did not know all the circumstances. Our desire to get out of the prison dominated our action." He and his friend managed to find a place on one of the Sherman tanks. There were so many Kriegies hanging on the tanks that it was impossible to tell their color anymore. Capt. Paul Kunkle tried climbing on one of the Shermans carrying a large pillowcase over his shoulder stuffed with rolls of toilet paper, socks, and food.

One of the Kriegies already on the tank told him there was not enough room for both him and the pillowcase. He dropped it without another thought and climbed aboard, but then one of the tank's crew told him he was too close to the cannon. He dropped off and then got on the back of the same tank where another crew member yelled at him: "Stick the aerial up your ass and hang on."

Lt. Bob Thompson, one of the Szubin Kriegies who had been captured at Anzio, decided to try to make it out with the task force. He was determined not to be a prisoner any longer. Somewhere he had found an M-1 rifle and two bandoleers of ammunition that he strapped across his chest. He felt he was ready for anything.

"I hid in some bushes, and late that night when the tanks started their engines to begin their trip back to the American lines, I climbed out of the bushes and tried to crawl up on one of the tanks, but so many of the prisoners had the same idea that the only place for me was on the hood of a half-track. I held onto the cannon of the half-track to keep from falling off, and the armored column started on their way. There were two Sherman tanks at the head of the column followed by about nine half-tracks. We drove through one little town about midnight and passed a couple of German soldiers on the street. They thought we were Germans, so they yelled their greetings, and we yelled 'hello' to them." So far, so good.

Lieutenant Jovanovic stood inside the Serbian compound, watching all the excitement and confusion on the American side. Suddenly, Lt. John Callaghan, an American with whom he had become good friends, came over to ask him to escape with him by going out with the task force. They should go together, Callaghan said.

"But I answered him, he should better think about it and not to climb a tank for a far and uncertain way back. Captain Baum managed it to come to Hammelburg, but it would be doubtful, if the way back would be that easy. . . . I tried to explain to him the dangers he would encounter. But he was determined to follow. He could not bear to stay any longer in this camp and wanted to go back, even if he would die. We embraced in friendship and shook hands and I wished him luck."

Jovanovic watched the column of tanks and half-tracks start up their engines while still more Americans tried to climb onto the vehicles. There were so many, he said, that they had to hold onto each other, and every vehicle was so jammed that he could no longer even distinguish the turrets of the tanks. "Everything went OK and according to schedule," Jovanovic recalled in 1977. "In vain I was looking for John, but I couldn't discover him in the crowd of people." He never saw Callaghan again.

Some of the men from Hammelburg thought they would stand a better chance of reaching the American front line if they tried to make it on their own. Lt. James Mills had spent much of the time since the Americans had burst through the barbed wire fence at the Serbian hospital checking on the progress of John Waters. When he was satisfied that Waters might live, he went to join the other Kriegies and was surprised to see many of them coming back into the camp looking angry and dejected.

When the other prisoners told him what the situation was, he decided that he was going to take advantage of his newfound freedom and try to escape by himself. As he walked toward the nearby woods, heading west, he looked over his shoulder and saw many other prisoners climbing all over the tanks and a few others following him in small groups.

Lt. Jay Drake had made the march from Szubin to Hammelburg and was determined not to remain a Kriegie any longer. He turned to his close friend Ed Lockert, who had also been at Szubin, and said, "Let's head west." Lockert said he was going back to the camp with all the others who were heading that way.

Two other men standing nearby, Robert Corbin and Dallas Smith, overheard the conversation and said they would like to go with Drake. All the trio had with them were their overcoats, gloves, and hats along with three loaves of bread and their most precious possession, a compass Drake had kept since being captured. They walked as fast as they could, determined to get as far away from the camp as possible before dawn. Then they planned to find a hiding place and sleep all day long.

Back at Hammelburg the heavy tanks began to maneuver to form a column to start heading back. Amidst all the noise and the growing darkness, no one noticed one of the task force's men lying wounded on the ground. Lt. Don Stewart, who was trying to get to one of the half-tracks, spotted him just as a Sherman started to back up toward him. Stewart, and then others, yelled at the tank to stop, but the noise was too great and one of the tank treads rolled right over the man's head, leaving just his legs and body and the mark of a deep tank tread where his head had been. Those who watched it happen never forgot the sight.

CHAPTER 11

TWO HOURS TOO LONG

THE JUDGMENT OF HISTORY SEEMS TO BE UNANIMOUS THAT TASK FORCE Baum stayed too long on the hillside outside of Hammelburg before trying to get back to American lines. "Amid the confusion, indecision, and grumbling at the Oflag, almost two hours passed," researcher Tobin Green says. Adding that to the two hours it had taken to reach the camp from the nearby hilltop put Task Force Baum much further behind schedule, giving the Germans even more time to prepare to move against them.

The Americans' chances of surviving the raid were growing slimmer by the minute. Everyone was frustrated and angry at the delay, and many viewed their survival as hopeless because of it.

"It was probably exhaustion that made Captain Baum sit on his tail for the next few precious hours," historian Charles Whiting writes, "while all about him in the darkened countryside the Germans prepared to deal him a death blow. Captain Abraham Baum simply wasted too much time at Hammelburg before he decided to move out." He also failed to post guards around their current position to detect any enemy soldiers who might be trying to sneak up on them in the darkness. Nor had he sent patrols to scout out any nearby German troop movements.

Baum was indeed exhausted by then and still suffering from previous battle wounds. He developed feelings of helplessness and guilt at having to leave so many men at Hammelburg to become POWs again. His task force was short of vehicles, gasoline, and ammunition. He doubted there was enough gas for his remaining vehicles to travel the 60 or so miles to reach American lines.

His men were equally worn out and discouraged and were still being harassed by so many of the prisoners pleading, even begging, to go along with them. Their tanks and half-tracks were so crowded with men clinging to them that some drivers could not see their way ahead or swivel their cannon and machine guns around.

And they too felt guilty at the thought of leaving men behind, the men they had come so far to set free. They had survived so much in the way of enemy attacks and lost so many of their own, and now they had to turn around and retrace their steps through enemy territory. The odds were not in their favor, and they all knew it. But their success or failure, indeed their survival, was the commander's responsibility, and "the young American captain from the Bronx hesitated too long about his next course of action. Two hours too long," Whiting argues.

Finally, sometime after 9:00 P.M., Baum called his subordinate commanders together and spread out a map on the hood of his jeep. "We can't go back the way we came," he told them, pointing to the west and south on the map. "The enemy who defended this area when we came in have had a chance to dig in. Why fight an entrenched enemy? I'm going around them. I'm going south to find the Seventh Army."

He told Lieutenant Nutto, still holding on despite his wounds, to lead his medium tanks and three of the half-tracks loaded with infantry on a reconnaissance patrol to see if Highway 27 leading to the west was open. When someone asked what they should do about any German roadblocks they might encounter, the answer was clear.

"We avoid them," Baum said. "We can't afford a firefight at night. Look at those half-tracks and tanks. They're covered with prisoners. We'd lose every one of them. We dodge roadblocks. We back up. We run around them. That's why I want Nutto to go out first, to find a clear route to the highway. Once he's found it, then we barrel-ass out of here."

Nutto's men started up their engines, shattering the night quiet, and began moving out. Baum gave the order to form the remaining vehicles in a single column to be ready to move as soon as they heard from Nutto. It was then 10:30 on the night of March 27, 1945.

Baum's two-hour delay worked to the advantage of the Germans, who made good use of the time, putting together several units in the area to block whichever direction the Americans decided to move. The 300 SS officer cadets had finished their forced march from the area around Gemünden and were ready to do battle at a point to the southwest of Baum's location.

Not far from them, a Major Diefenbek had rounded up a scratch force of combat engineers and anyone else he could find and was moving them slowly toward Baum's position from the south. Hauptmann Koehl, whose tank destroyers had started the battle against the Americans when they reached the hill overlooking the camp, had been refueled, fed, and rested and was eager to get back into action again.

By chance, a battalion of assault guns was passing through the town of Hammelburg on their way west from the Russian front. Their commander was either too timid, tired, or afraid to commit his troops to action, but a higher-ranking officer who happened to be in town on leave took over the outfit and agreed to join in the fight.

In the meantime, Colonel Hoepple, the military commander under General von Goeckel, set up radio communications between Hammelburg and other towns in the area through which the Americans might pass.

And finally, in the forest next to where Task Force Baum was organizing itself into a column, a lone German paratrooper whose name is not known moved toward the rear of the column. No one saw or heard him as he edged closer with his Panzerfaust.

Moments after Lieutenant Nutto led his reconnaissance patrol away from Baum's main force, the last tank in Baum's newly formed column exploded in a huge ball of fire and debris. The lone German had done his job well and he apparently escaped in the darkness. Baum ordered his outfit to spread out in a circular defensive formation and hoped he would hear good news from Nutto soon so they could move away from that area with its burning tank and the acrid smell of flesh from the incinerated crew members.

Nutto's reconnaissance unit was under observation by Hauptmann Hoepple from the moment it left the main force. As he watched its progress, he shifted his forces about to where it appeared they were heading. Nutto moved cautiously and stopped whenever he could not see clearly what was ahead. At those times, he ordered all engines turned off and he edged forward on foot by himself to assess what might be in front of them.

One of the times they stopped and Nutto got out, the men clearly heard the sound of German soldiers somewhere nearby. And they were singing, sounding as though they were drunk. The Americans did not dare make a sound as the enemy troops moved slowly past them and the strains of their singing slowly died out. The Germans had been sent to Bonnland, the second of two villages up ahead that Nutto's force would soon reach.

By 11:00 P.M., Nutto's men were passing through Hundsfeld, the first of the villages, which appeared to be empty. Nutto assumed that everyone who lived there was hiding in their cellars or had fled into the woods when they heard the tanks coming.

Actually, no one lived in either town; both had been long ago emptied of people and turned into infantry training centers for house-to-house close fighting. Shortly after Nutto's unit passed through the first town, the men spotted a roadblock ahead fashioned out of cut trees. Nutto stopped, radioed Baum, and asked what the captain wanted him to do.

Baum told him to do nothing until he got there, and then he drove as fast as he could in the dark to Nutto's position. When he saw the situation, Baum ordered Nutto to turn his unit around and go back to the first village and take the road heading toward the Reussenberg Woods, which were above the valley they were in.

When Baum got back to his main force, he was relieved to see that many of the POWs were heading back to the camp at Hammelburg. Baum and his men knew, as selfish as it was, that they had a greater chance of surviving and getting back to their lines if they were saddled with fewer prisoners hanging onto their vehicles.

Meanwhile, the Germans were carefully following Nutto's change of direction. They knew exactly where he was at all times and where he was heading. Hoepple ordered a platoon of combat engineers to proceed quickly to a hill near the Reussenberg Woods overlooking the road Nutto's unit was traveling on.

Referred to on maps as Hill 340, the Germans used it as a vantage point from which, within the hour, they saw Nutto's tanks. Within a few minutes, the Americans were close enough for the Germans to hear the sound of their engines and the clanking of their treads. It was the perfect spot for an ambush.

Nutto's men heard the sound of firing and saw a roadblock ahead at the same time. They stopped and radioed Baum, who came racing up in his jeep again. Baum quickly took in the situation and realized they could not continue in that direction.

"I guess we'll have to turn off here," he told Nutto. "This trail on the map heads west and will probably take us to the main highway at Höllrich." The town of Höllrich was four and a half miles distant, and the road to it had the advantage of winding its way through a forest that would provide protection from long-range artillery fire at least. It did not, however, provide any protection from the far-shorter-range Panzerfausts, or from machine-gun and rifle fire.

Nutto's reconnaissance unit kept moving as quickly as they dared down the narrow road in the darkness. But the movement soon turned into a running battle, with Kriegies still clinging to the vehicles.

Lt. Inge Herndon, one of those captured in the Bulge, hung on to one of the Sherman tanks at the head of the column. "The deck of the tank was crowded with extra tank tracks, jerricans of gasoline and water and clusters of 76mm shells," he recounted years later. "The tank drivers gunned their motors and began to move out. I felt exposed high up above the ground. As we moved out the cold wind blew in my face and I had an exhilarating and wonderful feeling of freedom."

Herndon never forgot the noise of the Panzerfausts that night. He continued: "One of the rockets swooshed by my head like a deadly Roman candle as it went past and exploded in the woods. I felt the heat and crouched down and hung on for dear life. If the round had been a few inches closer and had hit the tank all of us hanging on would have been killed."

That was too close for him. When the column slowed down a little later, Herndon jumped off the Sherman and ran back toward the rear of the column and leapt onto another tank. "Two other lieutenants and

I hung on and we stood on the narrow metal flange on the back. I felt relieved that I was no longer at the head of the column behind the German lines," Herndon recalled.

Chief Warrant Officer Harry Thompson, one of the Bulge Kriegies, was clinging to another Sherman with his best friend, Lt. John Everjohn, when the feeling suddenly came over him that the tank was going to be hit by German fire. "This thing's too nice a target for the Krauts with all these passengers, John," he shouted to his buddy. "We have a better chance to make it on foot. Come with me!"

But Everjohn did not want to get off the Sherman. He thought they would have a greater chance of making it out alive by staying with the column. "I begged him," Thompson said. "He told me he wanted to take his chances on the tank. We shook hands and I jumped off. The tank had gone only about one hundred yards when it took a direct hit. . . . Something just told me to jump off that tank." His friend and almost everyone else in and on the tank were killed.

Thompson had a narrow escape, but he was far from safe. Just as he saw the tank he had been on go up in flames, machine-gun and rifle fire broke out all around him. He remembered it in detail: "My escape was cut off. There was no place else to go. I started squirming along on my belly, just like the infiltration course back in the States had taught, except, in maneuvers, there was no one really trying to kill you. Bullets seemed to come at me from all sides. I cannot describe how scared I was. I think I would have just stopped and cried if I had not been so terrified. It seemed like some sort of cruel joke."

He kept moving and forced himself to crawl over the bodies of dead soldiers. He counted fifteen or sixteen, and the battle was still raging all around him. He made himself get up and run, as fast as he could, back toward Hammelburg.

Colonel Goode had also become increasingly pessimistic about the chances of success. He and his men were too weak and exhausted. He climbed on a tank and gathered the group of Kriegies around him. "We have to face it," he told them. "Most of us can't keep going. We should go back to the camp. We have tried our best. If we stick with the task force now, we'll weigh them down. We'll follow the road back toward the

Oflag. Those of you who are able to go on and are prepare to fight can stay with the column." Not many chose to stay. The rest slowly followed Goode, holding a white sheet above his head, back the way they came.

— —

Task Force Baum continued moving down the narrow roads and highways through the night, enduring more and more casualties from a determined enemy who set up one ambush and roadblock after another. If it had not been for the darkness, even more of Baum's men and vehicles would have been hit. It was after midnight by then, and when firing erupted at a roadblock up ahead, Nutto radioed Baum again to tell him he was at the base of Hill 427, the tallest hill in the area, and getting closer to the town of Höllrich.

The Germans had been able to keep both Nutto's advance unit and the main force under surveillance. They knew where the Americans were every minute and which directions they were heading on the twisting roads they took. As the Americans got closer to Höllrich, the woods ended and the men were more exposed to the possibility of ambush. But then they discovered that they would first have to get through the town of Hessdorf before they reached Höllrich.

Baum later wrote that everything had gone well for them until they crossed a bridge over a creek and drove into Hessdorf, where they ran into two German roadblocks formed by two trucks left across the road. The Kriegies jumped down from the tanks and pushed the trucks off to the side so the column could go through.

While they were doing that, the noise of the tanks' engines woke up the villagers, who panicked and put out white sheets and towels to show the Americans they had surrendered. Once the trucks were out of the way, the column raced on through Hessdorf, to the relief of the residents. The SS officer cadets came through in pursuit and, seeing the signs of surrender, shot some of the villagers on the spot.

Not long after passing through the town, Nutto, still in the lead, came to another fork in the road. He did not know which way to choose, but when he got out of his tank and walked ahead, he saw that one road was cobblestoned and the other unpaved. Given the choice, tankers always preferred the road with the harder surface. It gave better traction to tank treads.

Soon they passed a growing number of houses and buildings and found themselves in the narrow main street of Höllrich. Nutto walked ahead, alert for signs of an ambush. "He didn't want to be surrounded and cut off from the rest of the column. And everywhere was silence, always the oppressive silence. German civilians cowered within the houses, not daring to make a sound," *Raid!* tells us. They left the town and saw Highway 27 just ahead. Nutto radioed Captain Baum, who said he would be there with the main force in twenty minutes. Suddenly, two Panzerfausts fired at Nutto's unit, giving off enough light for Nutto to see at least one Tiger tank and a number of German infantry lying in wait for them. It was now 2:30 A.M. on March 28.

Nutto was standing in the open hatch of his tank when the rocket hit only a few feet away. "It was pitch black," he said, "no moon, blacker than crap. Then I saw the flare from the Panzerfaust and the goddamned thing hit the turret right where I was standing."

He was dazed but then began to feel one of the crewmen inside the tank pushing him out through the hatch. He did not have the strength to hold on and he fell over the side, landing on the ground in pain, both from the rocket attack and the fall. He started to crawl away and had to push his way over the body of one the Kriegies who had been hanging onto the tank.

Another explosion rang out and Nutto looked up to see Tiger tank fire hit a second Sherman, which burst into flames, flinging off all the POWs who had been on it. By then Nutto had managed to get to the side of the road, where he heard the sound of German voices. He glanced up to see several Germans climb into his tank and start the engine. He got very angry because it was his tank they were toying with, but there was nothing he could do about it.

Author Alex Kershaw reprints a story from Nutto: "I was lying there in the road, and bullets were ricocheting around me. Every time a bullet came close it kind of jolted me. Then this German officer comes up and sticks a [Luger] in my face and asks, 'Are you a Negro?' I almost said something stupid, but I hadn't shaved in a week and was covered in grease."

Nutto said he was not and tried to pull up one sleeve to show the German his white skin. Apparently satisfied, the German holstered his gun and walked away without another word.

"I guess he'd have shot my ass if I was," Nutto said years later. He ended up in a German military hospital in the city of Wurzburg.

Capt. Paul Kunkle, one of the Kriegies, was hanging onto a Sherman tank farther back in the column. When the firing started and the first two tanks were hit, the tank he was on backed up so fast to turn around that it crashed into a stone wall. If Kunkle had not pulled his feet up in the nick of time, both legs would have been crushed.

The tank commander yelled to the prisoners to get off the tank and make a run for it to save themselves. No sooner had Kunkle jumped when a shell from the Tiger tank ripped into his tank, slicing clean through the armor plating. He hid for a moment in a doorway, with shells and machine-gun fire ripping through the air all around him.

As the remaining tanks and half-tracks turned around and started back to where they came from, he jumped into the street and just managed to get a grip on the rear door of a half-track when someone pulled him onboard. He was one of the lucky ones that night. There is no record of how many Americans died during the ambush at Höllrich or how many took off to return to Hammelburg. Only fifty-seven were still with Task Force Baum.

Chief Warrant Officer Harry Thompson, who had survived the explosion of the tank he had just decided to leave, and who had crawled over more than a dozen bodies to get away from the firing, staggered back the dozen miles to Oflag XIIIB. Years later he recalled that journey: "I sprinted as fast as my emaciated legs would carry me, afraid a bullet would come firing through the dark at any moment. I ran straight over the flattened gates to my barracks, where I collapsed, exhausted."

Lt. Brooks Kleber, who had left with Colonel Goode's group, remembered in 1985 that "we walked back in the very ruts that the tanks sent to rescue us had made. I saw a German guard who told us, 'Get some sleep, fellows, you're had a tough night.' I was so exhausted, so emotionally drained, that I just went to sleep."

When Colonel Goode got back to Hammelburg, he was so furious at the inadequate size of the rescue force that he complained about it to General von Goeckel. "I want no further part of this foolishness," Goode declared. "Those [task force] people don't know what they're doing. I and most of my men prefer to stay here in the camp. Will you take us back, General?" The general nodded and Goode and those with him went silently back to their barracks.

Father Cavanaugh remembered coming back into the camp through the Serbian compound. "The joyous spirit that had animated the Serbs when we marched out five hours before was changed to silent gazing and dejection. There was scarcely a word spoken as we trudged along." They were told to go to their barracks and stay inside.

＿＿＿

When what was left of Nutto's reconnaissance unit turned around and started back toward Hessdorf, two of the SS officer cadets chased after them in the dark on a bicycle and managed to hit another tank with their Panzerfaust. Baum, racing toward Höllrich with his main force, heard the sounds of battle up ahead and knew that Nutto's force had run into an ambush. Baum realized they would have to find yet another way back to American lines.

Shortly after, he saw what was left of the recon unit racing down the road toward him. When both forces stopped, he was stunned to learn that he had lost at least two tanks and Lieutenant Nutto, his most experienced officer. He took stock of his situation and decided to make one more try to reach Highway 27 before sunrise by scouting out a back road around the town of Höllrich. This time he would go along in his jeep, riding behind two Shermans.

The road, more like a trail, was narrow and twisting and turning with deep woods on one side, and progress was slow. Suddenly, Baum sensed some movement ahead on the right, and a moment later a Panzerfaust fired and hit the first tank. Baum ordered his driver to stop the jeep and pull over to allow the second tank enough room to back up and turn around.

Baum suddenly found himself with a number of passengers crowding him in his jeep. They were the surviving crew members of the tank and a few Kriegies who had stayed with them. Together, the jeep and the remaining tank sped back the way they had come. Fortunately, no Germans followed them and they caught up again with the main force.

Baum knew then that there would be no escaping that night. He would have to find some place where they could hole up safely for the rest of the night and try again to get out in the morning. The situation was even more desperate now. His task force had only three assault guns, seven tanks, twenty half-tracks, and one jeep left, along with only 110 troops out of the 293 they had started out with. They had been on the go for over one hundred hours and were so exhausted they could barely keep awake. They also had an unknown number of wounded and about a dozen Hammelburg prisoners who had stayed with them.

Then he remembered the high ridgeline he had seen on his map and Hill 427, one mile to the east of Höllrich, as its highest point. He thought they would be safe from attack there on the top of the hill, the high ground, for the next few hours and maybe they could get some rest. When he reached there, he formed his vehicles into a protective circle.

Those who were too seriously wounded to be taken any farther would have to be left there in the hope that the Germans would get them proper medical care. They were placed in a large stone barn, the only building on the hill, and a large red cross was fashioned out of the brightly colored silk panels given to GIs to mark their positions so that friendly aircraft would not bomb or strafe them. It was draped over the roof of the barn. Baum then called his men together and checked on how much gas they had left.

"I had enough gas for a 38- to 40-mile trip," Baum said. "We siphoned gas out of eight of the half-tracks to give us a greater driving radius. We destroyed the eight half-tracks by burning them." It was 3:00 A.M. In four hours the sun would rise and Task Force Baum would have to get underway again.

Chapter 12

THEY SHOT THE CRAP OUT OF US

"And when I got ready to go, all hell broke loose." That was how Abe Baum remembered that morning on Hill 427 almost seventy years later. "And we were in column. We weren't prepared to fight. We were prepared to go. . . . We didn't get a chance to move. Oh, no, it was dark. We got daylight and *boom*. We didn't get a chance to move." It was "the fastest automatic fire I had ever seen." Lt. Lyle Bouck, one of the Hammelburg Kriegies captured in the Battle of the Bulge, put it more succinctly: "They shot the crap out of us," he said.

While the men of Task Force Baum had been getting a much-needed chance to rest before moving out, the Germans had been busily and brilliantly organizing troops around the base of the hill and then moving them ever so slowly up toward the top. In the hours before dawn, the Americans were completely surrounded, and none of them had heard a sound.

Some sources report that the column of Kriegies returning to Hammelburg led by Colonel Goode was still close enough to Hill 427 to hear the sounds of German tanks and troops moving toward the hill. Yet "none of Colonel Goode's men returning to the safety of the lager thought to send a runner back to warn CPT Baum of their discovery. Could they have all been so dispirited and exhausted from the last twelve hours of emotional ups and downs that they overlooked this critical point?" historian Richard Whitaker asks. For whatever reason, no word was sent to the men on the hilltop.

Oberst Hoepple, the military commander at Hammelburg, directed the entire complex operation, which involved Hauptmann Kuehl's remaining tank destroyers, the outfit that had first fired on the task force the day before as they had approached the POW camp. In addition, at least 80 of the 300 SS officer cadets who had marched so far and so fast to reach Hammelburg were in place with forty of the deadly Panzerfausts among them. They were located no more than 50 yards from the top of the hill.

The tank destroyers were to the northeast of Baum's men, six Tiger tanks to the north, another armored column to the northeast, with other self-propelled guns to the south. Oberst Hoepple was asleep at his headquarters in the Oflag when his aide awakened him at 7:30 A.M. with the news that it was then light enough to see the American tanks on the hill.

Hoepple stepped outside and examined the tanks through his binoculars. He telephoned Koehl and the other unit commanders to tell them to wait until the Americans started their engines. According to Whitaker, "No one was to fire until Koehl's antitank guns opened up, and then everyone was to fire at will!"

———

At 8:10 A.M., Baum called his officers to gather round and hear the orders for the day. They were very simple and direct: "We're not stopping for any roadblocks this time. We take them out. If we hit a defensive position, we overrun it. If we meet Tigers, we fight them. If we hit a wide stream, I want a half-track to go in as a bridge for the tanks. We go like a straight arrow until we run out of gas. . . . Remember, we've got to bowl over the Krauts. Mount up."

The officers ran back to their vehicles and Baum got in his jeep and told his driver to head over to the edge of the clearing. When he was sure everyone was ready, he raised his right hand with his index finger extended and made a circling motion with it, while yelling the traditional tankers' command to start their engines: "Turn 'em over."

The instant the motors started, the Germans opened fire with shells, machine-gun and rifle fire, and the Panzerfausts. It seemed as though the entire hilltop suddenly exploded in a giant ball of fire. The Germans had accurately lined up every target in their sights. Among the first to be hit was the large barn-like structure housing the wounded. The building was shattered instantly. No one survived. Baum had only enough time to send off one message: "Task Force Baum surrounded. Under heavy fire. Request air support." But it was already too late.

Raid! describes the devastation: "Within three minutes of Baum's order to move, the entire clearing seemed to be one single sheet of flame, every vehicle hit. The abrupt onslaught, the accuracy, the destruction wreaked in such a short period of time was beyond comprehension. It was then, almost as suddenly as the attack had begun, that it occurred to Baum that he had lost control of the situation, that he had lost his task force."

Just as quickly as the attack had begun, the shelling and firing stopped. The sudden silence was almost as overwhelming as the noise had been. The Germans stopped shelling the task force to allow the infantry to come in and finish the job. Baum saw them coming through the woods. As they got closer to the Americans, they started firing with their machine pistols from the hip, spraying bullets everywhere, not even bothering to take aim. There were so many targets to be hit, they did not have to narrow their fire to specific ones.

The only heavy return fire they received was from Sergeant Graham's three remaining assault guns, two of which were hit right away. "And he kept firing," Baum remembered, "and I finally yelled at him, 'Stop,' because once [he] stopped, they stopped, they stopped firing on us."

Finally, Baum shouted, "Every man for himself," as he headed toward the woods with Major Stiller and Technical Sergeant Sidles close behind him. Everywhere there was chaos and confusion, and those still alive, approximately eighty by then, broke up into small groups or fled individually and ran.

None of those who survived the attack remembered much about the details of their survival. Sgt. Robert Zawada recalled, more than sixty years later, that "when the Germans opened up, I bailed out of my half-track. Everybody did and I just went blank. I can never remember—What did I do? What happened? I started running and a shell exploded and I fell down on my shoulder and tried to get up and run again."

He saw something fly off and tumble over the ground and looked down and saw one leg was gone below the knee. Only a hideous, bloody mess remained. There was no pain yet, but blood was gushing out. He ripped off his necktie, wrapped it around the stump of his leg, and shoved his bayonet down inside the tie, making a tourniquet. He lay there, out in the open, with firing all around him and some of it very close, while watching other men surrender.

He panicked for a moment, wondering how he could physically manage to surrender. He could not stand up and he had to keep holding onto the tourniquet with both hands. "How do I put my hands up?" he asked himself, and the answer was all too obvious. He could not. He was trapped.

As German soldiers got closer, he saw one of them shoot a badly wounded black American soldier while accepting the surrender of white troops who were on their feet. Then the German saw Zawada and came toward him. "I was sure I was going to be shot," he said. The German looked at him, and then pulled on his arm.

Zawada looked up at the German. Neither man said a word. Then the German bent down and unbuckled his tourniquet, took the bayonet out, and threw it away. Then he rewrapped the tourniquet using the wooden handle of the entrenching tool GIs carried and left him there. Zawada passed out, and when he woke up hours later, he was lying on a stretcher back in the camp at Hammelburg.

Lieutenant Bouck wrote that the German soldiers "had us surrounded. . . . They lined us up and now they're trying to find who the POWs were that were liberated and who the tankers were. The next thing I remember, we're walking in a column back to the prison camp at Hammelburg."

Morale in the camp plunged even lower than it had been before, because now there were more of them in the camp with the addition of Baum's survivors. "They just crowded up our barracks more," one POW said. "You've got more guys and you're going to get less food."

Back near Hill 427, those of Baum's men who had not been wounded or captured, perhaps as many as fifty or sixty, ran into the woods to hide in the thick brush. The Germans brought up guard dogs from the camp to pursue the Kriegies.

According to Charles Whiting, "By midmorning the hunt was in full swing. Down on the road that ran south from Hammelburg, the Germans had placed tanks at intervals with patrols of infantry to link them up so that if the Americans ventured out of the thickly wooded Reussenberg area and tried to cross the road (which they must do if they wanted to take the quickest way back to their own lines) they would be picked up. Up on the hill, the SS men [the officer cadets], triumphant at the defeat they had inflicted on the Amis [Americans], worked deeper and deeper into the forest, led on by the excited, braying hounds."

The search for American soldiers went on throughout the morning, as the Germans continued to chase down and capture more of Baum's men and the Hammelburg Kriegies. One of the task force's medics, the German-born David Zeno, was on the run with an Italian POW who had escaped from another part of the Hammelburg camp in the confusion. He spoke enough English for him to follow Zeno's instructions on how they might best reach the road.

The Italian was as eager to escape as Zeno was, but Zeno had the more compelling reason not to be caught. He was a Jew and he knew his chances of surviving capture were none too good. Finally, they reached the end of the wood and saw the road just ahead, but before they could reach it, two German soldiers stood up from some bushes where they had been lying in wait. Zeno and the Italian had no choice but to surrender, but as the Germans stepped closer, Zeno received the shock of his life. He recognized one of them as a former schoolmate from his youth in Germany. Fortunately, the German did not recognize Zeno.

The other German-born member of Task Force Baum, the interpreter Irving Solotoff, was wounded in the German attack. He tried to get away but it was difficult with the backs of his legs slashed open by shrapnel. Leaving a trail of blood behind him, he realized he could not get far in that condition, and so he went over to the medics who were trying to treat the wounded.

The Germans quickly rounded them up while one of them searched each soldier. A mean-looking German sergeant opened Solotoff's wallet and found his mezuzah, a piece of parchment with verses from the Torah inscribed on it. He looked at Solotoff and asked him if he was Jewish. Solotoff said that he was and that he was the interpreter for the outfit.

The German said nothing for a moment, and then spoke in German, telling Soltoff to tell the other prisoners to empty their pockets and put everything on the ground. Then he gestured to the scenes of death and destruction around them and said, "What made you do this?" When

Solotoff replied that he did not know, the German shook his head several times with a sad expression on his face and walked away. Solotoff was safe, at least for the moment.

Sgt. Robert Vannett, one of Abe Baum's tankers, tried to hide out from the Germans behind what was left of the stone barn where all the wounded had been killed. But when he saw a number of others surrender as the Germans overran Hill 427, he too waved a white flag. The only alternative was to try to run, but there were too many Germans around by then.

To his amazement, one of the Germans took him over to his damaged but still intact tank, *Conquering Hero*. By using hand gestures, he indicated that he wanted Vannett to climb into the tank and turn it around so that it pointed toward the west. Vannett was reluctant to see the Germans use his tank; he considered resisting but then decided that they would shoot him on the spot if he refused.

He stayed in the tank for several hours until a German officer climbed aboard and told him to drive it back to the camp at Hammelburg, the second time he had driven that tank to the Oflag in two days. When he reached the camp, he climbed out and asked one of the Kriegies for a cigarette, but the man refused.

"For Christ's sake," Vannett yelled. "We gave you those cigarettes yesterday. They were ours."

"Tough shit," the prisoner said, leaving Vannett to wonder why he and the others in the task force had gone through so much to try to rescue guys like that.

Lt. Allen Moses of Task Force Baum managed to escape the destruction and death on Hill 427 along with two others named Celli and Kurelis. The three managed to get beyond the German perimeter and hid in a barn not far from a farmhouse. They watched the house long enough to see that an older woman was living there by herself.

The men decided to approach her and offer her some D-ration bars—the ones with chocolate that were so popular with Europeans—in return for some real food. They knocked on the door and Lieutenant Moses made the offer. The woman invited the three of them into a cheery kitchen with bright yellow curtains and a big black stove.

No one said a word as she made them a huge omelet and poured them glasses of milk. When they finished eating, they left, with still not a word spoken, and went back to the barn, where they wrapped themselves in hay and fell asleep. Their rest was short-lived. "When Moses awakened, he was looking straight into the bore of a machine pistol," according to *Raid!* "The two German soldiers kicked Celli and Kurelis, who woke with a start. The Germans stood over them and laughed at their dismay."

PFC Bob Thompson, one of the Kriegies who had come from Szubin with John Waters, decided to stay with the task force on Hill 427. An article published seventy years later quotes him as saying, "I had armed myself with an M1 Rifle and two bandoleers of ammunition, and was sitting on the back of one of the half-tracks waiting to move out again, when an armor-piercing shell hit the vehicle I was on. The shell tore up the half-track and threw me off on the ground."

He ran behind the stone building that housed the wounded and was still there moments later when it was hit and destroyed. He and several others with him were trapped. There was no way out. One of the men who was wearing white underwear tore off his undershirt, attached it to the tip of his bayonet, and waved it in the air. The Germans put the group in one of their surviving half-tracks and started back to Oflag XIIIB.

"As we were going back to the camp," Thompson recalled, "I began rummaging around in the half-track for food or anything else I could find, when I picked up a metal box that was about the size of a package of cigarettes. I opened the box and saw some diamond rings and diamond stickpins for men's neckties. I closed the box quickly, and stuffed it into my shirt before the German guard saw me."

When Thompson and the others arrived back at camp, they were placed temporarily in the German stable, which had a floor made out of thick dirt and sawdust. Thompson quickly dug a hole with his fingers and buried the box as deeply as he could. He never forgot that box, and twenty-two years later, in 1967, he and a friend went back to Hammelburg to try to find it. Through the American embassy, he made arrangements to be allowed to go back to the camp, which was still a German military base, and look for the diamonds.

The stable was still there, and the walls were still full of bullet holes from the battle, but the building was full with about twenty tons of coal. The Germans obligingly provided three workers and a truck, but when they removed enough coal to get to the spot where the diamonds had been buried, they were gone.

Four days after Thompson arrived back home, he got a letter from the embassy in Germany telling him that a resident of Hammelburg had heard about him digging up the floor of the stable. The man said a friend of his had worked for the US Army right after the war, cleaning out the stable, and had found the box.

The man had immigrated to Chicago and the person in Hammelburg said he would write to him and give him Thompson's name and address and tell him that he had come back to find the diamonds. "I have not yet heard from the man in Chicago," Thompson later wrote, "but after 22 years of waiting, I can always wait a little longer. In any event, we are still trying to locate the man and see if he will at least let me look at the box the diamonds were in." He died in 2014 at the age of ninety-two, having never again seen the diamonds, or the box they came in.

Abe Baum was one of those who survived the German assault and made it into the woods after yelling for everyone to spread out. Maj. Al Stiller was with him, along with one of the tankers, John Sidles. Behind them they could hear the Germans rounding up those who did not get away fast enough, or who were too dazed or wounded by the attack. Baum took out his tiny compass and led the others due west.

At one point all three men dropped to the ground when they spotted a group of six Americans running out of a wooded area into the open directly in front of some German troops. Five of the Americans immediately raised their hands in surrender, but the sixth one turned around and started to head back toward the trees. Just as one German aimed his rifle at the back of the man, the American stopped, raised his hands, and turned around. Baum silently congratulated the man on making a good move.

When the Germans and their captives left, Baum led the other two back into the woods, telling them to lie down, cover themselves with leaves, and wait until it got dark. The three exhausted and hungry men stayed there, not moving or making any sounds until a wagon came along.

As Baum told the story many years later, "There were three of us lying there in the woods. And up comes a buggy with two civilians. That's the home guard. And I'm looking up at them, and they're looking down at me.

"And I'm starting to fiddle underneath my Mackinaw for my .45. My hand was completely bandaged [from his wound at Gemünden]. I couldn't shoot the thing. And even if it wasn't bandaged, I couldn't hit the side of a barn with that .45. Anyway, he sees my predicament, puts his rifle down against the buggy, puts his hand on his hip, takes out a P38, a Luger, and shoots me." The bullet grazed his scrotum and went clear through his thigh. "You son of a bitch," Baum yelled at the man. "You went and shot one in my balls."

To Baum's amazement and anger, the German burst out laughing as though Baum had told him a great joke. As it turned out, the man had been born and raised in Bridgeport, Connecticut. His parents were German immigrants and he had gone to Germany in 1939, just before the war broke out, to, as he put it, serve his Fatherland.

He and the man with him started to take Baum, Stiller, and Sidles back to camp, but Baum could not walk any farther, even with help. His wounds were bleeding again and he was too weak to continue. Sidles tried to encourage him to keep up, but Baum told him to go ahead, and he and Stiller had no choice. "And they left me there on the ground," Baum said.

The two Germans took Stiller and Sidles back to the area around Hill 427, where the last battle had taken place; they joined about fifty other survivors there. A German officer looked over the prisoners and separated Stiller from the group because he assumed that, since Stiller was the highest-ranking American there, he must have been in command of the attacking force.

The Germans then searched the men, looking for weapons and souvenirs. When Sidles dropped a spoon out of his pocket, the German searching him said, "Pick it up. You'll need it, if you find anything to eat." The Americans were then marched back toward the camp.

When they reached the Oflag, they were ordered into the riding ring where Bob Thompson buried his box of diamonds. The place reminded Lt. Richard Baron of Madison Square Garden in New York City, where he had once seen a horse show. There were stables for horses on one side of the ring and bleachers on the other side.

At the top of the bleachers, there were several boxes for more distinguished viewers to watch events in greater comfort. The camp commandant, General von Goeckel, was there, along with some high-ranking prisoners. It looked as if they were comparing names on a list. Lieutenant Baron waved a collection of dog tags he had saved over his head until one of von Goeckel's aides called him over. Baron gave the man the dog tags and said, "These men are dead. Verifiably dead. I saw their corpses."

Shortly after that, the POWs were rounded up and marched to the railroad station in the town of Hammelburg. The men were taken by surprise at how well the guards treated them. When they arrived at the station, they were placed aboard a number of the old "forty by eight" boxcars, but this time they were not jammed inside.

Instead, only twenty men were placed in each car along with three guards. They had plenty of space to lie down on the straw, and the guards did not harass them at all. The men figured that the Germans were well aware that the war was almost over and so they wanted to avoid any problems with retaliation and revenge for cruel treatment.

When Sergeant Zawada, whose lower leg was torn off, regained consciousness, he found himself in the Serbian hospital at Hammelburg. "When I woke up, I was on an operating table and this guy at the end of the table was about six-four, and he had this big Russian-style beard, and he's standing there with a saw in his hand. My first thought was that this is like the Civil War and there's no anesthetics and this guy's going to start cutting at me like I'm a two-by-four. I screamed 'Ether! Ether! Ether!' and a guy behind me slammed a mask on my face and I went right out." The surgeon was Dr. Radovan Danich, who had operated on John Waters and who would save a number of other Americans.

Later that day, while other Kriegies were being put aboard the train, some German soldiers found Abe Baum barely conscious, still lying on the ground where he had been left. They placed him in a horse-drawn cart and took him back to the camp, to the hospital in the Serbian compound, which was now crowded with wounded men.

Wisely, Baum had tossed away his dog tags shortly after he had been hit. As he said many years later, "If the Germans knew who I was at that particular time [both Jewish and the commander of the task force], I might not be sitting here." The Germans continued to believe that Stiller, with his higher rank, had been the commander.

Baum was left on a wooden bench, exhausted, semi-conscious, in a great deal of pain, shivering from the cold and covered in mud and blood. Fortunately, he was soon spotted by Lt. William Dennis, who had been with the 101st Airborne and captured at Bastogne. Dennis had been a pharmacist and was assigned as a medic in Hammelburg.

He started taking off Baum's outer clothes so as to better examine his wounds, and then cleaned them with alcohol, which woke Baum up from the deep sleep he had fallen into. There were still Germans around and Dennis asked Baum in a soft whisper who he was. When Baum replied that he was the commander of the attack force, Dennis went to get the American doctor, Maj. Albert Berndt, who had been captured during the Bulge.

The first thing Berndt did was to rip off Baum's 4th Armored Division shoulder patches. He knew the Germans were still looking for the men in the task force, and so he told Dennis to put Baum down as one of the returned POWs. Then, just to make sure Baum remained safe, they moved him and a cot into a tiny room at the end of the hall where they kept medical supplies. The Germans never bothered to look in there.

Baum was weak from loss of blood but his wounds were not severe enough to require the skills of the Serbian surgeon, Dr. Danich, and so Dr. Berndt took care of him. He found bits of shrapnel in Baum's hand from his wounds received at Gemünden. Some pieces were embedded in bones and required a lot of digging to remove. The more recent bullet wound in his thigh was not as severe, but that was not what worried Baum.

"Do I still have nuts?" he asked Berndt. Assured that he did, Baum went to sleep. When he woke up, he could think of only one thing: how to escape. He went into the hallway looking for a way out, but Lieutenant

Dennis told him he was too weak to even leave his bed for a while. He could think about getting out when he got his strength back.

By late afternoon on March 28, when Baum was treated, he and the other wounded Kriegies in the Serbian hospital were just about the only Americans left in Oflag XIIIB. All those who could walk were headed to the east. Those who had been captured after the ambush on Hill 427 were being loaded aboard the boxcars headed for Nuremberg, but all the others had left several hours before the final battle of Task Force Baum took place.

Most of the men had gone to sleep on the night of the 27th, when they realized they were not free after all, but at 2:00 A.M., the guards had come stomping through every barracks, yelling at the men to line up outside. Many thought they were going to be executed on the spot, but instead they were marched down Hermann Goering Strasse out of the camp and down the road toward the town of Hammelburg.

Father Paul Cavanaugh remembered how they "plodded once again along a gravel road. The comparative ease of living behind barbed wire was replaced by the prisoners' march. From our experience we knew that forced marching under guard was not a comfortable way to live. There was a mist in the air and the chilly dampness disheartened us."

"I do not remember anything," Chief Warrant Officer Harry Thompson said years later, "except being half frozen. I looked at nothing except the road ahead. It was dark and I could not see a thing. As the day broke we marched past a great number of German soldiers getting ready to head for the front—the exact opposite direction from where we were going.

"Now we began our walk through hell. We marched across Germany for thirty-six days. . . . Little did we realize that so many officers in our group would never make it."

CHAPTER 13

NO NEWS OF BAUM

THE TRAIN CARRYING SOME OF THE KRIEGIES WESTWARD SCREECHED to a halt less than two hours after leaving the station at Hammelburg. The guards slammed open the doors and yelled "*Raus! Raus!*" for everyone to get out. The prisoners jumped down from the cars and followed the guards' gestures to run into the woods.

All of them heard the roar of the planes the instant the train went silent. They were American P-47 fighters roaring overhead, ready to tear the train to shreds with machine-gun and rocket fire. By that stage of the war, American fighter pilots roamed freely all over Germany looking for anything moving, even a single truck, to destroy.

By March 1945 it was almost suicidal to try to go anywhere in Germany on a train on a bright sunny day. The pilots found it great sport to hunt down a moving target like that and then to be rewarded with a massive explosion; the boiler on the locomotive would blow up as they flew down low through the column of smoke. It had become a game.

Some Kriegies from the train did not run into the woods. Instead they quickly put together some blankets to form a pattern indicating who they were, and they waved their arms frantically at the planes overhead. It worked. The pilots pulled up at the last moment before firing and then flew in circles over them and waggled their wings to indicate that they got the message. The POWs and their guards got back on the train and covered the rest of the 70-mile trip from Hammelburg in safety.

When the train stopped next, the Kriegies found themselves on the outskirts of Nuremberg. They were marched up a steep hill to a wide highway that looked down on the railroad yards. From there they were taken to the large open-air arena, capable of holding 150,000 people, where monster Hitler rallies had once been staged.

They were not there very long when they heard a low rumbling sound that grew louder and louder until the very ground beneath their feet felt like it was shaking. It was so loud that some of the men put their hands over their ears, but that hardly helped at all. They looked up to see squadron after squadron of B-17s that seemed to fill the whole sky. Most of the men had never seen so many planes at one time. It was an overwhelming and awe-inspiring sight.

But then the bombs started to fall, and they continued falling for a full thirty minutes with no interruption. It was one constant and continuing ear-splitting roar with fire and smoke, debris and bodies filling the air. The Kriegies were safe where they were. The targets were the railroad yards, where they had been not too long before, and the city itself.

When it was all over, when the bombs stopped falling and the planes disappeared back where they had come from, the dazed prisoners were told to sleep in the arena. The next day, to their amazement, there were enough railroad cars and track still intact for them to continue their journey to the east. They traveled another 40 miles to their new camp at Moosburg, which housed more than 100,000 POWs, perhaps the largest camp in all of Germany, and certainly one of the worst.

The other Kriegies from Hammelburg, the ones who had been awakened at 2:00 A.M. in their barracks the night before the attack on Hill 427, were kept marching through the night. In the days ahead, they would be broken up into different groups, the number of which is uncertain to this day.

They did not know it yet, but they would keep on marching for the next thirty-six days, and some for even longer, covering about 240 miles heading in the general direction of the same POW camp in Moosburg in southern Germany that the prisoners on the train were heading toward.

Those Kriegies who survived the long march to Moosburg would not be freed until April 29. But there were other groups from Hammelburg still trying to reach Moosburg when American forces caught up with them. They were not freed until May 2 and 3. Had George Patton not chosen to make his last gamble, all the American POWs at Hammelburg would have been liberated on April 6, only nine days after Task Force Baum was wiped out, when the Seventh Army reached them. And John Waters would not have been lying on a hospital bed, still in pain, wondering if he would ever be able to walk again.

Chief Warrant Officer Harry Thompson never forgot the first night and the next day of his long march from Hammelburg. "I still don't know how we managed to cover twenty-six kilometers [16 miles] that first day in our weakened condition. I guess you can do a lot of things you once thought impossible if you've got a gun barrel poking you in the back."

Father Cavanaugh was with Thompson's group. He remembered how they had marched for an hour at a time and sometimes were given a ten-minute break, which was never long enough to get their strength back. He also remembered how, at about 6:00 A.M. that day, he and the others heard the sounds of German tanks and troops moving past them in the darkness. The Germans were heading toward Hill 427 and their ambush of Task Force Baum.

An hour or so later, the marching Kriegies heard the sounds of battle behind them. They had no idea what was going on and wondered if it might have been a fully manned American advance breaking through the German line at Hammelburg. Had they just missed their chance at being free, they asked themselves.

But then it started to rain and there were more pressing matters to worry about. The dirt roads became muddy, the downhills became slippery, and the pace of the walk got slower and more precarious. By 10:00 A.M. on March 28, they had walked for eight hours with only a few ten-minute breaks. "We had had no sleep," Father Cavanaugh wrote, "and no food had been issued us, of course. The pace was slow, probably not much more than two miles an hour."

Finally, at about 1:00 A.M. the next morning, they were marched off the muddy road into a muddy field and told they would spend the night there. Thompson had managed to steal a few potatoes and some cabbage before they left Hammelburg. He later wrote about the produce's condition: "I tried to clean some of the dirt off the potatoes by rubbing them against my shirt as I walked. I couldn't get all the dirt off, but what the heck—I'm sure dirt has some nutrients in it."

And so it went, day after day, each one a soggy, exhausting, hungry repeat of the one before it. Finally, on the morning of March 31, a Saturday, the rain stopped and the sun came out. That was a blessing, but everything else remained the same.

George Patton was worried. And he had good reason to be. On March 29, three days after the Task Force Baum mission had gotten underway, the log for the 4th Armored Division read, "No news of Baum." The radio message Baum had tried to send immediately after the Germans attacked had not gotten through. Patton knew that Baum's men should have reported on their status by then, and he started to plan how he would account for the mission.

He worried that Waters might have been killed in the attempt to save him. When Patton later found out that Waters was badly wounded, Dwight Eisenhower's son, John, was with him. He later wrote that Patton had told him that "Waters had gotten his ass shot up. Patton then burst into tears. Later on, as we were leaving, he told me how much he owed my father. And he broke into tears again."

Reporters were beginning to get the sense of a story in the making. One of them had seen a battle map on the wall of the headquarters operations room, with a lone arrow going off to the southeast from Aschaffenburg to someplace called Hammelburg. When he started to ask what that was about, an officer pulled the map down from the wall and refused to answer.

Under increasing pressure to say something about the mystery raid, Patton told reporters on March 30 that the small force had been sent solely as a feint, to deceive the Germans into thinking that he was going to launch a major attack in that area. "I felt by hazarding a small force I would confuse the enemy completely as to where we were going. It did work, for they thought we were going to Nuremberg," Patton said.

As more details came out about the raid later, Patton insisted that he had no idea that Colonel Waters was there. He even made that point in a letter to his wife: "I had known of the camp there for a week, but did not know definitely he [Waters] was in it. I sent a force to capture it but fear that the force was destroyed. However, it was the proper thing to do." In another letter to Bea, he complained that reporters "were trying to make an incident of my attempt to rescue John. How I hate the press."

⁓

John Waters was still lying in his hospital bed at the Serbian hospital, still unsure if he would ever be able to walk again. He was too weak from his wound to flex his muscles or to even try to get out of bed. He worried about his future, knowing that if he was permanently disabled, his career in the army would be at an end. The thought was devastating. According to *Raid!*, "He was utterly unable to conceive of himself as a civilian, pursuing life outside the army."

Across the aisle from him, Robert Zawada was also confined to his bed, under strict orders to lie completely still, to make absolutely no movement at all. Any bodily movement, he was told, could cause the stump of his leg to start hemorrhaging. It was a long period of agony.

At the end of the barracks, in the tiny room in which he had been placed so the Germans would not find him, Abe Baum was healing enough that he was allowed out to talk to the other wounded. He spoke to all of his men there and spent a lot of time with Zawada, who was the most seriously wounded of all.

A few beds down from Zawada, Baum met a young black captain who had been captured in the Bulge and who had also lost a leg. When Baum tried to console him, the man smiled and said, "You don't have to console me. When I get back to Harlem, they'll know that I was in the war." After quoting the man in a 2013 interview, Baum added that "he was proud of the fact that he had lost a leg."

Baum walked over to the other side of the room and sat down on the empty bed next to Waters, and the two men began talking. Like all Kriegies, Waters wanted to know how the war was progressing. Baum filled him in with as much as he knew about the European campaign and how far the Germans had been pushed back on both the eastern and western fronts.

Waters also asked a lot of questions about Baum's mission to Hammelburg, and they both agreed that it was too small a force to liberate so many prisoners so far behind German lines. Neither man asked about or spoke of the suspicion that the real reason for the raid was to rescue Waters, which Baum knew to be true. "I didn't want to tell him it was," Baum said years later, "because I knew goddamn well he would feel sick over it." Baum kept what he knew to himself.

Easter Sunday, April 1, 1945, was truly a blessed day for the POWs who had been marching with few breaks and little food for the past four days. The guards told them the evening before that they would not march the next day. They would have a day of rest outside the little town of Heuchelheim. And there was more good news. They would soon receive Red Cross parcels of food.

"It was almost unbelievable," Father Cavanaugh wrote, "until we saw the German truck pull into Heuchelheim loaded with packages of food. . . . We each received a box for ourselves as the last day of March faded way." Capt. Roger Shinn remembered that the people of the little village were also generous with their food. They traded with the Americans, "but often they gave us things. We enjoyed some of their Easter baking and soft-boiled or fried some of their eggs—incredible luxury."

Before they finished what for them was a lavish meal, a "German guard gathered us in the woods, pulled out a box of bread, and gave it to us. He didn't try to trade, but we gave him a few cigarettes. . . . As we talked, he told us that his wife and child had been killed in Aachen. With no dreams or hopes left, he went on obeying his orders and wishing the war would end."

It being Easter Sunday, Father Cavanaugh arranged to hold a service in the tiny church in the town. Neither the guards nor the residents made any objections, and Cavanaugh was even allowed to walk from their camp into town to arrange for the service without a guard. "Walking down the streets of a German village without armed escort was a new experience for me," he later recollected. At 11:00 A.M., more than eighty American officers filled the church to overflowing and forgot for a moment that they were prisoners of war, and that the war was not yet over.

The war returned the next morning before daybreak when the guards roused them from sleep and gave them time to boil some water to make what passed for coffee. Then the men lined up in threes while the guards counted them to make sure none had gone missing. The German officer in charge then counted the guards and found that some of them were gone. But he made no effort to try to find them. Then he yelled *"Weiter marschiern"* (forward march) and another day began.

They covered another 16 miles that day and passed through a number of small towns and villages, seeing increasing evidence of destruction, even in such remote places. Thompson remembered "destroyed houses and businesses in nearly every village, and occasionally the smoking wreck of a shot-down aircraft, German or American. The damage in the villages now seemed worse than when we first started walking." And the farther they got into Germany, the more the destruction grew.

The next morning, the guards shouted them awake at 5:00 as usual and gave them an hour to boil some water, eat what little they still had for breakfast, and get ready for another day of marching. One thing changed, though, on the morning after Easter Sunday. The guards stopped counting them.

Thompson again: "I guess they figured we were so far inside Germany it would be foolish for us to try to escape and most likely be executed by the SS troops who seemed to be everywhere. Either that, or they realized, as we did, that the war was nearly over and when we were liberated any one of us could have a say in how they would be treated as POWs."

They kept walking through more little towns and past many farms where little kids often came out to the dirt road to see the strange procession going by and to raise their arms and shout "Heil Hitler!" On April 4 they came to Furth, the largest German city any of them had ever seen.

"When we entered the city," Thompson wrote, "I could not believe my eyes. There was damage, far more than I had ever seen. The city was demolished. . . . It seemed as though every house and all the buildings were just shells of what they used to be, old beautiful stone buildings. It was hard going through all that rubble." They found refuge that night in a large intact barn just outside the city and were told that the next day they would reach Nuremberg.

On the same day the Kriegies marched into Furth, nine days after Task Force Baum had begun its mission, George Patton finally found out what had happened at Hammelburg. He also found out that his son-in-law was badly wounded and might not still be alive. But there was nothing he could do about it yet. Not until the Seventh Army reached the camp, and that could take several more days of anxious waiting. But at least he knew there was hope that Waters might still be alive, thanks to the courage and endurance of one man who escaped to American lines.

Not all of those who survived the battle on Hill 427 were in the Serbian hospital or being marched deeper into Germany. A number of them had tried to escape. Most were killed or captured, but a few made it back to American lines. The one who apparently got there first, seven days later, on April 4, was one of Abe Baum's most capable fighters, T/Sgt. Charles Graham.

When Baum shouted that it was every man for himself after the Germans attacked, Graham got off the hill as fast as he could with four others from the task force. After going 2 miles, they ran into a German patrol; it captured the others but Graham hid out in the woods and got away. After the fourth day of heading back toward the American lines, he came face to face with a German corporal who had his P38 Luger pointed right at him.

In an interview with a reporter on April 10, four days after his escape (and shortly before Patton classified the mission as top secret), Graham described what happened next: "I also had my .45 pointed at him but it happened that he spoke good English and told me it was no use. I told him to put his down and I would put mine down. I told him I was heading for the front lines but I didn't say how many days I had been out.

"He then asked me to take his P38 and shoot a hole through his arm so that he could then go back to town and get evacuated. He said he had a wife and children. I knew that if I fired then I would draw the attention of troops in the vicinity so I took his pistol and told him to head out."

Before he left, the German told Graham to stay away from all towns, because each one had a home guard unit looking for escaping Americans, and to stick to the woods as much as possible. Graham did as the man suggested, but by the fifth day of not having anything to eat, he was so desperate that he decided to knock on the door of a farmhouse and ask for food. "I got halfway up the twelve concrete steps when I met the German farmer with three soldiers coming down. I wasn't hungry anymore," Graham recalled.

Luckily for him, it was dark and he was able to slip behind a wall. He decided not to try any more houses after that. On his sixth day, still without food, but with the sound of fighting nearby, he met three German officers in some woods, pulled his gun first, and asked them which troops were close by. When they told him the Americans were attacking, he let them go and slowly made his way toward the roar of tanks. He still had his .45 in his hand when a bunch of American infantry came into view.

They started shouting at him in German. "One called me a Kraut son of a bitch and yelled for me to come out. I told them I was American and they told me not to hand them that crap and to throw my pistol away. I walked on down towards them and showed them my dogtags but they weren't convinced and that's when I began to feel uneasy."

The GIs began firing questions at him, one after another, asking him things only a real American soldier would know—from baseball players to where he trained, his commanders all the way from division down to platoon level. He passed their tests and was sent back to their battalion headquarters where, after having no food for six days, he was given a cup of coffee and some pineapple, which promptly made him sick. But not too sick to tell the story of what had happened to Task Force Baum and to Lt. Col. John Waters.

A few others also managed to make their way back to American lines, arriving in the days following Sergeant Graham's return. One group of three, led by Lt. Jay Drake, decided to escape in the hours before the battle on Hill 427 began. Together with Robert Corbin and Dallas Smith, he headed out with three loaves of bread and a compass, believing they had at least a fifty-fifty chance of making it.

After an hour or so of stumbling through the woods full of other Kriegies trying to escape and almost as many German troops rounding them up, they decided they had better go into hiding until nightfall. They daubed mud over their faces and hands to make them less visible, burrowed under piles of leaves by a huge fir tree, and stayed there until 8:00 that night.

They agreed that it was safer to travel only by night and to sleep under cover during daylight hours. They also decided to avoid all roads and towns. On the second night, they saw a bridge over a river ahead. They were so close they could hear the German guards talking to one another, and so they moved quietly downstream to a point where they thought they could cross unseen.

"So we found some logs," Corbin said, "and the Germans had given us Polish overcoats; we took those Polish overcoats and put the logs through the sleeves and created a little raft. We took our packs, put them on there, and Dallas Smith, I'll never forget this, jumped in the cold water naked. He took that raft across the river. Then he came back to get our clothes."

They crossed two more rivers in the next two days and were totally exhausted, wet, and discouraged by then. On their third day, they came upon an abandoned farmhouse with a one-and-a-half-story barn alongside a railroad track within sight of a bridge across a river. They climbed into the hay loft, pulled the ladder up behind them, and went to sleep, grateful to be dry and indoors with a little warmth for a change.

When daylight came the next morning, they had a nasty surprise. A truck stopped about a quarter of a mile away and six German soldiers jumped out and proceeded to the little bridge the Americans had planned to cross. The Germans placed mines on the bridge, and when they finished, one of them walked over to the barn to take a look around.

"We crouched by the door," Drake said, "each armed with a short wood club, waiting for him to open the door. Just as he was about to round the corner, one of his men called out to him [to ask for a cigarette] and he returned to the bridge and they all left." Later that evening, when they came down from the loft, they saw lying in plain sight on the floor one of Corbin's US Army GI gloves. If the German had come inside the barn that morning, he could not have missed seeing it, and they would have easily been caught. This led Drake to issue a basic lesson in survival: never choose a hiding place without a back way out.

On the sixth morning, they found another place to hide in some woods and covered themselves up with pine needles, leaves, and even sticks and promptly fell asleep. Later, Drake was awakened by a noise, and when he peeked out from under his leaves, he saw a whole platoon of German soldiers climbing up the hill directly toward him, only about 6 feet away. Luckily for Drake and the others, it was a steep hill and the Germans were so intent on maintaining their footing that they did not look around. If they had, they might well have noticed three large piles of leaves in human form.

On their seventh day, the American trio suddenly ran into an armed German soldier directly in their path. He took one look at their uniforms and the clubs they held in their hands and said "Good morning" in German and moved on.

By their ninth day, Corbin wrote, "We were just really in terrible shape. We could only walk two, three or four hundred yards at the most and that would take us ten or fifteen minutes and then we would have to rest." Finally, they heard the sound of American engines and saw a big two-and-a-half-ton truck with the white star on the side roar by. Then a jeep came along with a GI in it. "And there we are," Corbin said, "Polish overcoats, ten days growth of beard, jumping up and down saying, 'Hey, here we are, we made it, we got back!'"

The soldier got out of his jeep, pointed his .45 at them, and said, "Who the hell are you?" After they answered his questions and showed him their dog tags, the man put away his gun and said American forces had been looking all over for them. Then he told them how far behind the American front lines they were. It turned out they had been safe for the past two and a half days without knowing it.

Another enterprising trio of Hammelburg Kriegies made it to safety a bit more brazenly and openly, perhaps because at least two of them were a bit older in age and higher in rank. They decided it was too dangerous to try to leave with Captain Baum's force and struck out on their own instead. And they left before Baum's outfit was ambushed on Hill 427, so they had no news of the success or failure of the mission to bring back with them.

Capt. Aloysius Menke decided that trying to hang on to one of Baum's moving tanks or half-tracks might not be the smartest thing to do. He thought he would be safer on his own trying to get back to the American lines. Two other officers, also from the 106th Division, Lt. Col. William Scales and 1st Lt. James Kelly, captured in the Battle of the Bulge, agreed with him. A close friend of theirs from the Serbian camp, Konstantin Jovanovic, asked to go with them too, and they agreed.

They ran off into the woods and kept on running for the next two hours, by which time Jovanovic realized that being a prisoner for the past four years had left him in no condition for such a physically grueling task. Reluctantly, they said goodbye, and the Serbian gave all the food he had jammed into his pockets to his American friends and headed back to Hammelburg.

By the second night, they came to a series of villages and stopped to consider how best to make it safely through them. The houses were all dark but they could hear an occasional barking dog. At first they thought it would be best to bypass the towns altogether and walk a long way around each one. But then Captain Menke came up with a better idea.

Instead of avoiding the towns, "the three would march right down the main drag of the village in a small column similar to any other group of soldiers in the darkness; no one would think twice. Menke figured the dogs are probably very used to the sound of boots in lockstep anyway. Marching single file, they stomped right up the street with hearts in their throats. There was no reaction from the populace, human or canine," according to one online history of the raid.

The next day they faced a different threat when they reached a bridge, still intact, spanning a 55-foot-wide river with a guard walking back and forth on their side. They looked in vain up and down the river for another place where they might be able to cross, but they found nothing. They had to cross that bridge, but how?

Kelly suggested that they simply charge the guard and knock him out or kill him if need be. But suppose the man had a chance to fire his rifle before they got to him? He could kill one or more of them, and the sound of the shot could bring other Germans on the run. Once again Captain Menke came up with a plan.

They would simply walk casually up to the guard and tell him they were POWs who had been working on one of the nearby farms and they were lost and wanted to cross the bridge to what looked like a familiar road on the other side. If he did not buy their story, then they could grab him and take his rifle. The others agreed to try it.

Menke "took the lead, carefully approaching the aged German with a relaxed but forlorn look on his face. He tried to explain using his hands and a [German] phrase here and there. Behind him, Kelly and Scales acted nonchalant. They pretended to yawn and look disinterested. The frightened old man let them pass, gesturing with his single-shot rifle, and they scampered away. About 100 yards away from the bridge, a shot rang out that whizzed over their heads. It might have been a face-saving measure."

Whatever it was, the three Kriegies dove for the ground, bracing themselves for more shots. When none came, they got up and ran as fast as they could deep into the woods. They staggered on for several more days until they were so weak from lack of food that they could not continue.

With no help in sight, Menke forced himself to go on until he came upon some troops of the Seventh Army. Once they were satisfied that he was who he said he was, an escaped POW, he led them back to the other two. They were sent to the Seventh Army headquarters at what was left of the city of Darmstadt, where they arrived on April 8.

By then a great deal more had happened to the other Kriegies in Nuremberg and Hammelburg, and at General Patton's headquarters, all of which had been set in motion by the destruction of Task Force Baum.

CHAPTER 14

THAT'S PART OF ME OVER THERE

THE AIR RAID SIRENS IN NUREMBERG WENT OFF AT 11:45 ON THE morning of April 5. The Kriegies who had been marching all the way from Hammelburg were sprawled out on a bare patch of ground on the southern edge of the city near railroad tracks and a large factory. They had been walking for more than nine hours so far, having been awakened at 2:00 A.M. Their guards marched them through what was left of Nuremberg, which was even more totally destroyed than Furth had been. There were hardly any people about and barely a single building still intact.

At last they stopped in a quiet place for them to eat whatever food they still had left. Chief Warrant Officer Harry Thompson remembered that he and his friend James Park "felt pretty lucky, since we had a couple of potatoes and grain in our pockets from the day before. We had stolen all our food from the barns where we stayed. . . . I traded some of the grain for half a cabbage, and then mixed the grain up with cold water to form oatmeal-like paste that tasted downright delicious—to me, at least."

As soon as the sirens sounded, the guards ran off, heading for the nearest shelters, leaving the POWs out in the open. The men knew they could be shot if they wandered off on their own and so they had no choice but to stay there. A moment after the guards left, a hundred or more workers from the nearby factory came running out of the building.

"Look at those Jerries run," a Kriegie yelled.

"Hey, look," another man shouted, "here come the planes."

A single ship dropped a flare directly over the factory, as a guide for the first wave of B-24 Liberators that followed.

"My God, we're on the target!"

Suddenly, the bombers were directly over their heads and started dropping 500-pound bombs.

"Make an act of contrition," Father Cavanaugh yelled before he flattened himself on the ground and pulled a blanket over his head, as if that could protect him from the falling bombs.

Antiaircraft guns, the German .88s, started firing from nearby positions, with shrapnel from their exploding shells falling back down to earth on them. "It was sheer chaos," Thompson later wrote, "eight-eight millimeter shells arcing into the sky and five-hundred-pound bombs screaming down and shaking the earth when they hit. It felt like an earthquake. We were both excited and scared stiff from being so close to the action."

The bombers came over in waves, one after another, each one preceded by a lead plane that dropped flares pointing to the target for that wave. And each flare and each bomb load seemed to get closer than the one before. Altogether there were eight waves of planes. The ground shook, the sky darkened, the factory disintegrated, and the flames from each explosion seemed to get closer and closer to the Kriegies. Many men were screaming, cursing, and praying out loud and wondering if they had come so far and endured so much only to die at the hands of their own people.

Thompson lay still, holding his head in his hands, but each time another bomb struck, he felt as if a giant hand was lifting him up into the air and pushing him back down into the dirt. And then a shower of dirt, rocks, and debris of all kinds, including parts of other men, fell on his back, sometimes covering him completely so that he felt as if he was being buried alive. When it finally ended, he stood up and looked around, his body still shaking as if the bombs were still falling. "The carnage was sickening. Dead and wounded men lay all around, some crying in pain, some with arms and legs blown off, bodies blown apart with intestines and organs on the ground, all covered in blood, either their own or that of stricken comrades. Some of us had bits of human flesh all over us," Thompson recalled a half century later. "War is so terrible—fifty years have passed and I can still close my eyes and see it all over again. What next, I wondered as we staggered away from that bloodbath."

He had pity for all the German women and children who had been suffering under the bombing for years. He felt, at least for that moment, that they did not deserve such a fate. Then he and his friend James started to tend to the wounded and the dead.

They reached deep down into a crater and pulled out what was left of an officer they knew whom they thought was wounded. But he was dead and his body seemed to be held together only by what was left of his uniform. They wrapped his remains in a blanket and Thompson said he wondered, not for the first time in the war, how and why he was still alive when this man was killed by a bomb only 10 feet from where he had been.

Father Cavanaugh ran from one body to the next, trying to help those who were still alive and anointing the dead, including the German officer in charge of the guards, who had not gotten away in time. The German's head was almost completely severed from his body. Cavanaugh gave him last rites also, because he had been kind to him.

There were so many bodies, many of them dead, but others alive and needing help desperately. He found young Lt. John Losh lying face down with his buddy sitting next to him. Losh's shirt was tightly wrapped around his stomach in an effort to keep his insides from spilling out.

"Do you think I'll be all right, Father?" Losh asked Cavanaugh.

"I sure hope you will be, Johnny," the priest replied.

He lay there for an hour while other Kriegies searched for a stretcher. He could not be moved otherwise. Finally, he was taken several miles away to a hospital for POWs, but he did not survive his wounds.

"Then there was Douglas O'Dell," Cavanaugh wrote after the war. "I found him sitting on a bomb crater while two men applied a dirty torn shirt sleeve as a tourniquet above his knee. The rest of his leg, with his boot still on it, lay a couple of yards away."

"Well, Father," O'Dell said. "It looks like I'm not going to make it." He gestured to his severed leg and said, "That's part of me over there." He was one of the lucky ones that day. He did make it.

An hour after the raid was over, the Germans rounded up the Americans and set out on the road again, to get away from the still-burning ruins of Nuremberg before more planes came over and dropped more bombs. They left behind 24 dead and 105 wounded Kriegies.

Meanwhile, Father Cavanaugh—together with three Protestant chaplains, three doctors, and over a dozen other POWs—stayed behind. They tried to do what they could for the wounded and placed the dead in neat rows in hopes they would be given decent burials. Each man was identified and tagged so that his next of kin might one day be informed of what had happened to him. The wounded were taken off to various hospitals in the area where an unknown number died in the coming days.

That afternoon, after all the wounded had been taken away, Father Cavanaugh and the other Americans "combed the area for the last time to make sure that no one was missed. Two cardboard boxes the size of bushel baskets were filled with human parts, legs, feet, arms and chunks of flesh. We placed these near the rows of dead that they might have proper burial."

The six German guards who had stayed behind with them then told them it was time to leave, and they marched them away from the ruins onto one of Hitler's gleaming autobahns, still in pristine condition, heading toward Munich.

Back in the Serbian compound at Hammelburg, Lt. Konstantin Jovanovic was certain that his four years of imprisonment were about to end. It was April 5, the same day the American Kriegies from Hammelburg were bombed at Nuremberg. The first thing he noticed was that their daily roll calls were stopped.

Hauptmann Muller, who had been their block superintendent for the past four years, still came around in the morning and the afternoon, but just to chat with them. Nothing more. The rest of the Germans stopped showing any interest in them at all, and more and more seemed to be disappearing each day.

Then on that April afternoon, American fighters swooped down and destroyed the German antiaircraft guns put in place around the camp after Task Force Baum had been beaten. The planes wiped out all the guns without doing any damage to the nearby camp, and when they finished, some of them flew back over the Serbian camp and wagged their wings in recognition of who they were.

Hauptmann Muller stayed with them during the air raid, sitting on the bunk of one of the prisoners. When it was over, he told them that they would no longer see one another and that the Americans were coming soon. Then he handed over the keys to the food storage rooms in case they got hungry before the Americans came.

"The Germans are curious peoples!" Jovanovic wrote thirty-two years later, in 1977, in his imperfect English. He was describing that scene when the German dutifully turned over his keys to his prisoners. After all, they were his responsibility. "His country is dedicated to the defeat, his future is uncertain, he don't know if he will still be alive tomorrow, but he thinks to the last moment of his duty and his mission."

Jovanovic said that he felt sympathetic toward the man who had been in charge of them since 1941, and that Muller looked very sad. After a long period of silence, Hauptmann Muller spoke again. "Tomorrow I will be where you are still today," he said to the Serbs. "For you begins the liberty, for me may be the end, imprisonment, uncertainty and who knows what insults or pain."

He continued, "I am no longer [of an] age where I can stand imprisonment, and I don't know about how it will end." He went on to tell the Serbs how he dreaded being in a prison camp and that he did not even have any warm socks to withstand cold weather. At that, one of the POWs opened a small box he had nearby and took out heavy woolen socks and handed them to Muller, who took them.

"It looked," Jovanovic wrote, "as if he [Muller] had tears in his eyes and his mouth was shivering slightly. Then he stood up and shaked [sic] hands with all of us, it was the first time, since we knew him. Then he fell into attention, gave us a military salute and went off without turning around. We all stood up and accompanied him outside. . . . After him, we have seen no more member of the German Wehrmacht. He was the last."

A few hours later, at 2:00 P.M., everyone in the camp at Hammelburg heard the sound of fighting in the distance rapidly getting closer. Before long they saw a column of American tanks coming from the direction of Gemünden, heading toward them. Abe Baum came out of his little windowless room at the end of the hospital building and watched as the tanks got closer.

They were from the 14th Armored Division of the Seventh Army, and there were a lot of them, with large numbers of infantry coming behind them. This was not another small task force like the one he had led. "When I heard the artillery," Baum said later," you know, the artillery, I felt that the whole Seventh Army was there."

Those Kriegies who could get out of their beds rushed to the hospital windows and saw some Germans taking down their flag and hoisting a white one in its place. Other German soldiers were quietly stacking their weapons in preparation for surrendering. Then Baum and the others heard that unmistakable sound he was so familiar with, the clanking of tank treads.

Before long the tanks with the infantry behind them hove into view and the lead tanks broke through the restored barbed wire fence and came to a stop outside the barracks. "So I go down," Baum said, "and the battalion commander of the tanks is starting to parade his tanks. And I go, 'What are you doing?' It happened to be a lieutenant colonel that I had trouble with in OCS." The man had tried to flunk Baum because he considered him to be insubordinate and a troublemaker.

Baum, at his diplomatic best, yelled at the commander, "You're out of your mind. You're going to have a counterattack any minute." Then he "decided to get the hell out of there because you could get hurt." But he was too late. The whole area was declared off-limits to anyone not in the attack force, perhaps because the tank commander wanted to get rid of Baum, and so Baum dejectedly went back inside his barracks.

A half mile away, the Serbs poured out of their compound when the Americans arrived, cheering and crying and even kissing the steel sides of the tanks. None of Baum's men had entered the Serbian compound when they had reached the camp, but the new Americans did. Lieutenant Jovanovic remembered that "the new Americans were different from the soldiers of Task Force Baum. They handed out plenty of cigarettes, canned foods and all kinds of sweets. They belonged to the main forces. . . . This time it were the real liberators."

Baum and the others in the hospital watched from their windows as an armored car sped through the camp gates, stopped while the driver asked directions of some Germans, and then pulled up fast outside the hospital. Baum went to the door as a major jumped out of the car and almost ran to the hospital.

When the man saw Baum, whom he did not know, he said he was Charles Odom, chief surgeon of the Third Army, and asked where Colonel Waters was. Baum was not aware of it at the time, but Odom was also Gen. George Patton's personal physician. When Baum pointed to one of the cots, Odom ran over to it. John Waters looked up at Odom and smiled.

"Funny meeting you here, Charles," he said.

"We've been worried about you, Johnny," Odom replied as he quickly examined Waters's wounds. "They did a damn good job on you," he said when he finished his examination, "but we want to get you back to a better facility and give you a thorough going over. I'll be right back."

Baum watched Odom rush back outside the barracks, proceed to his armored car, and say something over his radio. Baum was becoming increasingly angry that Odom did not ask anyone where he (Baum) or Major Stiller were, or even if they were still alive. It seemed clear to him that Patton had no concern with what might have happened to either man—or to the others who had been wounded on the raid.

In no more than a half hour, two L-5 reconnaissance planes landed in a field nearby. Shortly after, Major Odom came back inside the hospital barracks and supervised two medics who had come in on the planes as they moved Waters onto a stretcher. As they started carrying Waters away, Baum asked Odom where they were taking him and was told he was going to the 34th Evacuation hospital in Gotha, located about 110 miles northeast of Hammelburg. When Baum told Robert Zawada where Waters was being taken, the corporal said, "They got something against guys who lost their legs?"

Bitterness and resentment spread quickly among those left behind in the hospital barracks and grew in the coming days. Dr. Berndt and the other American doctors were also evacuated on that first day of liberation, and one of them said to an increasingly worried Zawada, "Don't worry, we'll get you out of here."

They did get him out, along with the other wounded, but it took four days, during which time they were left with no food and no medical help beyond one overworked medic. It was a mix-up, the reasons for which have never been explained, but those who were there never forgot how they were left behind when Waters was taken to a proper hospital.

Baum checked himself out of the camp hospital when he saw that no one was paying any attention to the men there. He jumped on the running board of a passing ambulance and then hitchhiked all the way to Gotha, where Waters had been taken because he was sure that General Patton would show up there before long. When he reached the hospital, the doctors there checked him out and pronounced him healing nicely with no problems or anticipated difficulties. He just needed to rest some more, which Baum was not used to doing for long.

Colonel Waters was also very relieved when the doctors at Gotha told him that he would be able to walk again and that no colostomy or any further surgical procedures would be necessary. As he described it, "not a single blood vessel, or a single bit of my plumbing had been injured; no vital bones had been hit or broken and my back door was in perfect shape. The sphincter muscle had not been cut so they didn't have to do a damn thing."

Patton went to see Waters at Gotha the next day, April 7. "Johnny is awfully thin," he wrote to his daughter, "but his morale is good and he is going to pull through." Patton was right in saying that his son-in-law's morale was good, but Waters had become worried about the reason why Patton had carried out the raid on Hammelburg.

Perhaps he overheard talk in the camp medical barracks, about others knowing that he was related to Patton. But for whatever reason, he had begun to feel uneasy about the reason for sending out Task Force Baum, and he was determined to ask Patton when he next saw him. He did not have to wait long.

"General Patton, did you know that I was in that prisoner of war camp?"

"No," Patton replied, "I did not know that you were there."

In that same postwar interview, Waters asserted his belief that Patton had not known that he was at Hammelburg, restating that belief several times, just minutes apart. "I firmly believe that he [Patton] did not know. . . . But I honestly think he did not know I was there. I can't conceivably see how he could know. . . . So I don't know how in the name of God he could have found out."

Waters explained the raid on Hammelburg in that interview by saying that "General Patton wanted to save all American prisoners of war and liberate them. That was his whole motive and his whole objective in doing this thing. He wasn't shooting for me. He just knew of this prisoner of war camp in his front and in his zone. He said, let's go and get these people out. They have been there long enough. So he went after them, and he did. He really went after them. It's too bad it wasn't a success."

Patton brought Waters up to date on his family and the progress of the war and then gestured to an aide standing by who read out loud Waters's commendation for the Distinguished Service Cross for his courage in North Africa. Then Patton took the medal out its case, looped it around Waters's neck, shook his hand, and left.

Baum was eager to see if General Patton would visit him after he saw Colonel Waters. Baum was pondering the same question that Waters had asked of Patton openly. But, of course, he already knew the answer: that Patton *had* known his son-in-law was in Hammelburg, which was why he had sent the task force there. The question on Baum's mind was whether he should bring it up, if for no other reason than to see what Patton would say.

While he was waiting for Patton, he had two other visitors, a major and a lieutenant from G-2, the intelligence section of the 4th Armored Division. They were there to debrief him about his mission. When he finished telling them in detail about what happened, they told him it was the largest defeat of a task force of that size in the history of the division. Baum had suspected that would be the case, but it was still disappointing to hear. And to know that the press would spread such a story, as well as his name as the mission commander, far and wide.

He need not have worried about that. Before they left, the major made a formal announcement: "Patton has classified this mission Top Secret. Speak to no one about it until it has been declassified."

Baum was sitting up in bed and his roommate, a badly wounded colonel, was lying down when a colonel entered the room and snapped "Attention!" Baum, of course, stayed where he was while the wounded colonel struggled to try to get to his feet. "Attention!" Baum snapped in an interview years later. "I'm in a hospital bed. What nonsense is that?"

Patton entered the room, told the colonel to get back in bed, and stood by while his aide walked up to Baum and read a citation: "For extraordinary heroism in connection with military operations against an armed enemy in Germany. On 26 March, 1945, Captain Baum led an armored task force in daring action into enemy territory to liberate Allied prisoners held by the Germans near Hammelburg, Germany. Enroute, as the column entered the town of Germunden [sic], Captain Baum was wounded by enemy rocket fire. Despite his wounds, he continued to lead the force throughout the day and the following night until he was again wounded during action on the outskirts of Hammelburg. Captain Baum's fearless determination, and his inspiring leadership, and loyal, courageous devotion to duty are in keeping with the highest traditions of the military service."

Patton pinned the Distinguished Service Cross to Baum's hospital gown and nodded to his aide to leave the room. Baum's first thought was that Patton had lied to him; he was not going to get the Medal of Honor as promised. He knew that required a detailed and extensive inquiry into the event, and Patton did not want any such investigation. So Baum settled for the DSC. "Not that I was interested in medals even, what they stood for," Baum later reflected. "Even though I was decorated four or five times prior to this."

The more important matter to Baum was how he might place the subject of the Hammelburg raid before Patton, because he knew that each man was wondering what the other was thinking about it. They made some cursory comments about the mission, during which time Baum thought that Patton seemed uncomfortable and tense.

"Do I call him on this?" Baum wondered, when pondering whether to ask Patton directly about the role of Colonel Waters in the planning of the raid. Then he answered his own question. "If I do, I'll be shafted. No, I'll leave it. If what happened becomes public, there would be a court-martial—a massive scandal."

In another explanation of his thinking during the meeting, years later he said, "Now, do I rock the boat and make a show of it? Or do I let it go by? Because we need him. Patton was needed to finish the war. He was needed. No other general, army general, was even able to shine his shoes when it came to tactics, when it came to the will to fight."

At one point in their conversation, Patton flattered Baum by saying, "You really did one helluva job. I always knew you were one of the best."

That was when Baum decided to speak out, but in a very guarded and diplomatic way. History has recorded two versions of the way Baum put the matter to Patton and the way Patton responded.

"You know sir," Baum said in one version, "it's difficult for me to believe that you would have sent us on that mission just to rescue one man."

"That's right, Abe, I wouldn't."

In the other version, similar in tone and purpose, Baum said, "I'm sure, General, you didn't send me to Hammelburg just to liberate your son-in-law." He then went on to tell a puzzled-looking Patton how successful the mission had been as a diversionary tactic, and how it had fooled the Germans into sending troops from other sections of their lines to deal with what they thought was a major attack.

"Yes," Patton replied, "it worked out very well. Sorry we couldn't spare more troops for you."

In both versions of the conversation, Baum's purpose was the same: to assure Patton that while he (Baum) knew the real purpose of the raid, the general could be sure that Baum would say no more about it. The secret was safe with him. The tactic worked. Patton immediately became less tense and the conversation took a decidedly lighter tone, with the two soldiers bantering back and forth like men of equal rank about tank tactics. Nothing more was said on either side about Task Force Baum.

After a few minutes, Patton showed signs of getting ready to leave, and he asked Baum what he wanted to do now. "I want to finish the war with my troops," Baum said. Patton shook his head and told him he could not go back to the front, because the Geneva Convention forbade former POWs from serving again in the same area where they had fought before. The only war he could be allowed to fight was the one against the Japanese. Baum was quick with his reply.

"First," he told Patton with his usual lack of deference to higher rank, "I was never officially registered as a POW by the Germans. They never knew I was there."

"That'll help," Patton said.

"And second, you're George S. Patton, aren't you?"

Patton smiled and asked his aide to get the commanding officer of the hospital there. The man came into the room so quickly that he must have been hanging around outside the door.

"Lose Baum's papers," Patton told the man. "I'm going to send someone to pick him up." There would be no paper trail left behind, no evidence that Baum had ever been in the hospital. And no record that Patton had ever been involved. It was a win-win situation for everyone—except for the Kriegies from Hammelburg who had been killed or wounded and the rest who were still being marched eastward to Nuremberg.

CHAPTER 15

DER KRIEG IST KAPUT

"I could see birds, but couldn't hear them singing," Chief Warrant Officer Harry Thompson wrote in 2002 about that first day after the bombing of Nuremberg. "Many noises I used to hear I no longer hear, my eardrums shattered by the concussion of all those bombs." The men were exhausted, and still stunned by the massive bombardment that some of them had survived, and so were the guards.

They were also even hungrier than usual, and the column was allowed to stop near a farmhouse 3 miles beyond Nuremberg. An elderly lady gave Thompson some water and asked him in broken English where his home in America was. When he said Texas, she beamed and told him proudly that her son lived in a little town in Texas he had barely heard of.

When she asked him if he knew her son, he answered yes without any hesitation. She smiled with delight and gave him a piece of cheese, "probably all the food that they had. I felt badly about that afterwards," Thompson wrote. "She seemed so nice and seemed proud to have a son living in the states. I felt pretty guilty for lying to her and wished that I really had known her son so that I wouldn't have had to lie. . . . They were the first Germans to treat me nicely since I was captured."

The next morning, April 6, the guards were so exhausted that they let the Kriegies sleep until noon before getting them up. Even as late as it was, they allowed the men to leisurely eat whatever they could find before heading out again at 3:00 that afternoon on another long march. As the men gathered together in formation, it became clear that there were not nearly as many of the original bunch from Hammelburg as there had been. In addition to the casualties from the bombing, some had apparently decided to head out on their own.

But there were also new men with them, brought together from other groups, including some American airmen who had tried to escape from another column and were recaptured and put in with them. The army POWs were amused by how shocked the air crews were at all the destruction they saw, which of course had been caused by their bombing and strafing attacks.

Capt. Roger Shinn wrote that "their view of combat from the air was so remote that they never comprehended what it was like on the ground. They knew of course what their bombs accomplished; yet the actual sight of the destruction was shocking."

Being killed by their own planes, which seemed to be everywhere overhead, soon became a major worry. "During our march south," Lt. Brooks Kleber told an interviewer in 1985, "we were buzzed by American planes. The word went out not to act like scared rabbits when they came by, as they might think we were Germans. We were told to stand in the road. The next day, I was at the head of the column when American planes appeared overhead. They circled around and around, then they peeled off for the attack. We had no Red Cross things [panels signaling that they were POWs]. We looked just like a bunch of stragglers. As the plane got over us, he waggled his wings and flew off. That was a dramatic moment for me."

The men from Hammelburg made up just one of many columns being marched through Germany, and few of them knew where they were headed. That included the German guards. They did not know where they were going either. The group from Hammelburg had been intended to go to camps just a mile or so from where they were bombed, but the Germans decided to abandon those camps. They were too close to where there might be more air raids.

The POWs already there were marched out, joining other groups on the roads trying to stay ahead of the American advance. The strict German order seemed to be breaking down. Both German soldiers and civilians were treating lines of passing Kriegies with markedly less hostility and, in some cases, were even friendly. Both sides knew the end of the war was in sight.

"We would take wood from woodpiles," Lieutenant Kleber said, "potatoes from farms, and when the farmers came out to complain, the guards would say, 'You can't talk like that. They are *American* prisoners.'" One evening, trucks bearing Red Cross parcels arrived in the little town of Feucht, where the men had stopped for the night.

Father Cavanaugh saw the trucks arrive "just after we had been served a substantially thick soup of potatoes and meat from a washtub in the alley. Civilians were anxious to trade bread and other solid food for cigarettes and coffee. A black market flourished at the entrance to the alley and, when that became too embarrassing to the guards, over the wooden fences along the streets."

Over the next day or two, the Kriegies noticed that their numbers were dwindling ever further—down from 500 to 400 according to Father Cavanaugh. They also saw more evidence of other POW columns by the refuse they had left behind. "Every few kilometers, along otherwise clean and rubbishless roadsides were scattered for several hundred yards sardine cans, cheese boxes, milk tins, chocolate, and cigarette wrappers from America," the chaplain attested. When the Hammelburg Kriegies finished their Red Cross parcels, they left their own trail of trash as evidence that more Americans had been there.

On April 9, four days after the bombing in Nuremberg, the POWs and the guards were so exhausted that they stayed in place the entire day, even though the American artillery was getting so much closer that the shells sounded as though they were landing no more than a half mile away.

They made up for it the next day, getting on the road by 6:00 A.M. and marching as fast a pace as they could. They only stopped when a German general appeared and the guards formed the POWs in a large circle around him. He told the men that he was in command of the district they were marching through and that he had received orders from Hitler to kill all prisoners. Despite his orders, he added, no POW would be killed in his jurisdiction, which left the men wondering what would happen to them when they got to the next district.

Thompson remembered that afternoon when they stopped in yet another village. "I traded my fountain pen for an egg from one of the guards. After dark I managed to steal a few more potatoes and another head of cabbage. Was that all the Germans had left to eat?" In one of the villages, Father Cavanaugh was able to hold a service in a local church and was invited to dinner at the monastery, where he and the monks were served the same food the men were eating—potato soup. "But to sit at a clean table and eat from porcelain dishes made the soup taste much better than having it dumped into a tin can from an iron pot and eaten at the edge of a barnyard."

The next day, April 12, the guards announced that they would have the day off. And not only that, the guards heated a 50-gallon drum of water and told the men they could boil their socks in it as a special treat.

Thompson slipped into a nearby barn, where he caught and killed a pigeon. Then he took off his shoes and socks, placed the gutted pigeon in one sock and a potato in the other, and tossed them both in the boiling water along with hundreds of other socks. "The dirty sock water made for a pretty nasty broth, but the pigeon and potato were edible all the same, even if the pigeon and potato tasted like dirty socks," he later wrote. It was his first hot meal since leaving Hammelburg. His socks then smelled like a dead pigeon, he said, but it was well worth it.

On April 8, the day after Patton had visited Baum in the hospital at Gotha and told him he would send him back to his unit, a P-47 pilot who had been shot down nearby showed up and led Baum out to another L-4 reconnaissance two-person plane. Patton was fulfilling his promise to send Baum back to his outfit. "I got into the Piper Cub," Baum remembered, "and I say to him, a little short guy, 'There's a field hospital over here that I would like to go to. I know a nurse over here.'"

When the plane reached the landing field at the hospital, the pilot said to Baum, "I can't land it." Apparently he had never flown an L-4 before.

"You can't land it? You can't land this Piper Cub?"

"No," the pilot said.

"So he starts down," Baum told an interviewer, "and as he starts down another plane nearly crashes into us. They get out of their plane. We get out of our plane. We go towards one another. Finally, we stop."

"Baum, what are you doing here?" a man Baum recognized yelled at him. "The same thing you are, General," Baum said, and then he turned around and walked away without saying anything else or even saluting. It was a general who had had a run-in with Baum in the earlier fighting in France and had tried to get Baum court-martialed. No doubt remembering how useless it was to try to get the best of Baum, the general also turned around and walked away. Baum did not say whether or not he found the nurse he was looking for.

Baum finally reached the headquarters of his old outfit, the 4th Armored Division, by the middle of April. They were outside of Chemnitz by then, in eastern Germany, preparing to invade Czechoslovakia. Creighton Abrams and Hal Cohen were amazed and delighted to see him. "I can't get over it," Cohen said. "We sent this son of a bitch off to certain doom and he came back."

After Baum quickly told them the highlights of his time away, he asked what had been happening to them, and Cohen told him that he too had been a POW but only for twenty-four hours. He had been caught on April Fool's Day while being treated in a field hospital for his hemorrhoids. As he told Baum, "Now, it is one thing to surrender to superior forces in the field when there is no more food or ammo. It is another thing to be plucked from a sitz bath with your ass dripping wet."

The Germans put Cohen in a farmhouse along with some German wounded and two German nuns, and before long he heard the sounds of fighting getting closer. He knew the usual GI approach was to toss grenades inside buildings before going in to see who had been there.

Cohen yelled out in his thick Georgia accent that he was an American colonel and that there were only dead and dying Germans and two nuns inside the farmhouse. The front door was flung open, but instead of throwing in hand grenades, an American soldier stepped inside and said, "I believe y'all really is an American colonel. I'm a Georgia boy myself."

One day after Baum got back to his outfit, he was promoted to the rank of major. A few days after that, the division surgeon, Dr. Morris Abrams, came to see him because he had no paperwork clearing Baum for returning to active duty. Abrams gave him a quick exam and pronounced him fit, but suggested that he take it easy for a bit longer. He should have known that Baum never listened to advice like that, no matter who gave it.

A few days later, the unit came under heavy artillery fire, the kind that led everybody to dig deep into their foxholes and stay put. Baum, however, stood up, went forward to the front line, and then walked slowly out in the open from one platoon to another, as if daring an enemy shell to hit him. None did, but word of his behavior reached Dr. Abrams, who ordered a further examination of Baum, thinking that there had to be something wrong with a man who put himself in such danger for no reason at all.

But there had been a reason. Baum was testing himself, to find out if he had lost his nerve. He needed to know that he could still be an effective combat leader. Creighton Abrams and Hal Cohen understood that reason and told the surgeon, but he still insisted that Baum had to be given a further examination. He knew, however, that Baum would not listen to him and that he had to have a higher authority behind him, and so he went to General Hoge, who ordered Baum to appear at his headquarters.

"I knock on the door," Baum said, describing his visit to Hoge's headquarters, "and the door opens, and there's Hoge sitting there. On one side is Morrie Abrams, the division surgeon, and the division psychiatrist . . . and Hoge says, 'They just told me what you did and they feel you need a rest.'"

"I don't need a rest," Baum said. "I want to finish the war with the troops. And I argued with them. I mean, I'm pretty cocky, you know, at that time. And I argued with them." Hoge understood what Baum had been trying to do by taking his walk in the midst of an artillery barrage. He knew what Baum was trying to prove to himself and was satisfied that Baum did not need psychiatric care. But neither of the doctors was convinced and they argued that, at the least, Captain Baum needed to have some R&R (rest and relaxation) before rejoining his outfit. Hoge finally gave in and agreed to send Baum to the Riviera for eleven days, a decision that did not go unchallenged by Baum.

"I don't want to go," Baum said to Hoge. "I want to finish the war with the troops." Reflecting on the moment years later, he said, "And here

I'm fighting with him because he wants to send me to the French Riviera, the epitome of recreation." Baum knew that he would not win that fight, but he kept it up for as long as he thought Hoge, for whom he had great respect, would take it, and then submitted to the inevitable.

"I get on the plane," Baum said years later. "On the plane is this lieutenant colonel that wanted to court-martial me [for insubordination months before Hammelburg]. I had to stay in the same room with him in the hotel. So, finally, I get on a plane and I go back."

He was on the plane heading back to the front when the pilot told him he had just received a radio report announcing that the Germans had surrendered. It was May 8, 1945. The war in Europe was over. Baum said he was happy about it, but keenly disappointed that he was not back at the front when it happened. "I really belonged with my men."

Three days after Patton visited Colonel Waters in the hospital in Gotha, Waters was flown to Paris, where he was taken to the First General Hospital. "I was fortunate," he said. "They kept the wound open and gave me a chance to get some nourishment and get my strength back." It was not a sightseeing visit. It was still very difficult for him to get up and about.

He stayed in the Paris hospital for three weeks and was then flown to the Walter Reed US Army Hospital in Washington, DC. He remained in the hospital for the next five months while his wound finally began to heal internally. Following that, he was able to live outside the hospital, but he had to return every week for the following six to seven months to have the wound opened and drained.

The war in Europe as well as the war in the Pacific both ended while he was still being treated and recovering from his wound. However, in everything that John Waters wrote and told interviewers about his experiences over the following years, he never once blamed or implicated Patton as being in any way responsible for what happened to him. Nor did he ever suggest that Patton knew that he was a POW at Hammelburg.

Rumors about a mysterious raid on a POW camp at somewhere called Hammelburg continued, the result of Europe-based American press hearing reports over German radio. As more information began to appear, as more rumor fed on rumor and some details about the failed raid became known, Patton tried to suppress them. When that did not work, he tried to blame others. It was, he claimed, the fault of General Eddy and General Hoge for sending out too small a force to accomplish the mission.

That did not satisfy the war correspondents, and they pressed for more information. On March 30 Patton held a press conference in which he stated: "There has been a blackout on an operation we pulled about 60 miles from this point. There was a prisoner of war camp containing at least 900 Americans, mostly officers, both ground and air. . . . I felt that I could not sleep during the night if I got within 60 miles and made no attempt to get that place. I felt that by hazarding a small force I would confuse the enemy completely as to where we were going. It did work, for they thought I was going to Nuremburg. I don't know whether that force has been captured or what. If they have the Third Army [Patton's army] luck, they might get through."

Later that evening Patton wrote a sobering note in his personal diary that he did not share with the press. "The German radio announced today that the American troops that had been sent on a special mission to Hammelburg had been captured or destroyed. We have no confirmation of this state, but, on the other hand, we have not been able to locate them either from the air, due to bad flying weather, or by radio. It is therefore probably that they are lost."

For a while he continued trying to blame others for the failure of the mission, charging that they had refused to send a large enough force to do the job, and to divert attention from the real purpose of the raid, to rescue his son-in-law. In his official diary he wrote, "There were two purposes in this expedition: first, to impress the Germans with the idea that we [Patton's Third Army] were moving due east, whereas we intended to move due north, and second, to release some nine hundred American prisoners of war who were at Hammelburg. I intended to send one combat command of the 4th Armored but, unfortunately, was talked out of it by Eddy and Hoge . . . so I compromised by sending one armored company and one of armored infantry."

He was even cagey about the mission and still blaming others for its lack of success in letters to his wife as late as April 5. "I heard there was a prison camp at Hammelburg. Forty miles east of Frankfurt so I decided to liberate it. My first thought was to send a combat command (1/3 Div) but I was talked out of it by Omar and others." As his biographer, Carlo D'Este, notes, Patton tried to blame everyone but himself for the failure at Hammelburg.

In addition to trying to shift the blame to others, Patton also continued to try, in those early days after the raid, to justify the mission as being a clever feint to divert German troops from his Third Army in its sudden shift to the north. In that approach he tried to convince the press, and everyone else paying attention, that liberating prisoners from Hammelburg was only a secondary purpose of the mission.

He was able to persuade some people that the real purpose of the raid had been to serve as a decoy. Some even believed his claim that it was a great success. In 1965 the noted Patton scholar Martin Blumenson described the raid as "a well-executed feint, a fine piece of generalship."

At the time, however, in the spring of 1945, the press continued to dig deeper into the Hammelburg raid and the rumors that Patton's son-in-law had been a POW there. But then Patton was saved for a while by a major event back home in the States that eclipsed everything else that was happening in the war. Every headline and every radio broadcast spoke of little else.

President Franklin D. Roosevelt died on April 12, and the nation went into mourning. Patton was relieved when he heard the news. He knew that reporters would stop searching for what he had done in the little town of Hammelburg, at least for a while.

"What the hell!" he exclaimed. "With the President's death you could execute buggery in the streets and get no further than the fourth page [in newspaper coverage]." He could not have asked for better or more diverting news than that, and the stories about Hammelburg did indeed disappear from newspapers and broadcast reports for a time.

Then, on April 18, just six days later, he was having breakfast and reading *Stars and Stripes*, the GI newspaper, when he saw that he had been nominated for promotion in rank to four-star general. "Well, I'll be," he said. He had reached the greatest, highest goal he had ever dreamed of.

His excitement did not last long, however, when he came to realize that Omar Bradley and others whom he considered inferior to himself in leadership had been promoted to four-star rank the previous month. That night he wrote in his official diary, "While I was, of course, glad to get the rank, the fact that I was not in the initial group and was therefore an 'also ran' removed some of the pleasure."

His staff prepared to celebrate his promotion by presenting him with two four-star pins, a large four-star flag, and a bottle of Four-Star Hennessey cognac. In addition, his "aides set to work repainting the large placards that adorned the general's convoy transports, and the next time Patton arrived at his staff briefing room, he found his lieutenants broken into squads of four men apiece. George was genuinely flattered," historian Jonathan Jordan writes.

Five months after Hammelburg, and four months after the surrender of Germany, the story of Patton and his raid would once again become the subject of speculation by reporters. There was so much renewed interest that Patton felt obliged to hold a press conference to dispel the stories being circulated.

On October 4, 1945, a correspondent for the *Boston American* newspaper, Austen Lake, wrote an article based on the news conference. Two days later the *New York Times* picked up the story with a piece entitled "Costly Prison Drive Explained by Patton." The raid on Hammelburg was described as an "incomprehensible mystery mission," until "we later discovered that this stalag held General Patton's son-in-law."

At the press conference, Patton held up, one in each hand, his personal and his official diaries and said both of them showed that he did not know that his son-in-law was there until nine days after the mission had ended. Of course, he did not let any reporters examine his diaries. He told them that the sole reason for his sending the task force to Hammelburg was because of his fear that the American officers being held there "might be murdered by the retreating Germans."

After that brief flurry of renewed interest in October, there is no record of any further active pursuit of why Patton authorized the mission to Hammelburg. It began to look as though he had gotten away with it. But by then he was being pilloried by the press for quite different reasons.

———

The Kriegies from Hammelburg learned about the death of President Roosevelt from their guards, who spread the word on April 13, one day after it happened. "We didn't know whether to believe it," Captain Shinn said. "The guards were always so hopelessly ignorant of war news, even when they were friendly enough to tell us what they knew, that we were skeptical that they would have the news from America. But everyone in Germany knew when Roosevelt died. And soon we were convinced that the report was true. It was a jolt to us."

Father Cavanaugh refused to believe it until a parish priest in the German town of Zell convinced him that the report was true by naming the new president, Harry Truman. The priest told him that everyone, both German and American, should pray for the dead president and the new one, which they did in a well-attended mass led by Cavanaugh in the local church.

The Hammelburg Kriegies were still spread out in various groups, all making their way toward Moosburg over a number of secondary back roads. The pace of marching was slower and the guards seemed even less alert and certain of where they were going. "I wonder if they even had a destination for us," Harry Thompson later wrote, "or just intended to walk us around until the war ended. . . . Our troops were so close they did not know which way to take us. It's funny—the closer our troops got, the nicer our guards became. We all now were getting the hell scared out of us. The American army was right behind us. Some artillery shells were landing no more than fifty to one hundred yards behind us."

Some Kriegies, like lieutenants Lyle Bouck and Alan Jones, decided that they had marched long enough and that they would hide out somewhere and just wait for the American army to show up. One morning they stayed behind in a nearby ditch when their column moved out, and then the two headed off in the direction they had come from.

After a few days, they became so desperately hungry that they took a huge risk and knocked on the door of a farmhouse. As quoted by author

Gerald Astor, Jones said, "The woman let us in, fed us bread, jam and milk. There was a German staff sergeant, recuperating from the Russian front there. We all talked in English, and I still had on my lieutenant's bars and insignia, but nobody tried to turn us in. When we left, they gave us each a half a loaf of bread." By the next day, they had joined up with another group of POWs.

Another Kriegie, on his own, knocked on the door of a small cottage, and when a woman answered, he asked her in German if he could trade soap for bread. Before she could answer, a voice inside the house yelled in a Brooklyn accent, "No, we don't want any soap today, come around some other time." It was another Kriegie who had gotten there first.

On April 17 one group of Americans from Hammelburg reached the Danube River. Father Cavanaugh remembered looking up and down the river for as far as he could see and not spotting a single bridge left intact. The German guards seemed baffled; obviously no one had told them the bridges had all been destroyed, some by American planes and others by the Germans blowing them up to slow down the American advance. After conferring among themselves for a while, they moved the prisoners downriver to a point where they were ferried across in small boats. Everyone kept their eyes on the clear blue sky, dreading the sight of planes, but none came and they all made it across the river.

The Kriegies from Hammelburg marched in their different groups for fifteen more days before being liberated. They settled each night near a town, sleeping in barns, searching everywhere for food and scratching constantly due to an outbreak of lice. Trucks full of Red Cross parcels caught up with them periodically, usually leaving them with enough food to barter with the locals, who became increasingly friendly and willing to help as the end of the Third Reich drew ever closer. They increasingly heard Germans say, "*Der Krieg ist kaput*," the war is lost.

The sounds of artillery fire seemed to follow them everywhere they went, indicating that even though German civilians realized that all was lost, the German army was still fighting. But not the guards. One night they broke into a German bar and drank a fifty-liter barrel of schnapps, leaving them all drunk. The next morning they staggered out late to move the POWs on. They were clearly hungover, and some of them handed their weapons to the Kriegies to carry for them during the day's march. Later in the day, when the guards had sobered up enough, the Americans gave them their guns back minus the bullets, an omission the guards never noticed.

Some men from Hammelburg made it to the POW camp at Moosburg (Oflag VIIA) in southern Bavaria, where they were liberated on April 29, along with some 110,000 other prisoners from a number of other countries, including 30,000 Americans. It was the largest German POW camp of the entire war. Col. "Pop" Goode was one of those freed that day. It is not known if he still had his bagpipe. Maj. Al Stiller was there too, and in relatively good shape even though he had lost some thirty pounds since his capture.

After a brief battle with SS troops on the outskirts of the camp, the American tanks broke through the barbed wire and were engulfed by thousands of cheering Kriegies. "They rushed to greet their liberators. So many flowed over and around the tanks . . . that even the huge Sherman tanks completely disappeared beneath a mass of jubilant humanity. 'You damn bloody Yanks. I love you,' shouted a six-foot-four Australian as he threw his arms around a driver. A weary bearded American paratrooper climbed onto a tank and kissed the tank commander as tears streamed down his cheeks. Italians and Serbs, tired and drawn, jammed around the vehicles. . . . A U.S. Army Air Forces lieutenant kissed a tank. 'God damn, do I love the ground forces,'" he said.

Two days later, on May 1, a jeep bearing two large flags of rank rolled into the camp. "A tall soldier was standing in the passenger side," Lt. Joseph Lovoi of the Army Air Force, who had been shot down over Austria, wrote. "He was helmeted and stood very straight. As he got within 50 yards of the open front gate we recognized him. It was General Patton, looking like a cowboy with his six-shooters strapped to his sides."

Patton's jeep was surrounded by thousands of dirty, malnourished, cheering men, and when the senior Allied officer, a group captain in the RAF named Willets, approached Patton and saluted, Patton replied loudly enough for all to hear, "It is we who salute you and all these brave men."

Patton then pointed to the German flag and shouted, "I want that son-of-a-bitch cut down, and the man that cuts it down, I want him to wipe his ass with it." The crowd went wild when the American flag was raised and even louder when trucks began arriving in the camp with all sorts of food, including donuts served by two pretty blond American girls.

Lieutenant Lovoi said that he felt completely drained, and he sat down on the ground and said out loud, "Well, thank God it's over."

But it was not yet over for other groups from Hammelburg who were still on the march by May 1. They woke up that morning to find themselves in the midst of what Father Cavanaugh described as "a blinding snowstorm and biting wind." More Kriegies dropped out of the march, huddling together in barns or taken in by German families who were now hoping for good return treatment from the American army when it arrived. More guards drifted away as well, and those remaining seemed not to notice or care about the number of Kriegies who had disappeared.

On May 2 the group Father Cavanaugh and Harry Thompson were with stopped in the lovely and still-intact town of Gars am Inn located on the Inn River, where the only bridge out of town had been blown up minutes before by Germans. The senior American officer with the group told the Kriegies to scatter themselves around the town so the guards would have trouble rounding them up again.

Father Cavanaugh and many others were taken in by residents of the town. He was fed cake and coffee, had his first bath in months, and was given a pair of clean socks. He had been wearing the others for six months. "At half past four o'clock a convoy of ten American tanks lumbered down the steep slope into Gars. Not a round was fired," Cavanaugh recalled.

That same day the group Lt. Alan Jones was with stopped briefly at another town. "Our senior officers told us it can't be much further. But some, like me, said, 'To hell with it. We're not going on.' We sat down on the curb. I wasn't there more than a few hours when I looked up and there was a young kid, carrying an M-1, chewing gum. Then I saw more and more of our kind of steel helmets. . . . Seventeen days later, I was aboard a steamer, bound for the U.S."

The war was finally over for the men from Hammelburg.

CHAPTER 16

A HELL OF A WAY
FOR A SOLDIER TO DIE

GEORGE PATTON DREADED THE END OF THE WAR. ONE OF HIS FAVORITE sayings, repeated often in letters and private conversations, was that "The only way for a soldier to die is by the last bullet in the last battle of his final war." But he was still very much alive when the Germans surrendered on May 8, 1945, and it left him distraught, depressed, and discouraged.

Five months later, on October 22, he wrote to his son at West Point, "The great tragedy of my life was that I survived the last battle. It had always been my plan to be killed in this war." He knew there would be no other wars for him and that his career as a fighting general was over for good. For Patton war was "a pleasant adventure. . . . I love war and responsibility and excitement. Peace is going to be hell on me."

His nephew, Fred Ayer Jr., who was with him much of the time during his last months, described him as a sad, discouraged, and disillusioned man and commented after his death two months later that "perhaps it was better for him that Uncle George died when he did, even if not by the last bullet of his last battle."

Patton's biographer, Carlo D'Este, argues that he was just as poorly prepared for peace in 1945 as he had been in 1919 when the First World War ended. But he had been a lot younger then. And could still have the hope that another war would come along. Not so in 1945. "He seemed unable to accept the fact that the war was over, that he had fought his final battle, and that the remainder of his life would inevitably have to take a different direction."

Patton's son later wrote that "for Georgie, the shock of peacetime . . . was intensified. Because he was happy in war, his happiness a sort of steady state in which his swings between feeling good and feeling bad were only incidental anomalies in a prevailing condition of total engagement in life. Without a world war to give them a vast and appropriately awesome arena in which to play out, he could not expect to survive very contentedly or very long."

"Another war has ended," Patton wrote in his diary when Japan surrendered in August, "and with it my usefulness to the world. For me, personally, it is a very sad thought." To Bea, he wrote, "It is hell to be old and passé and know it."

He also worried about his continued usefulness to his family. Did they need him anymore? Did they even want him around anymore? In a letter to Bea, he said, "Sometimes I feel I might be nearing the end of this life. I have liberated J. [John Waters] and licked the Germans, so what else is there to do?" In another letter to her, he complained that "I have not heard from any of you since John was rescued so I suppose that having done that, my usefulness has ended."

He learned that his niece and lover, Jean Gordon, still in Europe as a Donut Girl, was having an affair with a much younger officer. Another important part of his life was being closed off for him and there was not a thing he could do about it, other than to transfer the officer as far away as possible. But he was sure that would not bring Jean back. And did he even want her back by then? There is some evidence that they met and quarreled a few weeks after the surrender of Germany, but there is no indication that he ever saw her again after that.

On June 7, a month after the end of the war in Europe, George Patton came home for the first time in nearly three years. It was for what he called "a goddamn bond-raising tour," to make a series of public appearances and rousing speeches to sell more war bonds. It was a smashing success for the sale of bonds, but it got him into trouble again for saying the wrong thing at the wrong time to the wrong audience.

As he stepped off the plane outside of Boston, his wife and children noticed how old, tired, and worn he looked. But he stood straight and tall as he smiled and waved at all the people who were there to greet him. It was estimated that the crowd lining the 25-mile drive into the city, with Patton standing the whole time in an open car, was as large as one million people.

His first speech was at a rally at the Hatch Band Shell on the Charles River, where at least 20,000 people listened and cheered. Among them was a group of 400 wounded soldiers from his own Third Army. As Patton spoke, he stood even more erect and saluted them as he said, "It is a popular idea that a man is a hero because he was killed in action. Rather, I think a man is frequently a fool when he gets killed. These men are the heroes."

The words came out wrong. It was not what he had intended to say, and he certainly did not intend to disparage the dead, but that night at a ceremony at the Copley Plaza Hotel in Boston, he compounded the problem. During his speech, while tears streamed down his face, he said of the ultimate sacrifice that so many men had made, "When we mourn for such men who have died, we are wrong because we should thank God that such men were born."

He went from Boston to huge rallies in Denver and Los Angeles. In the latter 100,000 cheered and roared their approval at the Rose Bowl and the Coliseum, where he appeared with another American hero, Jimmy Doolittle. Patton's tour resulted in the sales of millions of dollars of war bonds, and when it was over, he went to Washington to lobby for a role in the Pacific war.

Meanwhile, anger and disapproval were building over his comments in Boston about those who were killed in the war. When his comments were published, they brought about "howls of protest against his perceived insensitivity from the Gold Star parents of those killed in action," according to D'Este. "Telegrams and letters poured into the War Department, addressed to Marshall and Stimson," which did not help his effort to have an active command in the Pacific. And besides, everyone in the War Department knew that MacArthur would never agree to share the publicity with someone like Patton.

D'Este notes that no one else in the army seemed to want him either. Mark Clark, commander of American occupation forces in Austria, said he did not want that "sonofabitch" anywhere near his command. "Patton was perceived as a loose cannon whom no one wanted. Even Eisenhower had written to Marshall that Patton was a 'mentally unbalanced officer.'"

Patton finally accepted that he would have no role to play in the Pacific theater, and so he hoped to get assigned as commander of the Army War College. Or at least to train troops somewhere in the US, but to no avail. Those in command could not even agree to retire such a public hero. What to do with him? The one assignment he did not want, according to his son, was to return to Europe to become the military governor of the area of southeastern Germany under the control of his old outfit, the Third Army. But that was what he got.

Before he left to return to Europe, he had a little time alone with his daughters, Ruth Ellen and Bea. They were in Bea's house in Washington and their mother had gone upstairs. "Well," Patton said in a normal conversational tone, "I guess this is goodbye. I'm not going to see you girls again. Keep an eye on your kid brother." Ruth Ellen, in describing the scene, said that both girls replied at once, "What are you talking about? The war is over. You'll be home in a few months for good. Of course we'll see you again."

"No," he said just as calmly as before, "my luck has all run out. I've used it up. You're born with a certain amount of luck. It's like money in the bank, and you spend it and it's gone. A front-line soldier spends it faster than a rear-echelon cook. I've been very lucky, but I've used it all up. The last few shells that fell near me, each time was closer. I've had increasingly narrow escapes. It's too damned bad I wasn't killed before the fighting stopped, but I wasn't. So be it." That was the last time they ever saw him.

Occupation duty in Germany was tedious for a warrior like Patton, but it did provide him with an easy opportunity to get into trouble again. And to see his name in the headlines once more, though not very favorably. As the military governor of a large area of southeastern Germany, Patton was responsible for denazification, removing former Nazis from positions of power and replacing them with Germans not linked to the regime. It was also his job to provide food and basic services to the millions of people living in his area of responsibility, including Germans and thousands of Jewish survivors of concentration camps.

He began getting more bad press when he insisted that it was foolish to get rid of what he considered to be the best and most intelligent Germans of them all by removing Nazis from positions of power. This led quickly to the charge that he was pro-Nazi, which he denied by pointing out that he had killed more of them than anyone else had.

But with the war over, Patton argued for quickly rebuilding a strong Germany to help thwart what he described as the growing Soviet menace to the Western world. He wanted to keep American troops in Europe so they would be ready to fight a new war that he would lead against Russian domination. "We could beat the hell out of them," he said. Perhaps there was a chance of another war for Patton after all, if he could manage to have his views prevail before the majority of American troops were rotated back home.

The other area in which he ran afoul of the press was his disparaging comments about Jewish survivors in the camps in his area. He began referring to them publicly as "a sub-human species without any of the cultural refinements of our time" and "lower than animals." After visiting one concentration camp, he described the inhabitants as "the greatest stinking bunch of humanity I have ever seen." He also began describing Russians in the same derogatory terms, referring to them as "a scurvy race and simply savages."

At the same time, he was describing Germans as the only decent people left in all of Europe and said that joining the Nazi party in the Hitler era had been no different than Americans choosing to be Democrats or Republicans. That comment may have been the last straw. Many Americans expressed outrage at such a view, and editorial columns and letters to the editor sections of American newspapers were full of calls for firing Patton. Once again he had gone too far.

Eisenhower came under increasing pressure to "do something" about Patton to quiet the continuing outrage from the public and the press. On September 29 Patton reported as ordered to Eisenhower's headquarters in Frankfurt, where he and Ike were cloistered for two hours, during which Patton was told to keep his mouth shut. Eisenhower also relieved him of command of his much-loved Third Army and kicked him upstairs to command the Fifteenth Army. Those who saw Patton emerge from Eisenhower's office described him as looking "pale-faced and shaken."

Patton's new command was nothing more than a paper army, an administrative unit whose job was to write a history of the war in Europe. He was devastated. Eisenhower had refused to simply fire Patton and force him to retire, thinking (no doubt correctly) that such a move could make a martyr of him among some Americans. Patton said later that he considered resigning but then thought better of it. He would stick it out, like a good soldier. "Still," he wrote, "it is rather sad for me to think that my last opportunity for earning my pay has passed." He received a good bit of sympathy in some newspapers back home and was praised in some quarters for daring to speak his mind, particularly about what he saw as the growing threat to the West from Russia.

The *New York Times* (as quoted by D'Este) took a perhaps more perceptive and understanding view. "Patton has passed from current controversy into history. There he will have an honored place. . . . He was obviously in a post which he was unsuited by temperament, training or experience to fill. It was a mistake to suppose a free-swinging fighter could acquire overnight the capacities of a wise administrator. His removal by General Eisenhower was an acknowledgement of that mistake."

Patton took over his new command, such as it was, but spent much of his time hunting, riding, and traveling to Paris, Brussels, Stockholm, and other European cities to receive an array of medals, awards, and even honorary citizenships. Then he decided to go home for the Christmas holidays and while there to try once again to get a stateside assignment, preferably as commander of the Army War College. He also decided that if he could not get a better command than his paper army, he would retire.

Arrangements were made for him to leave Europe on December 10, fly to England on Eisenhower's plane, and then sail home aboard the battleship USS *New York*. On the morning before he was due to leave Europe for good, his aide, Gen. Hobart "Hap" Gay, noting how depressed the general was, suggested that they go pheasant hunting. Patton thought that was a great idea; he planned to take some pheasant feathers home to Bea so she could have a pheasant feather hat made, like the one she had loved so much when she had been his bride.

Patton and Gay were on the outskirts of Mannheim, Germany, in a huge 1938 Cadillac limousine, Model 75. Their driver, PFC Horace Lynn Woodring, known as "Woody," had been Patton's driver for the past four months and was a graduate of the Army Chauffeur Training School. Patton liked him so much that he had asked him to be his chauffeur in civilian life when he retired. Woodring had agreed. Gay sat up front next to the driver and Patton was in the rear seat on the passenger side. Because it was a limousine, the distance between the rear and front seats was large and Patton was leaning forward, sitting on the edge of his seat and talking to Gay, when Woodring saw two half-ton GMC army trucks approaching them from the opposite direction. Suddenly, one of the trucks turned into his path.

"I saw him in time to hit my brakes but not in time to do anything [else]," Woodring claimed. "I was approximately not more than twenty feet away from him. The GMC barely hit us with its right front fender and hit us solid with the right side of the bed."

Neither Gay nor Woodring, nor the driver of the truck, were hurt, but Patton, leaning so far forward, hit his head on the edge of the partition behind the front seats. "It took all the skin from the General's forehead," Woodring wrote in his official report of the accident, "for approximately three inches above his eyebrows and three inches across, partially scalping him." The force of the impact propelled Patton forward, and he ended up crumpled in Gay's lap.

"Work my fingers for me," Patton asked Gay, who moved the general's fingers back and forth several times. "Go ahead, Hap," Patton said again after a moment, "work my fingers." He felt nothing. He was paralyzed.

Patton spent the next two weeks in the US Army hospital in Heidelberg, where he lay "immobilized in traction, at times in a head and neck brace, at times with metal hooks inserted into his cheekbones and drawn tight under ten pounds of pressure." Bea was flown to Germany along with a leading neurosurgeon. They were met at the airport by Woodring, chosen deliberately by Patton to show him that he did not blame him for the crash.

"What chance have I to ride a horse again?" Patton asked the neurosurgeon.

"None," he replied without hesitation.

"In other words," Patton said, "the best that I could hope for would be semi-invalidism."

"Yes."

A few days later, he said to an old friend, "This is a hell of a way for a soldier to die." On another day, while he was in and out of consciousness, his wife, Bea, heard him say enigmatically and wistfully, "I guess I wasn't good enough." He said it as though he were talking to himself, she said, and she interpreted it as expressing his disappointment at not being killed in action.

"Georgie's fate," his grandson wrote almost fifty years later, "lingering paralyzed and in bed, helpless as a child," must have been seen by Patton as some kind of rebuke or chastisement for not having been good enough. Whatever he had been thinking, George Patton did not die with a sense of fulfillment and certainly not of happiness. Jean Gordon said after his death, "I think it is better this way for Uncle Georgie. There is no place for him anymore, and he would have been unhappy with nothing to do."

Every day he told the nurses that he was going to die, and that he was ready to die. "Why don't they just let me die?"

And finally, on December 21, 1945, he told the nurse who was attending to him, "I am going to die. Today." And he did.

For more than seventy years, conspiracy theories have alleged that Patton was killed on the orders of Stalin, to keep him from continuing to try to stir up a war with Russia while the American and British armies were still in Europe in large numbers. The latest is the popular 2014 book by Bill O'Reilly and Martin Dugard, entitled *Killing Patton: The Strange Death of World War II's Most Audacious General*. However, most academic historians, as well as Patton family members and his close associates at the time, continue to believe that it was accidental. In 1979 General Gay, who had been riding in the front seat, wrote to Woodring, "Of course, it was purely accidental. In fact, as you know, the trip was not planned until late that morning," implying that there had not been enough time to arrange for such a crash in advance.

In 1985 Patton's son, a retired major general, and daughter Ruth Ellen Totten were asked whether they thought their father's death was an accident or murder. With his sister nodding in agreement, General Patton said, "We don't feel there was a conspiracy. I know for a fact that it was not an assassination attempt." "No, it wasn't murder," Totten said. "He wasn't murdered." Like the lure and legend of Patton himself, suspicions about the nature of his death will no doubt linger for many more years to come.

Abe Baum, newly promoted to major, was on his way back to the States shortly after Germany surrendered to take a thirty-day leave. Then he was shocked and angered to learn that he had been assigned to duty at an infantry post at Camp Claiborne in Louisiana.

It was bad enough, he said, to be sent to the infantry, but he was not about to go to Louisiana, which he considered "the worst fucking place in the world in the army." He vowed he would not go there, and so he got on the phone to his former division commander, Gen. John Wood, who then ran a replacement depot at Fort Knox, Kentucky.

When he told General Wood about his assignment, Wood said, "Forget about the orders. Report to me." When Baum arrived at Wood's headquarters in Fort Knox, they talked about their days in France together. Wood said, "You know, Abe, I could keep you here—give you a battalion. Maybe in three or four months make you a lieutenant colonel. But I know you don't want that. I want you to go over to the armored school and teach those dummies over there how to fight tanks."

When Baum got to the armored school, he was disappointed to find that his students were officers from the Pacific theater who were now recovering from wounds, along with new OCS candidates. None of them knew anything about tanks. As Baum put it in his colorful way, "They didn't know their ass from a hole in the ground about tanks." Then he received another disappointment when he reported to the colonel in charge, who said he was glad to have a man with experience in tanks and ordered Baum to write a field manual about them.

"A field manual?" Baum yelled. "I never even graduated high school. What kind of crap is this? Give me a field manual and get me out in the field with the troops."

The next day he was out in the field trying to teach the men about tanks when word came that the Japanese had surrendered. World War II was over. Baum decided to suspend classes, and he sat down with his students under a big tree, where he proceeded to joke and banter with them about life in the army. That stopped when a major saw what was going on and chewed Baum out in front of his students for not doing their formal training. Baum told him that when he (the major) had taken his first enemy town and shot up his first enemy tank, then he could come back and talk to him that way, and he walked away without being dismissed or even saluting. The next day General Wood transferred the major to another camp.

Baum was discharged from the army not long after because of wounds received in the raid on Hammelburg. He went back to New York and started a business with his father that he called, in proud recognition of the rank to which he had risen, the Major Shirt Company.

He liked to stay in touch with those he had spent the war with and enjoyed telling his parents, with whom he was still living, about them. Baum's mother was particularly taken with the stories about Creighton Abrams. "I'm living with my parents in a six-story walk-up in the Bronx," Baum told an interviewer. "So I call him up and say, 'Hey, I'd like you to spend the weekend. My mother would like to see you.'" Abrams and his wife came and apparently had a memorable visit.

In 1947 Baum was sought out by Moshe Dayan and Teddy Kollek, two major leaders in the fight for Israeli independence in the war against their Arab enemies, and asked for his military advice. Dayan later wrote that "after a few minutes of conversation [with Baum] at our New York meeting, I recognized in him a soldier who knew what he was talking about. . . . He preached the supreme importance of speed and mobility in battle."

In 1981 Baum, together with two others, wrote a book about the Hammelburg raid, calling it *Raid! The Untold Story of Patton's Secret Mission.*

In 2005 Baum and his wife and children joined a reenactment tour in Germany covering the route taken by Task Force Baum. The group, including German serving officers and a few other American survivors of the raid, were greeted almost as heroes by the later generations of people living in the towns the mission had fought their way through.

Abraham Baum died in March 2013 at the age of ninety-one at his home in Rancho Bernardo, California. A friend wrote, "He was a real mensch; he lived by duty, family, country and God. But Abe could needle you and you'd look up and see a grin on his face. And you knew he got you again." He was buried at Arlington National Cemetery with full military honors.

Lt. Col. John Waters, Patton's son-in-law, was still a patient at Walter Reed US Army Hospital in Washington, DC. "It took me a year from the time that I returned—was returned back from overseas—before I went back on active duty," he later wrote. It is sadly ironic that his only wound in two wars was received during his father-in-law's attempt to rescue him. He eventually rose to four-star rank, having served as commandant of cadets at West Point, a corps commander in Europe, and head of the Continental Defense command. In 1955 he became chief of the military mission to Yugoslavia, where he located and became close friends with the Serbian surgeon who had saved his life in Hammelburg, Dr. Radovan Danich.

He also served in the war in Korea. Waters retired in 1966 and died in 1989 at the age of eighty-two. His time in Korea was very difficult for his wife, Bea, who found herself once again waiting and worrying that he might be killed or wounded again, as she had in World War II. "Now she faltered," George Patton's grandson wrote. "She didn't look well, complained of chest pains, resisted consulting a doctor." She died in 1952 at the age of only forty-one.

When her sister and her mother were clearing out her things after the funeral, "they were stunned to find quantities of alcohol hidden about her bedroom. They hadn't thought she drank at all. They'd thought she was coping okay." As her sister, Ruth Ellen, later said, "It isn't only soldiers who are casualties of war."

— —

Col. Creighton Abrams celebrated the surrender of Germany by having a wild party with his men, including Lt. Col. Harold Cohen, in a captured German hotel. It went on into the early morning hours, when Cohen and the others had enough partying, leaving Abrams still in a happy mood. He got into his jeep, test fired the mounted machine gun, and took off at high speed on the curving mountain roads with MPs in hot pursuit.

"In due course," his biographer wrote, "the inevitable happened—the road kept going, but Abrams' jeep did not. Instead, he rolled it down (well, partway down) the mountain, in the process putting a gouge in his leg that was worthy of about thirty-six stitches when they finally brought him down." It was the only wound he ever received in all his years of military service in three wars. He later served in Korea, spent five years in Vietnam, then became the US Army Chief of Staff. He died in 1974 at Walter Reed while still on active duty. In 1980 the army unveiled its new tank, which it called the M-1 Abrams.

Harold Cohen left the service after World War II, having earned four Silver Stars, three Bronze Stars, as well as decorations from Poland, England, France, and Luxembourg. He died in 2006 at the age of eighty-nine in Tifton, Georgia, where he had built up a highly successful business called Tri-State Systems.

The German commandant of Oflag XIIIB, General von Goeckel, was captured when Hammelburg was liberated by American troops. At first he was threatened with execution for allegedly having killed a number of POWs. When that was found not to be true, and the former POWs spoke in support of him, he was sent to a POW camp for the next two years. During his confinement his wife supported herself by selling goat's milk on the black market, going from door to door. The general retired in 1981 to a town not far from Hammelburg.

The American army continued to occupy the camp at Hammelburg until 1956, eleven years after the end of the war. They renamed it Camp

Denny Clark, after an American medic killed in the war. One part of the camp was used as a prison for Nazi party members while the rest housed a large number of German refugees who had fled the advancing Russians.

After the Americans gave the camp back to Germany, it became what it had been before the war and still is today, a major training camp for the German Army. The buildings that remain today look rather much as they did in 1945, though in better condition and without the barbed wire fences enclosing them. A museum on the grounds has on display the same kind of German tank destroyer that did so much damage to Task Force Baum, as well as an American M3 half-track, of the kind used on the mission. One section of the camp that continues to be immaculately maintained is the cemetery for those of all nationalities who died as POWs there during World War II.

Improbable as it may seem to find much of anything hilarious about spending years in a prisoner of war camp, there was a popular American TV comedy series called *Hogan's Heroes* based on Hammelburg. The program was a hit from 1965 to 1971, a longer run than America's part in World War II. It also became very popular in Germany in the 1990s. Dubbed in German, it was called "A Cage Full of Heroes" (*Ein Kagig voller Helden*).

Of course, to those who were at Hammelburg, either as POWs or as members of Task Force Baum, there was nothing funny about Patton's last gamble. "Those of us who were inside POW Camp Oflag XIIIB at Hammelburg will never forget Patton's ill-fated raid," Chief Warrant Officer Harry Thompson wrote fifty-seven years later, in 2002. "I do not know how many POWs were killed. I saw many dead POWs though there were quite a few who had made it to the woods.

"I have no idea how many prisoners returned to camp or how many were killed or just lost in the woods, too starved and weak to return or advance. . . . Many of us still suffer the aftereffects of the noise and horror of the day." At the end of his account of his experiences at Hammelburg, Thompson wrote that when the war ended, he had been so happy to be back home but then realized that "everything was not as rosy as I had hoped. Night and day, I relived my captivity. Even to the present day."

Lt. William Falkenheiner wrote as late as 2014, referring to his days as a POW, that "not a day passes that I do not in some way recall some portion of the past."

Gen. Omar Bradley put it best when he wrote after the war had ended, "The shooting war may be over, but the suffering isn't." The effects of Patton's last gamble stayed with the men from Hammelburg and from Task Force Baum for the rest of their lives.

CHAPTER 17

THE JUDGMENT OF HISTORY

When Abe Baum was asked, sixty years after World War II ended, what he thought of George Patton, he said, "Well, I wouldn't want him as a relative. But under the circumstances, his performance was outstanding. Today, if there was a need for a Patton, I would go with him."

When he was asked whether he thought the mission to Hammelburg had been a success or a failure, he hedged just a bit and said, "It could go two ways. You can say that it was a success. And in another way, you can say it was a failure. . . . We failed on the POWs. But the success part was the fact that we did so much damage and created confusion with the Germans and allowed the 4th Army Division to go really without any—without too many casualties. It was a half-assed success, basically, that's it."

If the goal of the mission had been to liberate all the prisoners, not just John Waters, then it obviously failed and dismally so. No POWs were set free and safely brought back to American lines, and Waters lay seriously wounded as a result of the raid. Many years later General Waters said about the mission that "it could have succeeded if a larger force had been sent. General Patton was written up in the *Saturday Evening Post* that this was the only mistake he ever made in the war; sending a boy [too small a force] when he should have sent a man."

Patton repeated that point later on in his diary: "I can say this, that throughout the campaign in Europe I know of no error I made except that of failing to send a combat command to Hammelburg." One of his basic rules of warfare was to never send a boy to do a man's job. He had always believed that "the larger the force and the more violence you use in the attack . . . the smaller will be your proportionate losses."

Patton later claimed that he had wanted to send a larger force but was dissuaded from doing so by Eddy and Hoge. "I intended to send one combat command in the 4th Armored [about 4,000 troops] but, unfortunately, was talked out of it by Eddy and Hoge . . . so I compromised by sending one armored company and one company of armored infantry."

In another diary entry, he placed the blame elsewhere for sending too small a force. In the immediate aftermath of the failed raid, he blamed Bradley. "So far I have made only one mistake, and that was when I lost two companies of the 4th Armored Division in making the attack on Hammelburg. I made it with only two companies on account of the strenuous objections of General Bradley in making any [effort] at all. Had I sent a combat command as I had first intended to do, this mistake would not have occurred."

Had Patton's last gamble worked and the mission succeeded, he would no doubt have boasted that the reason it had been so successful was his wisdom and brilliant planning in sending only a small force, overruling the objections of everyone else who insisted on sending a combat command.

The mission to Hammelburg was not only undermanned, but also poorly prepared under the pressure of very little time to make adequate provisions. Along with the shortage of maps (only fifteen could be gathered in time for the 293-man unit), there were also hardly any compasses. They were needed, not only to get to Hammelburg, but to help the POWs make their way back from there to American lines should they be detached from the raiding party.

In addition, they could not carry with them nearly enough fuel to get to Hammelburg and back, nor were there enough vehicles to carry back the hundreds of POWs thought to be there. As a result, the Kriegies had faced the choice of trying to get back to American lines on their own, difficult to do in their weakened condition, or giving up and going back behind the barbed wire so soon after they thought they had been liberated. The raiding party had also not been equipped with extra weapons to hand over to those POWs who might have wanted to fight their way back to American lines.

In short, they constituted too small and poorly prepared and equipped a unit to carry out their assigned mission.

How has history judged Patton's last gamble? Most historians have criticized it for failing to achieve its mission, but some have pointed to what they see as secondary benefits that, in their view, made the mission and its losses acceptable.

Carlos D'Este takes the negative view, concluding that "Hammelburg was the least defensible decision he ever made, and nearly as self-destructive as the slappings [in Sicily]. His denials notwithstanding, the raid not only branded Patton a liar but tarnished the very fabric on which his fame had rested—that his troops came first, and everything possible must be done to insure their survival. Instead, he sent 307 men on a mission whose implicit purpose was the rescue of his own son-in-law."

Rick Atkinson, in *The Guns at Last Light*, his book about the war in Europe, also takes a critical view. "Patton had abused his authority, issuing reckless, impulsive orders to indulge his personal interests. As in the slapping incidents in Sicily, his deportment, compounded this time by mendacity, was unworthy of the soldiers he was privileged to lead."

However, Martin Blumenson, who served as a historian with Patton's Third Army during the war and later wrote a biography of Patton and edited his papers, took a far more positive view. In 1955, while serving in the Adjutant General's Office, as Chief of Military History of the US Army, he wrote what was apparently the first public paper to discuss the mission. It is also the most generous statement on the effects of the raid.

Entitled "The Hammelburg Mission" and published in the May 1955 issue of *Military Review*, Blumenson's article stated that "despite failure, the Hammelburg mission had accomplished much. It had disrupted the entire Aschaffenburg–Hammelburg sector. It had damaged military trains, destroyed antiaircraft guns, deranged troop schedules, disabled gun units, and provoked general uncertainty and confusion.

"In addition, the task force caused the Germans to draw additional forces to the Hammelburg area—thereby making Patton's feint successful. The effect of sending the task force deep into German territory weakened further the deteriorating German morale.... As a typical Patton maneuver—a cavalry action combining audacity and a willingness to gamble—it deserves to be remembered."

Historian John Toland also subscribed to this positive view of the results of the mission. "The mission to Hammelburg was a complete failure," he wrote in 1963, "but the gallant force had accomplished something quite different, and even more important than Patton intended. Task Force Baum had left a path of destruction in its wake. Every town it had passed through was in a state of confusion and hysteria. The German Seventh Army still did not know what had happened."

Patton never admitted to the truth, and his secret was kept by those who knew better—his subordinates Hoge, Eddy, Abrams, Stiller, Cohen, and Baum. It was not until 1967, all of twenty-two years later, that Creighton Abrams, then a general, wrote that Major Stiller had told him at the time of the raid what its true purpose was.

Of course, none of his superiors at the time was willing to publicly rebuke Patton for a failed mission for which they might also be judged guilty by association. Or simply on the assumption that as his superior officers, they must have given their permission for the raid to take place. Bradley, Eisenhower, and Marshall all made quiet disapproving comments but none openly reprimanded Patton. Bradley said that "failure itself was George's own worst reprimand," but he wrote later that "he [Patton] did not consult me. Had he done so, I would have forbidden" the Hammelburg raid.

It was not until 1981 that Abe Baum coauthored a book on the raid, pointing out its failings and weaknesses. Other biographies have been written about Patton with no mention of the Hammelburg raid, nothing to tarnish the golden image of Patton as the ultimate warrior.

What did the Kriegies themselves think of Patton's last gamble? They were the ones who suffered death and wounds, both in the attack by Task Force Baum and in the aftermath of its failure, when most of them were sent on long marches to the east, facing even greater hardships and bombings by American planes. Those who survived were not liberated until a month after the raid on Hammelburg. Those few who were still there were freed a week later.

Capt. Roger Shinn, one of those who was marched all the way to Moosburg, described his feelings twenty-seven years later, when he wrote, "Generally, it was considered an ill-conceived attempt. None of us could justify the deaths of American soldiers for such a mission." Shinn concluded that it was "a glaring and unjustifiable error in judgment and sacrifice of life."

Lt. Brooks Kleber, who also made it to Moosburg, remembered his overwhelming sense of letdown after climbing into one of Abe Baum's half-tracks and thinking that he was finally free only to find himself a POW again. When, a month later, he was finally liberated at Moosburg, he found that "the exultation of being liberated was muted by this surrealistic nightmare of that night at Hammelburg."

"Was it worth it?" Harry Thompson asked long after the war. "If Patton had succeeded, he would have been considered an even bigger hero and hailed for his strategic genius. History would have glorified his gamble. As it was, the entire task force was lost, failing to liberate any POWs. What a shame so many POWs and task force troops had to die."

George Patton took his last gamble at Hammelburg, and the POWs and the men of Task Force Baum lost.

ACKNOWLEDGMENTS

Trying to accurately reconstruct an event that occurred more than seven decades ago would not be possible without the help of those who work to keep memories alive: the dedicated people who collect, catalogue, record, and classify the data of history and make it available to those of us who try to write about the events.

I am grateful to the archivists, librarians, historians, website developers, veterans' associations, oral-history collectors, and previous authors who preserved the events of the Hammelburg raid during World War II. They are the keepers of history who take us back in time. And there would be no history to keep, no memories to record, without those who made that history at places like Hammelburg and who were willing to relive their pasts and all they endured to talk about their experiences to interviewers.

The following online sources were useful to me in the writing of this book, and they will be of help to readers who want to learn more about Task Force Baum and the raid on Hammelburg. They also provide more descriptions of the conditions in the two POW camps discussed, those at Szubin, Poland, and Hammelburg, Germany. These websites about the Hammelburg mission and the Kriegies (American POWs, from the German *Kriegsgefangener*) from Szubin are continuously being updated as more information from and about survivors is gathered.

The first one to consult is Task Force Baum: The Hammelburg Raid, http://taskforcebaum.de/index1.html. The site contains a number of links to both German and American sources and includes photos and maps; a precise, to-the-minute timetable of events before, during, and after the raid; a schedule and descriptions of reenactments and reunions that have taken place; and an archive of primary and secondary sources. The site was developed and is maintained by Col. Peter Domes, a former serving officer in the German Army who has studied the raid on Hammelburg for many years.

Another informative site is the Oflag 64 Association at http://www .oflag64.us. It contains a full and rich history of the American officers who were confined to the POW camp at Szubin. The fascinating contents include the personal stories of the prisoners, a collection of photos of the camp and the prisoners, complete issues of the association's continuing quarterly newsletter, a database of the interned POWs, and links to articles and interviews of former Kriegies.

A third useful site is a travel guide to Hammelburg: History of the Real Stalag 13, http://www.uncommon-travel-germany.com/stalag_13 .html. It contains photos, maps, and drawings of the camp at Hammelburg from its origins through World War II and up to the present. It includes descriptions of the officers' and enlisted men's camps, the conditions in which they lived, the raid on the officers' camp, and the final liberation of the last POWs. The site provides tourist information for today's visitors and also discusses the popular American television series *Hogan's Heroes*.

I am happy to acknowledge the National WWII Museum in New Orleans, Louisiana, for providing online access to a videotaped interview with Abe Baum (http://ww2online.org/view/abe-baum/segment-1). The interview was conducted in 2013, the year in which Baum died at the age of ninety-one. Baum answered questions about every aspect of the raid. In 2010 Baum gave a lecture at the museum in which he described his experiences before, during, and after the Hammelburg raid (see http:// www.ww2online.org/view/abe-baum).

The National WWII Museum also conducted an interview with Robert Zawada, the member of Task Force Baum who lost his leg after the battle on Hill 427, and who was in the same hospital back in Hammelburg with Abe Baum and John Waters (see http://www.ww2online .org/view/bob-zawada/segment-15). I am grateful to Christine Badger of Transcription Professionals in Evanston, Illinois, for her transcription of these interviews.

No story of the Hammelburg mission, and the life and times of George Patton, would be complete without the many print sources listed in the bibliography. That list includes the few books written specifically about the raid, which were published almost four decades ago, at a time when many survivors were still alive and able to contribute their experiences.

In 1970 the British historian Charles Whiting published *48 Hours to Hammelburg*, and in 1981 *Raid! The Untold Story of Patton's Secret Mission* was published, and penned by Abe Baum and Richard Baron, a survivor of the camp, along with military writer Richard Goldhurst. For the life and career of George Patton, I found the 1996 biography by Carlo D'Este, *Patton: A Genius for War*, to be an authoritative source.

For those who want to learn more about General Patton's personal life and family, I recommend *The Pattons: A Personal History of an American Family*, published in 1994, by Patton's grandson, Robert H. Patton, and *The Button Box: A Daughter's Loving Memoir of Mrs. George S. Patton*, written in 2005 by his daughter Ruth Ellen Patton Totten.

I would like to thank Robin Rue of Writers House for her many years of patient encouragement and guidance; Kevin Leonard of The Leonard Group, for cheerfully accessing the photos on short notice; Dave Reisch and Ellen Urban of Stackpole Books for their careful attention to this project; and, of course, my wife, Sydney Ellen, who continues to make everything better, including this book.

Notes

Chapter 1. I Have Just Pissed in the Rhine

Page 1 "Time out for a short halt" Toland, 283–84.
Page 1 "I have just pissed in the Rhine" D'Este, 703.
Page 1 "Thus, William the Conqueror" D'Este, 712–13.
Page 1 "I've studied military history all my life" D'Este, 690.
Page 1 "the eighth wonder of the world" D'Este, 713.
Page 2 "Just look at that . . . God, how I love it" D'Este, 634.
Page 2 "don't tell anyone, but I'm across" Whiting, *48 Hours*, 41–42.
Page 3 "Brad, for God's sake" Whiting, *48 Hours*, 42.
Page 3 "This operation is stupendous" D'Este, 714.
Page 3 "When asked where the fast moving Patton was" Jordan, 504.
Page 4 "Patton was a hero" Keane, 121.
Page 4 "the most fascinating yet enigmatic military escapade" Green, 1.
Page 5 "Your nerves, hell, you are just a goddamn coward" Whiting, *48 Hours*, 21.
Page 5 "the strongest words of censure" D'Este, 536.
Page 5 "Patton is *indispensable*" D'Este, 536.
Page 6 "I am convinced that my action" Ayer, 136.
Page 6 "I think he was suffering a little battle fatigue himself" D'Este, 538.
Page 7 "the most controversial military decision" D'Este, 714.
Page 7 "stupid and selfish" Frankel and Smith, 42.
Page 7 "began as a wild goose chase" Whiting, *48 Hours*, 50.
Page 7 "doomed from the start" Jordan, 499.

Chapter 2. One Last Chance to Be a Hero

Page 8 "When I was a little boy" D'Este, 456.
Page 8 "I must be the happiest boy in the world" D'Este, 43.
Page 8 "Aunt Nannie" D'Este, 35–36.
Page 9 "A man who has been the indisputable favorite of his mother" Schultz, 295.
Page 9 "The accursed infant" D'Este, 76–77.
Page 9 "How did such a beautiful woman" D'Este, 337.
Page 9 "scared to death" St. John, 4.
Page 9 "I thought he was an ogre" Totten, 122.
Page 9 "Dear God, please let that son of a bitch" D'Este, 337.

Page 10 "From now on" Ayer, 40.

Page 10 "of gold" Ayer, 19.

Page 10 "something arrogant [and] aristocratic" Whiting, *48 Hours*, 20.

Page 10 "the Pattons' private life" Whiting, *48 Hours*, 20.

Page 11 "nearer God" Blumenson, "Patton Legend," 3.

Page 12 "You had better send me a check" Blumenson, *Patton Papers*, 1:939.

Page 13 "I am better than they are" Jordan, 20.

Page 13 "I belong to a different class" D'Este, 73.

Page 13 "dirty little Jew" Patton, 124.

Page 13 "My personal opinion" Blumenson, *Patton Papers*, 2:759.

Page 14 "seemed to have been motivated" Whiting, *48 Hours*, xviii.

Page 14 "The last thing he remembered" Blumenson, *Patton Papers*, 2:7.

Page 14 "never forget Georgie's face" D'Este, 49.

Page 15 "Georgie was mad at Ma" Robert Patton, 233.

Page 15 "It's lucky for us" Robert Patton, 234.

Page 15 [Note on Jean Gordon] Robert Patton, 288.

Page 16 "the remainder of his life" D'Este, 77.

Page 16 "curse steadily" Ayer, 35.

Page 16 "Patton was always interested" Blumenson, *Patton Papers*, 1:8–9.

Page 16 "Do you know why I made" D'Este, 369.

Page 17 "I still get scared" D'Este, 469.

Page 17 "It was quite simply" D'Este, 323.

Page 19 "Patton's men strapped the bodies" Blumenson, "Patton Legend," 5.

Page 19 "trembling with fear" Groom, 53.

Page 19 "Let's go!" D'Este, 259.

Page 19 "I felt a great desire to run" D'Este, 259.

Page 20 "During the interwar period" Blumenson, "Patton Legend," 7.

Page 21 "an officer of outstanding physical and mental energy" [and following] Jordan, 907, 916, 938.

Page 21 "A snappy move" Robert Patton, 244.

Page 21 "All that is needed now" Robert Patton, 248.

Page 21 "The eyes of the world" George Patton, 253.

Page 22 "With sirens shrieking" Atkinson, *Army at Dawn*, 401.

Page 22 "Patton sure scares" Atkinson, *Army at Dawn*, 402.

CHAPTER 3. THAT IS SOME SORRY ASS

Page 25 "that he would make" Blumenson, *Patton Papers*, 2:665.

Page 25 "We are headed" Blumenson, *Patton Papers*, 2:884.

Page 25 "It certainly lifts a dark feeling" Robert Patton, 261.

Page 26 "I don't know you" Atkinson, *Army at Dawn*, 187.

Page 26 "You can't" Robert Patton, 215.

Page 26 "cigarettes long gone" Atkinson, *Army at Dawn*, 201.

Page 26 "fast, agile deathtrap" Atkinson, *Army at Dawn*, 187.

Page 26 "Crewmen tumbled from the hatches" Atkinson, *Army at Dawn*, 203.

Page 27 "just peeking out" George Patton, 7, 8.
Page 27 "I was very much pleased" D'Este, 446.
Page 27 "they just outnumbered" George Patton, 12–14.
Page 27 "I had noticed some Arabs" Whiting, *48 Hours*, 15.
Page 28 "we will win the war" Whiting, *48 Hours*, 15.
Page 28 "The Germans were bringing in Italians" Parnell, 21–23.
Page 29 "directed Eddy to send" Blumenson, *Patton Papers*, 2:665.
Page 29 "George wants a special expedition" Whiting, *48 Hours*, 57.
Page 29 "Hoge had never liked Patton" Baron, Baum, and Goldhurst, 7.
Page 30 "were reluctant to do this" Blumenson, *Patton Papers*, 2:665.
Page 30 "You little son-of-a-bitch" D'Este, 531.
Page 31 "The general wants it to go on" Whiting, *48 Hours*, 59–60.
Page 31 "Pick up the phone" [and dialogue that follows] Toland, 290.
Page 31 "I want you to put this little task force together" Baron, Baum, and Goldhurst, 6–7.
Page 31 "This is going to make the MacArthur raid" Whiting, *48 Hours*, 58.
Page 31 "What's so darned important" Whiting, *48 Hours*, 62.
Page 32 "The 'Old Man' wanted" Whiting, *48 Hours*, 62.
Page 33 "General Hoge, I'd like to tell you something" Sorley, 90.
Page 33 "If we have to go that far" Baron, Baum, and Goldhurst, 7.
Page 34 "Prepare your battalion" Baron, Baum, and Goldhurst, 8.
Page 35 "I'm telling you in plain talk" Baron, Baum, and Goldhurst, 9.
Page 35 "Hal Cohen" Baron, Baum, and Goldhurst, 10.
Page 35 "I don't want any dammed hemorrhoids" Whiting, *48 Hours*, 10.
Page 35 "That is some sorry ass" Baron, Baum, and Goldhurst, 11; Baum video interview.
Page 36 "I have my orders" Baron, Baum, and Goldhurst, 11.

CHAPTER 4. WHEN WILL THIS END?

Page 37 "We lived in dormitories" Cochran, 45.
Page 37 "almost less a prison than a haven" Shinn, 86.
Page 38 "I admired him" Parnell, 29.
Page 38 "The bird is going to sing" Cochran, 47.
Page 38 "We had an incredible amount of activities" Cochran, 46.
Page 39 "barley was added" Drake, 9.
Page 39 "You worried about food" Cochran, 46.
Page 40 "could 'tame' almost any German soldier" Parnell, 31.
Page 40 "the first thing we would do" Corbin, 17.
Page 40 "Those poor bastards" Parnell, 30–31.
Page 40 "And so another month begins. When will this end?" Atkinson, *Guns at Last Light*, 569.
Page 41 "Morale got lower" Cochran, 47.
Page 41 "There's a POW camp" Baron, Baum, and Goldhurst, 12.

Page 42 "The general wants me to get a taste of combat" Baron, Baum, and Goldhurst, 13.
Page 42 "Don't think you can get rid of me" Baron, Baum, and Goldhurst, 14.
Page 43 "What the hell" Sorley, 93; Baron, Baum, and Goldhurst, 14.
Page 43 "knew what the war was about" Whiting, *48 Hours*, 72.
Page 44 "he soon displayed" Astor, 228.
Page 44 "If I was younger" [and following, through "three majors in a state of shock"] Baum video interview.
Page 45 "Naturally, I was afraid" Astor, 229–30.
Page 45 "Harold was, let's put it, street smart" [and following] Baum video interview.
Page 46 "was not usually as good as the Germans'" Astor, 230.
Page 46 "I wouldn't have as good a division" Astor, 230.
Page 46 "sure enough, I blow up" Astor, 230.
Page 48 "Suddenly, as if in a vision" Whiting, *48 Hours*, 78.
Page 48 "It's suicide" Baron, 26.
Page 49 "Task Force Baum would have to avoid" Green, 8–10.

CHAPTER 5. THE JEEP WAS RED WITH BLOOD

Page 50 "The town was reported not to have much in it" Green, 13–14.
Page 50 "Chicken, this is Shit," Baron, Baum, and Goldhurst, 29.
Page 50 "I've got to get through there fast" Baron, Baum, and Goldhurst, 30.
Page 51 "Get that tank out of there" Baron, Baum, and Goldhurst, 31.
Page 51 "Pancake saw that Powell's jeep was red with blood" Baron, Baum, and Goldhurst, 31–32.
Page 52 "We're late" Whitaker, 22.
Page 52 "It's important to General Patton" [through "We've got to get there first"] Baron, Baum, and Goldhurst, 38.
Page 52 "I wasn't too happy about it" Sherman, 2.
Page 52 "After hearing this" Whitaker, 22.
Page 52 "The foot soldiers ran" Whiting, *48 Hours*, 84.
Page 53 "It's no good" Baron, Baum, and Goldhurst, 37.
Page 53 "They weren't able to completely clean the area" Baum video interview.
Page 54 "The whole episode" Zawada video interview.
Page 54 "We had blizzards" Parnell, 43–44.
Page 54 "Old men, old and younger women" Parnell, 43–44.
Page 55 "I had a long Polish overcoat" Drake, 10.
Page 55 "The unfortunate part" Corbin, 18.
Page 55 "We saw them move off" Shinn, 103.
Page 56 "a conglomerate group" Shinn, 100.
Page 56 "which he took seriously" Shinn, 108.
Page 57 "He was an inspiring sight" Shinn, 109.
Page 57 "within minutes, they had opened their doors" Corbin, 21.
Page 57 "As a small boy passed" Shinn, 104.
Page 57 "We could have bought half of Germany" Corbin, 21.

Page 57 "knew the war was lost" Parnell, 47.
Page 58 "a haunting sensation" Shinn, 119–20.
Page 58 "Toughest day yet" Atkinson, *Guns at Last Light*, 570.
Page 58 "Survivors studied their own stool" Atkinson, *Guns at Last Light*, 570.
Page 58 "the German colonel" Parnell, 51.
Page 59 "Siggelkow was our favorite town" Shinn, 126.
Page 59 "We feasted" Shinn, 126.
Page 59 "You were just put in there" Parnell, 47.
Page 60 "Why have a man shot" Parnell, 47.
Page 60 "We have had a long and hard trip" Shinn, 128.

CHAPTER 6. SOMEBODY KNEW WE WERE COMING

Page 62 "When we entered a town" Whiting *48 Hours*, 88.
Page 62 "German officers hurrying along" Baron, Baum, and Goldhurst, 84.
Page 63 "Moses hated jumping" Baron, Baum, and Goldhurst, 84.
Page 63 "Somebody knew we were coming" Baum video interview.
Page 63 "It was three o'clock" Domes, "Hammelburg Raid," 5–6.
Page 63 "The American casualty was left behind" Domes, "Hammelburg Raid," 6.
Page 64 "Now that pisses me off" Baron, Baum, and Goldhurst, 86.
Page 64 "This sure isn't a secret" Baron, Baum, and Goldhurst, 85.
Page 65 "I ignored it" Baum video interview.
Page 65 "That must have been Lieutenant Nutto" Domes, "Hammelburg Raid," 7.
Page 65 "Is this the high old time" Baron, Baum, and Goldhurst, 88.
Page 67 "Hammelburg was in bad shape" Parnell, 48.
Page 67 "They looked scruffy" Whiting, *48 Hours*, 29.
Page 68 "Approximately 200 men" International Red Cross, 2.
Page 68 "compared to the worst US Army barracks" Falkenheiner, 12.
Page 68 "The normal daily menu" International Red Cross, 6.
Page 69 "You have millions of my sons" "History of the Real Stalag 13," 8.
Page 70 "All prisoners of war" Green, 49.
Page 70 "Goode straightened up" Whiting, *48 Hours*, 32.

CHAPTER 7. LET'S JUST GET THE HELL OUT OF THIS PLACE

Page 71 "Last night I sent an armored column" Blumenson, *Patton Papers*, 2:666.
Page 71 "would catch hell" Jordan, 495.
Page 71 "I'm in trouble again" Jordan, 496.
Page 71 "I was quite nervous" Blumenson, *Patton Papers*, 2:666.
Page 72 "Bradley, frowning" Jordan, 498.
Page 72 "he didn't know his son-in-law was interned" Jordan, 499.
Page 72 "[Patton] did not consult me" Bradley, 415.
Page 73 "I estimate there must have been" Whiting, *48 Hours*, 91.
Page 73 "One after another" Whiting, *48 Hours*, 91.
Page 73 "Message received" Baron, Baum, and Goldhurst, 92.
Page 74 "Working in a reconnaissance platoon" Baron, Baum, and Goldhurst, 93.

Page 75 "Pin 'em down" Baron, Baum, and Goldhurst, 94.

Page 75 "go over the bridge and seize it" Baum video interview.

Page 75 "Nutto watched as the stunned platoon leader" Whitaker, 23.

Page 75 "the rocketlike projectile" Baron, Baum, and Goldhurst, 95.

Page 76 "You want to go back?" Baron, Baum, and Goldhurst, 96.

Page 76 "We don't quit" Baron, Baum, and Goldhurst, x.

Page 76 "Let's just get the hell out of this place!" Domes, "Hammelburg Raid," 8.

Page 76 "What do you think the turning point was" Baum, 3.

Page 76 "I remember the sense of absolute frustration" Parnell, 49.

Page 76 "For the newly captured prisoner of war" Cavanaugh, 24.

Page 77 "This train ride lasted at least a week" Falkenheiner, 11.

Page 78 "It was a small piece of brown bread" Falkenheiner, 11.

Page 78 "many of the men" Cavanaugh, 35.

Page 78 "At each station" Whiting, *48 Hours*, 36.

Page 79 "Every step was a torture" Cavanaugh, 81.

Page 79 "The heavily wired gates" Cavanaugh, 81.

Page 79 "What a mess!" Harry Thompson, 111–13.

Page 80 "There were times" Cavanaugh, 86.

Page 80 "Two roll calls a day" Cavanaugh, 92.

Page 80 "the class became" Cavanaugh, 116.

Page 80 "unbelievably infantile" Whiting, *Death of a Division*, 146.

Page 80 "both the enlisted men" Kelly.

Page 80 "severe nervous breakdowns" Harry Thompson, 115–16.

Page 80 "Day by day" Cavanaugh, 99–100.

Page 81 "I can't tell you what a horrible feeling" Corbin, 22.

Page 81 "We were all plagued" Falkenheiner, 14.

Page 81 "I picked them up" Cavanaugh, 118–19.

Page 82 "thought to himself" Baron, Baum, and Goldhurst, 77.

Page 82 "They reviewed every rank" Baron, Baum, and Goldhurst, 78.

Page 82 "the differences a small thing" Harry Thompson, 125.

Page 82 [Father Cavanaugh's schedule] Cavanaugh, 124.

Chapter 8. Now They Know Who We Are

Page 85 "Chaos reigned in the narrow streets" Whiting, *48 Hours*, 105–6.

Page 86 "Put them on the road" Baron, Baum, and Goldhurst, 98.

Page 87 "Surrender" Baron, Baum, and Goldhurst, 99.

Page 87 "This isn't where I'm supposed to be" Baron, Baum, and Goldhurst, 100.

Page 88 "We started to interrogate him" Baum video interview.

Page 88 "with as much dignity" Baron, Baum, and Goldhurst, 102.

Page 89 "I was leaning over the front" Zawada video interview.

Page 89 "a fiasco having them run around" Baum video interview.

Page 89 "All of a sudden" Baum video interview.

Page 90 "He knew how badly" Baron, Baum, and Goldhurst, 104.

Page 90 "told me that he was a small boy" Whitaker, 24–25.

Page 91 "pointed to some second floor windows" Whitaker, 25.
Page 91 "Now they know who we are" Baron, Baum, and Goldhurst, 104.
Page 93 "Tell him he'll be a lot sicker" Baron, Baum, and Goldhurst, 106.
Page 93 "I don't know how to get to Hammelburg" Baron, Baum, and Goldhurst, 107.
Page 94 "I didn't trust him" Baum video interview.
Page 95 "The answer was an excited yes!" Whitaker, 25.
Page 96 "the courtesies of the officer profession" Whiting, *48 Hours*, 108.
Page 97 "I have two hundred men" Baron, Baum, and Goldhurst, 112.

CHAPTER 9. THIS OFFICER MUST BE SAVED

Page 98 "That's the way a tank battle starts" Cavanaugh, 130.
Page 98 "The rumble of guns" Cavanaugh, 130.
Page 99 "We did not believe" Harry Thompson, 134.
Page 99 "General Patton's boys are getting close" Cavanaugh, 130.
Page 99 "An American task force" Whiting, *48 Hours*, 121.
Page 100 "It would be foolish" Whiting, *48 Hours*, 122.
Page 100 "*Die Amerikaner sind da*" Jovanovic, 5–6.
Page 100 "All of a sudden" Parnell, 51.
Page 101 "My God, they're raiding the mess" Baron, Baum, and Goldhurst, 114.
Page 101 "Canned goods" Baron, Baum, and Goldhurst, 115.
Page 102 "We were very much disturbed" Whiting, *48 Hours*, 104.
Page 103 "The tank's interior" Whiting, *48 Hours*, 124.
Page 104 "Now that we're here" Baron, Baum, and Goldhurst, 123.
Page 105 "Since no more can get here" [through "prone on the floor"] Cavanaugh, 131.
Page 106 "I kept pushing the task force" Whiting, *48 Hours*, 130.
Page 107 "there is no point" Parnell, 52.
Page 107 "My poor German" Parnell, 53.
Page 108 "had the bullet been" Baron, Baum, and Goldhurst, 127.
Page 109 "This officer must live" Baron, Baum, and Goldhurst, 128.

CHAPTER 10. MISSION ACCOMPLISHED!

Page 110 "I expected then" Whiting, *48 Hours*, 131.
Page 111 "Yellow tracers" Jovanovic, 7.
Page 112 "they are aiming at me!" Jovanovic, 8.
Page 112 "The silhouette of the American helmet" Shinn, 128.
Page 112 "Men were dropping" Whiting, *48 Hours*, 135.
Page 113 "I could see it" Jovanovic, 8.
Page 113 "Got a cigarette, buddy?" Baron, Baum, and Goldhurst, 128.
Page 113 "I had violent hiccups" Parnell, 55.
Page 114 "Just as I finished" Cavanaugh, 132–33.
Page 114 "Liberated prisoners" Cavanaugh, 133.
Page 114 "It was not only the glorious hope" Shinn, 139.
Page 115 "It was like Times Square" Whitaker, 27.
Page 115 "We had to push them off" Whiting, *48 Hours*, 138.

Page 115 "elated at the fact" Kershaw, *Longest Winter*, 21.

Page 116 "It was the last message" Whiting, *48 Hours*, 139.

Page 116 "They appeared tired" Falkenheiner, 15.

Page 117 "We came to bring you back" Baron, Baum, and Goldhurst, 133.

Page 117 "That way is west" Harry Thompson, 135.

Page 118 "My duty was clear" Cavanaugh, 136.

Page 118 "We are not free yet" Kershaw, *Longest Winter*, 217.

Page 118 "We did not know where the American forces were" Shinn, 141.

Page 118 "Baum had put the cards on the table" Baron, Baum, and Goldhurst, 135.

Page 119 "We're better off here" Baron, Baum, and Goldhurst, 135.

Page 119 "A friend and I decided" Falkenheiner, 16.

Page 119 "Stick the aerial" Baron, Baum, and Goldhurst, 137.

Page 119 "I hid in some bushes" Bob Thompson, 1.

Page 120 "But I answered him" Jovanovic, 11.

Page 120 "Everything went OK" Jovanovic, 11.

Page 121 "Let's head west" Drake, 17.

Chapter 11. Two Hours Too Long

Page 122 "Amid the confusion, indecision" Green, 22.

Page 122 "It was probably exhaustion" Whiting, *48 Hours*, 140

Page 123 "the young American captain" Whiting, *48 Hours*, 141.

Page 123 "We can't go back" Baron, Baum, and Goldhurst, 140.

Page 123 "We avoid them" Baron, Baum, and Goldhurst, 140.

Page 126 "I guess we'll have to turn off" Baron, Baum, and Goldhurst, 147.

Page 126 "The deck of the tank" [and following quotes] Herndon, 5–6.

Page 127 "This thing's too nice" [through "sort of cruel joke"] Harry Thompson, 136–37.

Page 127 "We have to face it" Kershaw, *Longest Winter*, 216–17.

Page 129 "He didn't want to be surrounded" Baron, Baum, and Goldhurst, 149.

Page 129 "It was pitch black" Kershaw, *Longest Winter*, 215.

Page 129 "I was lying there in the road" Kershaw, *Longest Winter*, 216.

Page 130 "I sprinted as fast" Harry Thompson, 137.

Page 130 "we walked back" Cochran, 48.

Page 131 "I want no further part" Whiting, *48 Hours*, 147.

Page 131 "The joyous spirit" Cavanaugh, 136.

Page 132 "I had enough gas" Whiting, *48 Hours*, 154.

Chapter 12. They Shot the Crap Out of Us

Page 133 "And when I got ready to go" Baum video interview.

Page 133 "the fastest automatic fire" Herndon, 6.

Page 133 "They shot the crap out of us" Collins, 7.

Page 133 "none of Colonel Goode's men" Whitaker, 29.

Page 134 "No one was to fire" Whitaker, 29.

Page 134 "We're not stopping for any roadblocks" Kershaw, *Longest Winter*, 218.

Page 135 "Task Force Baum surrounded" Domes, "Entire Schedule," 16.
Page 135 "Within three minutes" Baron, Baum, and Goldhurst, 165.
Page 135 "And he kept firing" Baum video interview.
Page 135 "Every man for himself" Green, 26.
Page 135 "when the Germans opened up" [and following] Zawada video interview.
Page 136 "had us surrounded" Collins, 7.
Page 136 "They just crowded up" Collins, 7.
Page 136 "By midmorning" Whiting, *48 Hours*, 159.
Page 137 "What made you do this?" Baron, Baum, and Goldhurst, 176.
Page 138 "We gave you those cigarettes" Baron, Baum, and Goldhurst, 175.
Page 139 "When Moses awakened" Baron, Baum, and Goldhurst, 176.
Page 139 "I had armed myself" [and following] Collins, 2.
Page 141 "There were three of us" [and following] Baum video interview.
Page 141 "Pick it up" Baron, Baum, and Goldhurst, 174.
Page 142 "These men are dead" Baron, Baum, and Goldhurst, 179.
Page 142 "When I woke up" Zawada video interview.
Page 143 "If the Germans knew" Baum video interview.
Page 143 "Do I still have nuts?" Baron, Baum, and Goldhurst, 185.
Page 144 "plodded once again" Cavanaugh, 140.
Page 144 "I do not remember anything" Harry Thompson, 144.

CHAPTER 13. NO NEWS OF BAUM

Page 147 "I still don't know" Harry Thompson, 145–46.
Page 147 "We had had no sleep" Cavanaugh, 141.
Page 147 "I tried to clean" Harry Thompson, 146.
Page 148 "No news of Baum." Whitaker, 221.
Page 148 "Waters had gotten his ass shot up" D'Este, 716.
Page 148 "I felt by hazarding a small force" Atkinson, *Guns at Last Light*, 575.
Page 149 "I had known of the camp" Atkinson, *Guns at Last Light*, 575.
Page 149 "He was utterly unable" Baron, Baum, and Goldhurst, 187.
Page 149 "You don't have to console me" Baum video interview.
Page 150 "I didn't want to tell him" Baum video interview.
Page 150 "It was almost unbelievable" Cavanaugh, 149.
Page 150 "but often they gave us things" Shinn, 146.
Page 151 "Walking down the streets" Cavanaugh, 149.
Page 151 "destroyed houses and businesses" Harry Thompson, 149.
Page 151 "I guess they figured" [and following] Harry Thompson, 149–50.
Page 152 "I also had my .45 pointed at him" Lake, 6–7.
Page 153 "One called me a Kraut" Lake 7.
Page 154 "So we found some logs" Corbin, 26.
Page 154 "We crouched by the door" Drake, 21.
Page 155 "We were just really in terrible shape" Corbin, 31–33.
Page 156 "the three would march" Kelly, 16.
Page 157 "took the lead" Kelly, 16.

CHAPTER 14. THAT'S PART OF ME OVER THERE

Page 158 "felt pretty lucky" Harry Thompson, 151.
Page 158 "Look at those Jerries run" Cavanaugh, 155–56.
Page 159 "It was sheer chaos" Harry Thompson, 152.
Page 159 "The carnage was sickening" Harry Thompson, 154, 160.
Page 160 "Do you think I'll be all right, Father?" Cavanaugh, 159.
Page 161 "combed the area" Cavanaugh, 165.
Page 162 "The Germans are curious peoples!" [and following material] Jovanovic, 17–18.
Page 163 "When I heard the artillery" Baum video interview.
Page 163 "So I go down" Baum video interview.
Page 163 "the new Americans" Jovanovic, 19.
Page 164 "Funny meeting you here" Baron, Baum, and Goldhurst, 190.
Page 164 "They got something against" Baron, Baum, and Goldhurst, 190.
Page 164 "Don't worry, we'll get you out of here" Zawada video interview.
Page 165 "not a single blood vessel" Parnell, 56.
Page 165 "Johnny is awfully thin" Whiting, *48 Hours*, 176.
Page 165 "General Patton, did you know" Parnell, 56–58.
Page 166 "Patton has classified this mission" Baron, Baum, and Goldhurst, 196.
Page 166 "I'm in a hospital bed" Baum video interview.
Page 166 "For extraordinary heroism" Baron, Baum, and Goldhurst, 197.
Page 167 "Not that I was interested in medals" Baum video interview.
Page 167 "Do I call him on this?" Kershaw, *Longest Winter*, 250.
Page 167 "Now, do I rock the boat" Baum video interview.
Page 168 "That's right, Abe" Baron, Baum, and Goldhurst, 198.
Page 168 "I want to finish the war" Baum video interview.
Page 168 "you're George S. Patton" Baron, Baum, and Goldhurst, 199.
Page 169 "Lose Baum's papers" Baum video interview.

CHAPTER 15. DER KRIEG IST KAPUT

Page 170 "I could see birds" Harry Thompson, 162.
Page 171 "their view of combat" Shinn, 157–58.
Page 171 "we were buzzed by American planes" Cochran, 49.
Page 172 "We would take wood from woodpiles" Cochran, 49.
Page 172 "just after we had been served" [through "wrappers from America"] Cavanaugh, 169–70.
Page 173 "I traded my fountain pen" Harry Thompson, 166.
Page 173 "But to sit at a clean table" Cavanaugh, 174.
Page 173 "The dirty sock water" Harry Thompson, 168.
Page 173 "I got into the Piper Cub" Baum video interview.
Page 174 "I can't get over it" Baron, Baum, and Goldhurst, 200.
Page 174 "it is one thing to surrender" Baron, Baum, and Goldhurst, 200.
Page 174 "I believe y'all really is an American" Baron, Baum, and Goldhurst, 201.
Page 175 "I knock on the door" [through "and I go back"] Baum video interview.
Page 176 "I really belonged with my men" Baron, Baum, and Goldhurst, 202.

Page 176 "I was fortunate" Parnell, 56.
Page 177 "There has been a blackout" Blumenson, *Patton Papers*, 2:667.
Page 177 "The German radio announced" Blumenson, *Patton Papers*, 2:667.
Page 177 "There were two purposes" George Patton, 275.
Page 178 "I heard there was a prison camp" D'Este, 718.
Page 178 "a well-executed feint" Green, 32.
Page 178 "What the hell!" Green, 53.
Page 178 "Well, I'll be" Jordan, 509.
Page 179 "While I was, of course, glad to get the rank" George Patton, 304.
Page 179 "aides set to work" Jordan, 510.
Page 179 "incomprehensible mystery mission" *New York Times*, "Costly Prison."
Page 179 "might be murdered" *New York Times*, "Costly Prison."
Page 180 "The guards were always so hopelessly ignorant" Shinn, 160.
Page 180 "I wonder if they even had a destination" Harry Thompson, 169.
Page 181 "The woman let us in" Astor, 439.
Page 181 "No, we don't want any soap" Cavanaugh, 190–91.
Page 182 "They rushed to greet their liberators" Lankford, 4.
Page 182 "A tall soldier" Nichol and Rennell, 283–84.
Page 182 "It is we who salute" Nichol and Rennell, 283–84.
Page 183 "a blinding snowstorm" Cavanaugh, 197.
Page 183 "At half past four o'clock" Cavanaugh, 202.
Page 183 "Our senior officers" Astor, 439.

Chapter 16. A Hell of a Way for a Soldier to Die

Page 184 "The only way for a soldier to die" Ayer, 1.
Page 184 "The great tragedy of my life" Blumenson, *Patton Papers*, 2:800, 693, 695.
Page 184 "perhaps it was better for him" Ayer, 243.
Page 184 "He seemed unable to accept" D'Este, 745.
Page 185 "for Georgie" D'Este, 745–46.
Page 185 "Another war has ended" Blumenson, *Patton Papers*, 2:736.
Page 185 "It is hell to be old" D'Este, 756.
Page 185 "Sometimes I feel I might be nearing the end" Groom, 393.
Page 185 "I have not heard from any of you" Blumenson, *Patton Papers*, 2:694.
Page 185 "a goddamn bond-raising tour" Robert Patton, 254.
Page 186 "It is a popular idea" Robert Patton, 254.
Page 186 "When we mourn for such men" D'Este, 747.
Page 186 "howls of protest" D'Este, 747.
Page 187 "Patton was perceived as a loose cannon" D'Este, 751.
Page 187 "I guess this is goodbye" Totten, 349; St. John, 1–2.
Page 188 "We could beat the hell out of them" Groom, 394.
Page 188 "a sub-human species" [through "simply savages"] Blumenson, *Patton Papers*, 2:754, 712.
Page 189 "pale-faced and shaken" Whiting, *48 Hours*, 190.
Page 189 "it is rather sad" Whiting, *48 Hours*, 190.

Page 189 "Patton has passed from current controversy into history" D'Este, 775.

Page 190 "I saw him in time to hit my brakes" Blumenson, *Patton Papers*, 2:818.

Page 190 "It took all the skin" Blumenson, *Patton Papers*, 2:818.

Page 190 "Work my fingers for me" Robert Patton, 280.

Page 190 "immobilized in traction" Robert Patton, 280.

Page 191 "the best that I could hope for" Blumenson, *Patton Papers*, 2:825.

Page 191 "This is a hell of a way for a soldier to die" Ayer, 263.

Page 191 "I guess I wasn't good enough" Robert Patton, 283.

Page 191 "Georgie's fate" Robert Patton, 283.

Page 191 "I think it is better this way" Blumenson, *Patton Papers*, 2:856.

Page 191 "Why don't they just let me die?" Robert Patton, 281.

Page 191 "Of course, it was purely accidental" Lande, 276.

Page 192 "We don't feel there was a conspiracy" St. John, 3.

Page 192 "the worst fucking place in the world" [through "'My mother would like to see you'"] Baum video interview.

Page 193 "after a few minutes of conversation" Dayan, 97.

Page 194 "He was a real mensch" Wood, 4.

Page 194 "It took me a year" Parnell, 74–75.

Page 194 "Now she faltered" Robert Patton, 290.

Page 194 "they were stunned to find" Robert Patton, 290.

Page 195 "In due course" Sorley, 97.

Page 196 "Those of us who were inside" Harry Thompson, 138–39.

Page 197 "not a day passes" Falkenheiner, 20.

Page 197 "The shooting war may be over" Bradley, 211.

CHAPTER 17. THE JUDGMENT OF HISTORY

Page 198 "Well, I wouldn't want him as a relative" Baum video interview.

Page 198 "It could go two ways" Baum video interview.

Page 198 "it could have succeeded" Parnell, 57.

Page 198 "I can say this" George Patton, 331.

Page 199 "the larger the force" Schafer, 4.

Page 199 "I intended to send one combat command" George Patton, 275.

Page 199 "So far I have made only one mistake" Blumenson, *Patton Papers*, 2:668.

Page 200 "Hammelburg was the least defensible decision" D'Este, 717.

Page 200 "Patton had abused his authority" Atkinson, *Guns at Last Light*, 575.

Page 200 "despite failure, the Hammelburg mission had accomplished much" Blumenson, "Hammelburg Mission," 30.

Page 201 "The mission to Hammelburg" Toland, 301–2.

Page 201 "failure itself was George's own worst reprimand" Bradley, 415; Atkinson, *Guns at Last Light*, 575.

Page 202 "Generally, it was considered an ill-conceived attempt" Shinn, 142.

Page 202 "the exultation of being liberated" Cochran, 49.

Page 202 "Was it worth it?" Harry Thompson, 139.

BIBLIOGRAPHY

PRINT SOURCES

Astor, Gerald. *A Blood-Dimmed Tide: The Battle of the Bulge by the Men Who Fought It.* New York: Donald J. Fine, 1992.

Atkinson, Rick. *The Guns at Last Light: The War in Western Europe, 1944–1945.* New York: Holt, 2013.

Ayer, Fred. *Before the Colors Fade: Portrait of a Soldier, George S. Patton, Jr.* Dunwoody, GA: Norman S. Berg, 1971.

Baron, Richard, Abe Baum, and Richard Goldhurst. *Raid! The Untold Story of Patton's Secret Mission.* New York: Putnam, 1981.

Blumenson, Martin. "The Hammelburg Mission." *Military Review* 35 (May 1955): 26–31.

Blumenson, Martin. "The Patton Legend: How It Started and Grew." *Army* 54, no. 7 (June 2004): 24–29.

Blumenson, Martin. *The Patton Papers.* 2 vols. Boston: Houghton Mifflin, 1974.

Boston Herald. "Gen. Patton's Niece, Suicide." January 9, 1946.

Bradley, Omar. *A General's Life: An Autobiography.* New York: Simon & Schuster, 1983.

Cavanaugh, Paul. *Pro Deo et Patria—For God and Country: The Personal Narrative of an American Catholic Chaplain as a Prisoner of War in Germany.* Lexington, SC: Palmetto Bookworks, 2004.

Chawkins, Steve. "Abe Baum Dies at 91: Decorated WWII Officer." *Los Angeles Times*, March 23, 2013.

Cochran, Alexander. Interview of Brooks Kleber. *Military History* 1, no. 4 (February 1985): 43–49.

Dayan, Moshe. *Moshe Dayan: Story of My Life.* New York: William Morrow, 1976.

D'Este, Carlo. *Patton: A Genius for War.* New York: Harper Collins, 1996.

Eanes, Greg. *Battle Baby at the Bulge: The POW Experience of Claude Hodges.* Crewe, VA: The Eanes Group, 2014.

Frankel, Nat, and Larry Smith. *Patton's Best: An Informal History of the 4th Armored Division.* New York: Hawthorn Books, 1978.

Groom, Winston. *The Generals: Patton, MacArthur, Marshall, and the Winning of World War II.* Washington, DC: National Geographic, 2015.

Hart, James. "Was George S. Patton Murdered? New Light on an Old Conspiracy." *Military Heritage*, December 15, 2014.

Jordan, Jonathan. *Brothers, Rivals, Victors: Eisenhower, Patton, Bradley, and the Partnership That Drove the Allied Conquest in Europe.* New York: NAL, 2011.

Keane, Michael. *Patton: Blood, Guts, and Prayer.* Washington, DC: Regnery History, 2012.

Kershaw, Alex. *The Longest Winter: The Battle of the Bulge and the Epic Story of WWII's Most Decorated Platoon.* Boston, MA: DaCapo Press, 2004.

Kershaw, Alex. *The Liberator: One World War II Soldier's 500-Day Odyssey from the Beaches of Sicily to the Gates of Dachau.* New York: Crown, 2012.

Lande, D. A. *I Was with Patton: First-Person Accounts of WWII in George S. Patton's Command.* Minneapolis, MN: Zenith Press, 2002.

New York Times. "Costly Prison Drive Explained by Patton." October 6, 1945.

New York Times. "Gen. John Knight Waters, 82: Fought in World War II and Korea." January 13, 1989.

New York Times. "Nazi Camp Victims: Colonel Waters, Son-in-Law of Patton, Wounded as He Tries Break to Guide Rescuers." April 8, 1945.

Nichol, John, and Tony Rennell. *The Last Escape: The Untold Story of Allied Prisoners of War in Europe, 1944–1945.* New York: Viking, 2003.

Parnell, William C. *John K. Waters: An Oral History.* North Charleston, SC: CreateSpace, 2012.

Patton, George S., Jr. *War as I Knew It.* Boston: Houghton Mifflin, 1947.

Patton, Robert. *The Pattons: A Personal History of an American Family.* New York: Crown, 1994.

Schultz, Duane. *Intimate Friends, Dangerous Rivals: The Turbulent Relationship Between Freud and Jung.* Tarcher, 1990.

Sherman, Pat. "Sixty Years Later, Task Force Baum Succeeds." *San Diego Union-Tribune*, December 2, 2008.

Shinn, Roger Lincoln. *Wars and Rumors of Wars.* Nashville and New York: Abington Press, 1972.

Sorley, Lewis. *Thunderbolt: General Creighton Abrams and the Army of His Times.* New York: Simon & Schuster, 1992.

Thompson, Harry. *Patton's Ill-Fated Raid.* Corinth/Denton, TX: Historical Resources Press, 2002.

Toland, John. *The Last 100 Days.* New York: Random House, 1965.

Totten, Ruth Ellen Patton. *The Button Box: A Daughter's Loving Memoir of Mrs. George S. Patton.* Columbia: University of Missouri Press, 2005.

Washington Post. "Gen. Patton's Niece Ends Life Surrounded by His Pictures." January 9, 1946.

Whiting, Charles. *48 Hours to Hammelburg.* New York: Ballantine, 1970.

Whiting, Charles. *Death of a Division.* New York: Stein & Day, 1981.

Wood, Beth. "Decorated World War II Hero Abraham Baum Dies at 91," *San Diego Union-Tribune*, March 21, 2013.

Online Sources

Baum, Abe. Interview at the National WWII Museum, New Orleans, LA, 2013. http://ww2online.org/view/abe-baum/segment-1.

Bischoff, Laura A. "Bob Corbin: Former Ohio House Legislator, WWII POW Dies." *Dayton Daily News*, February 22, 2013. http://www.daytondailynews.com/news/bob-corbin-former-ohio-house-legislator-wwii-pow-dies/eKG1uv3OsgLs6qbgrTdYPI.

Collins, Elizabeth. "One More Battle: Battle of the Bulge Heroes Fight for Survival in Nazi Captivity." *Soldiers*, January 2015. http://soldiers.dodlive.mil/2015/01/one-more-battle.

Corbin, Robert. "Prisoner of War Story." Unpublished manuscript, 1988. http://oflag64.us/ewExternalFiles/corbin_robert-story.pdf.

Domes, Peter. "The Hammelburg Raid." Unpublished manuscript, 2003. http://oflag64.us/ewExternalFiles/oberstleutnant_peter_domes-the_hammelburg_raid-eng.pdf.

Domes, Peter. "Entire Schedule of Hammelburg Raid." Last updated September 22, 2013. http://www.taskforcebaum.de/schedule/schedule.html.

Domes, Peter, and Martin Heinlein. "The Book." Last updated April 14, 2017. http://www.taskforcebaum.de/projekte/book.html.

Drake, Jay A. "On the Other Side: Guest of the Third Reich." World War II Stories: In Their Own Words. Last updated February 17, 2012. http://carol_fus.tripod.com/army_hero_jay_drake.html.

Falkenheiner, William C. Personal statement. World War II Veterans Concordia Parish, Louisiana. June 10, 2014. http://concordialibrary.org/2014/06/william-c-falkenheiner.

Goode, Paul R. A Debriefing of Colonel Paul R. Goode, SAO at Oflag 64 and Oflag XIII-B. War Department General Staff, G2 Military Intelligence Service. May 17, 1945. http://oflag64.us/ewExternalFiles/roster_of_american_pows_at_oflag.pdf.

Green, Tobin. "The Hammelburg Raid Revisited." Washington, DC: The Strategic Studies Institute, Johns Hopkins University Paul H. Nitze School for Advanced International Studies (SAIS). July 7, 1994. http://www.dtic.mil/dtic/tr/fulltext/u2/a281238.pdf.

Hendrikx, Peter. "The Death of General George S. Patton." http://www.osssociety.org/pdfs/Patton.pdf.

Herndon, Inge Jr. "The FReeper Foxhole Remembers Task Force Baum—The Hammelburg Raid." January 16, 2003. http://www.freerepublic.com/focus/vetscor/823677/posts.

"History of the Real Stalag 13." War History Online, n.d. https://www.warhistoryonline.com/war-articles/history-of-the-real-stalag-13.html.

Hopkins, Nicholas. "A Poor Defense: Sherman Tanks in WW2." University of Illinois Archives. November 22, 2013. http://archives.library.illinois.edu/blog/poor-defense-sherman-tanks-ww2.

International Red Cross. Report: OFLAG XIII-B. Military Intelligence War Department. November 1, 1945. http://www.taskforcebaum.de/oflag13/report1.html.

Jovanovic, Konstantin. Letter Hanns-Helmut Schnebel, Librarian, Infantry School, Hammelburg (as reproduced by Peter Domes). January 20, 1977. http://oflag64 .us/ewExternalFiles/letter_from_konstantin_jovanovitsch.pdf.

Keiler, Jonathan. "Top Secret Missions: Liberating General George S. Patton's Son-in-Law." Warfare History Network, December 9, 2016. http://warfarehistory network.com/daily/wwii/top-secret-missions-liberating-general-george-s -pattons-son-in-law.

Kelly, C. J. "The Hammelburg Raid." Last updated May 11, 2017. http://hubpages.com/ education/The-Hammelburg-Raid.

Klassen, Carolyn, and Rebecca Nieto. "Finding Aid for Roger L. Shinn Papers, 1920–2010." April 20, 2016. The Burke Library Archives, Columbia University Libraries, Union Theological Seminary. http://library.columbia.edu/content/dam/ libraryweb/locations/burke/fa/uts/ldpd_11447037.pdf.

Kleber, Brooks. "Patton Raids the POW Camp at Hammelburg." n.d. http:// www.94thinfdiv.com/pow.pdf.

Lake, Austen. Interview with Captain Baum (Task Force Commander) and Sergeant Graham (Task Force Member). April 10, 1945. http://taskforcebaum.de/documents/ baum/interview.html.

Lankford, Jim. "The 14th Armored Division and the Liberation of Stalag VIIA." US Army History Center. January 20, 2015. https://armyhistory.org/the-14th -armored-division-and-the-liberation-of-stalag-viia.

Military Intelligence Service War Department. "American Prisoners of War in Germany." November 1, 1945. http://oflag64.us/ewExternalFiles/american_pows _in_germany-mis_docs.pdf.

Moore, Don. "Harry Long Was a POW with Patton's Son-in-Law." First published in *Charlotte Sun* (Port Charlotte, FL), February 2003. https://donmooreswartales .com/2010/04/16/harry-long.

The Oflag 64 Item, March 2, 1944. http://www.oflag64.us/ewExternalFiles/1944.3.2.pdf.

Pioneer Press (St. Paul, MN). "Did You Know That 'Hogan's Heroes' Was Based on a German POW Camp Actually Called 'Stalag 13?'" July 28, 2014. http://www .twincities.com/2014/07/28/did-you-know-that-hogans-heroes-was-based-on -a-german-pow-camp-actually-called-stalag-13.

"Salute to Lt. Col. Harold Cohen on His Receipt of Distinguished Service Cross." *Congressional Record* 142, no. 64 (May 9, 1996): H4787–88. https://www.gpo.gov/ fdsys/pkg/CREC-1996-05-09/html/CREC-1996-05-09-pt1-PgH4787-3.htm.

San Diego Union-Tribune. "Decorated WWII Hero Abraham Baum Dies at 91." March 21, 2013. http://www.sandiegouniontribune.com/obituaries/sdut -abraham-baum-decorated-veteran-2013mar21-story.html.

Schafer, Joe. "The Hammelburg Raid Redux." August 28, 2014. https://github.com/ jschaf/mccc/blob/master/battle/hammelburg.md.

Spartanburg (SC) Herald-Journal. Harold Cohen obituary. August 16, 2006. http://www .legacy.com/obituaries/spartanburg/obituary.aspx?n=harold-cohen&pid=88808392.

St. John, Jeffrey. "Reflections of a Fighting Father." 1985. http://.www.pattonhq.com/ textfiles/reflect.html.

"Stiller, Alexander." *Military Times* Wall of Valor (database). http://valor.militarytimes
.com/recipient.php?recipientid=32928.

Sudmeier, Jim. "William Nutto." 2017. http://jimsudmeier.com/william-nutto.

Thompson, Bob. "Bob Thompson's Account of the Raid at Oflag XIIIB." 2002. http://
oflag64.us/ewExternalFiles/thompson_bob_account-diamonds_story-with
_photos.pdf.

Whitaker, Richard. "Task Force Baum and the Hammelburg Raid." *Armor*, September–
October 1996. http://oflag64.us/ewExternalFiles/whitaker-richard-tfb-article.pdf.

Zawada, Robert. Interview at the National WWII Museum, New Orleans, LA, 2013.
http://www.ww2online.org/view/bob-zawada/segment-1.

INDEX